Narrative Humanism

Narrative Humanism

Kindness and Complexity in Fiction and Film

Wyatt Moss-Wellington

EDINBURGH
University Press

Edinburgh University Press is one of the leading university presses in the UK. We publish academic books and journals in our selected subject areas across the humanities and social sciences, combining cutting-edge scholarship with high editorial and production values to produce academic works of lasting importance. For more information visit our website: edinburghuniversitypress.com

© Wyatt Moss-Wellington, 2019, 2021

Edinburgh University Press Ltd
The Tun – Holyrood Road
12 (2f) Jackson's Entry
Edinburgh EH8 8PJ

First published in hardback by Edinburgh University Press 2019

Typeset in 11/13 Monotype Ehrhardt by
IDSUK (DataConnection) Ltd

A CIP record for this book is available from the British Library

ISBN 978 1 4744 5431 5 (hardback)
ISBN 978 1 4744 5432 2 (paperback)
ISBN 978 1 4744 5433 9 (webready PDF)
ISBN 978 1 4744 5434 6 (epub)

The right of Wyatt Moss-Wellington to be identified as author of this work has been asserted in accordance with the Copyright, Designs and Patents Act 1988 and the Copyright and Related Rights Regulations 2003 (SI No. 2498).

Contents

Acknowledgements	vi
Introduction	1

Part I Humanist Hermeneutics

1. Reading the Human Drama in Film and Fiction	13

Part II Social Narratology

2. Foundational Functions of Fiction	45
3. Affective Functions of Fiction	56
4. Connectedness and Character	73
5. Mental Work and Memory	98
6. Ethics and Conclusions	116

Part III Genre Case Study: The Suburban Ensemble Dramedy

7. An Introduction to the Millennial Suburban Ensemble Film	129
8. Discussions: Affect, Sociopolitics and the Ensemble Narrative	146

Part IV Close Reading Case Study: *Parenthood*

9. *Parenthood*: A Humanistic Close Reading	181
Afterword	208
Bibliography	214
Index	241

Acknowledgements

Thank you first and foremost to Sophia Harris, David Kelly and to the staff at Edinburgh University Press, without whom there would be no book. Thank you also to all those who offered love, support and kept me intellectually honest over the past few years, in particular Kim Wilkins, Rebecca Johinke, Lili Paquet, Peter Marks and Bruce Isaacs (among many others). Thanks to Kathryn Millard, Joseph Kupfer and John Frow for their helpful feedback. Finally, thank you to my family and friends for support while I have been engaged with this research, thinking, writing, and deliberating – I owe you all a beverage.

Introduction

We are all story addicts. We might go to bed with a book or film, or wake up to the news; our immersion in micronarratives on the internet has scarcely made a dent in television use; the expansion of television into epic serialised narratives made for intensive or 'binge' consumption tells of an increasing appetite for fictive immersion throughout the day; narratives in songform now follow us relentlessly throughout the urban environment; and we tell of our lives by ordering autobiographical memories into comprehensible narratives. Much of our day is, thus, engaged in storied activities, a phenomenon that some have positioned as a contemporary Western 'addiction' or 'obsession' with narrative (Landy 2011: 497). Although we perform multiple acts of sustained creativity in our lives, which arguably have further-reaching impact on participants – childrearing and teaching, for example – we single out the fictive storyteller for special regard and loftier status, in many cases aspiring to similar creativity, while ignoring our own quotidian creative practices. So why should this activity, concocting and disseminating creative fictions, matter to us so much? As Dennis Dutton writes:

> Human beings across the globe expend staggering amounts of time and resources on creating and experiencing fantasies and fictions. The human fascination with fiction is so intense that it can amount to a virtual addiction. (2009: 109)

Joseph Carroll has pointed out that many evolutionary interpretations of the genesis of art fail to account for the insatiable need to create and consume narrative, our story 'addiction' (2004: xxi). Considering the widespread use of narrative arts in the daily life of a majority, it would not be right to characterise this addiction as pathological; instead, it appears to be foundational to human sociobiology, one of those very few qualities that can truly be considered pancultural. Once investigated, we begin to witness the diversity of uses we have found for the storytelling instinct, and they are terrifically manifold.

The following volume largely concerns the utility and the ethics of narrative. Specifically, it looks at our motivations for storytelling, and the way we might extend research in human sociobiology to ask ethical questions: how we ought to live. As such, I begin with an attempt to come to grips with what, precisely, a narrative is, and ground a sense of narrative purpose in human history and development. Following from these foundations, I introduce two central concerns: what humanistic narrative and humanist hermeneutics might look like. From the start, however, it is necessary to be careful in delineating the confines of sociobiological speculation and literary Darwinism: given that we find new uses for old adaptations (exaptation occurring at a complex cultural level, for instance), we cannot explain all human behaviours via portrayals of their origins (Buller 2005; Turvey 2014: 49), and further, evolutionary theory contains no prescriptive value and cannot tell us *how* to act. Accounting for these dilemmas is one substantial component in the project I am calling 'narrative humanism'.

I take a broad view of story. Story is a communicative act that specifically implies a chain of causality, and story as we popularly know it is any series of descriptors, transmitted via any sensory means, which can be read as causal, or 'a chain of events in cause–effect relationship occurring in time and space' (Bordwell and Thompson 2003: 69). In effect, stories mimic how we think: due to our necessary abstraction of the world into causal patterns, if we receive any communication from another, we intuitively attempt to unpack its concept of causality.[1] Likewise, when concocting imagery, using tools from the written word to a stage prop, the storyteller suggests 'a set of perceptual processes that the reader then uses to construct a particular idea or experience' (Mar and Oatley 2008: 178). For example, we may neuroaesthetically react to the ornamentality of an abstract painting and thus be drawn to consider it, but once considered we apply meanings based on a pattern of causal understandings, by which we know the world – thus our relationship with the artwork, and how we explain its meaning to ourselves, although abstract, is 'storied', founded on narrative. It is also an implicitly human narrative we are attempting to read, as we discern and empathise with emotional states the artist moved through in their creative process: 'the relationship between embodied simulation-driven empathic feelings in the observer and the *content* of art works, in terms of the actions, intentions, objects, emotions, and sensations portrayed in a given painting or sculpture' (Gallese 2010: 446). That is, artworks and still images tell all kinds of stories: stories of the emotional and interior process of their creation, stories of the kind of person we are when we react to them, or the culture we mutually exist within, a prompting to conceptual causality that ignites a reasoning that fortifies or puts into question our values. So even if an image does not suggest a narrative in itself, it connects to other narratives, or reductions to pertinent causal details – self-narratives, cultural narratives and so on – to become meaningful.[2] Likewise, if we describe to an acquaintance two separate and seemingly unrelated objects, merely by offering them in succession we have suggested a story: our friend cannot help but attempt to read their relationship, and effectively put together a narrative in their mind which will suggest a causal perspective on the world. Our pattern-recognition faculties beget a storied understanding of the world.

Fiction 'is a particularly useful simulation because negotiating the social world effectively is extremely tricky, requiring us to weigh up myriad interacting instances of cause and effect' (Oatley 2008: 43). Not only is storied behaviour vital to retaining complex social structures, but we may also be more likely to *remember* the exertion of piecing together causality, and thus recall information or analysis gleaned from emotionally stimulating narrative. Causal narrative's use in stimulating memorability can also be observed in the mnemonic link system – the practice of constructing a story to memorise unconnected items. These are accounts of the uses and perhaps the origins of *fictive* storytelling. Laura Ashe (2015) dates literary fiction to 1155, we often refer to Greek theatre as the birth of a specifically Western formalised narrative practice, and Palaeolithic cave paintings from sites across the globe, dated as old as 40,000 years, contain narrative information; however such accounts refer only to literary and artistic histories, which have the benefit of a visual record. There is, of course, no way to timestamp the birth of oral storied imaginings.

There are equivalent non-fictive paradigms of causal storytelling. In the construction of memory into autobiographical self-narrative, for instance, there is evidence to suggest that writing one's story assists trauma recovery (see Joshua M. Smyth's [1998] summary of such findings in 'Written Emotional Expression: Effect Sizes, Outcome Types, and Moderating Variables'). However, research conducted by James W. Pennebaker and Anna Graybeal in 2001 also found that:

> individuals who showed an overall increase in the use of causal words (e.g., 'because,' 'cause,' 'reason') and insight words (e.g., 'realize,' 'know,' 'understand') demonstrated comparatively larger and more significant health improvements than those who did not increase their use of causal words. (91–2)

This contrasted with predominant use of emotional words, which they found 'only weakly related to health' (91). Similarly, Amanda Barnier and Penny Van Bergen offer a rundown on the individual and relational health benefits of sharing autobiographical memory stories in '"Remember when we . . . ?" Why Sharing Memories is Soul Food' (2014), in particular highlighting the research of Robyn Fivush.[3] Developing causal narratives appears to be essential for our mental health – it is the provision of meaning by which we may feel in control of our environment, and ourselves, and know how to act accordingly. Perhaps the more causal attributions we make also, the more likely our account is to acknowledge complex multicausality, and capitulate to the interrogation of distilled and discrete causal theories which are essentially tied into a composite account; we know by their multifariousness that such accounts do not summarise the world, but provide a few of the many explanations we require to make collective meaning from its boundless causal convolutions. However, in this book I am mostly concerned with fictional narratives, and while life narratives and fiction are both storied behaviours, the similarities may well end with their founding causal structure, or as Peter Lamarque suggests in his article 'On the distance between literary narratives and real-life narratives' (2007), their most superficial aspects. However, divorcing the two completely would be inappropriate, neglecting how each informs the other. Katherine Nelson (2003: 125–36), as well as Qi Wang and Jens Brockmeier (2008: 45–64), describe the interdependence of autobiographical memory and collectively produced narratives; Dan P. McAdams discusses the influence of biographical genres (in particular redemptive biographies which fortify generativity) in *The Redemptive Self: Stories Americans Live By* (2006); while Tilmann Habermas and Susan Bluck (2000) describe how life narratives begin in adolescence, which could also be seen as a primary age for developing and negotiating awareness of cultural narrative absorption.[4] In cinema studies, the debate on what constitutes documentary filmmaking shows us just how difficult it can be to separate fictive and non-fictive storytelling acts (Eitzen 1995). The following analysis acknowledges how freely we can exchange between fictive and non-fictive storytelling, while at the same time noting distinctions between the two. Ultimately, though, all comparisons between fictive and real-life narratives reveal just how deeply storytelling behaviours are ingrained in our cognition: it is the 'structure of sense' (Burkert 1979: 5) particular to humans.

Further to the causality account of storied behaviours, in Alan Palmer's conception of narrative explored through 2004's *Fictional Minds*, we concoct a psychological map of other autonomous agents and their intentions, and use our resultant understanding of motivational interactivity to navigate the complex social world. Raymond A. Mar and Keith Oatley see this process as the same as any kind of psychological simulation, which has two functions: to 'provide information by offering a model when access cannot be direct' (2008: 174), as in another's mind and motivation, and 'to understand, and to some extent predict, the behavior of systems made up of many processes in interaction' (175), as in the complex social world. In theoretical discourse the understanding of narrative as a network of causal intentionality also reaches back to Kenneth Burke's grammar and rhetoric of motives, which, while innovative in its time, in Jerome S. Bruner's view suffers from a negligence of 'character' (1986: 20); there is something indubitably human missing from such a mathematical approach. Perhaps a multiplicity of motivational causalities in fiction, by which we must work to extend the bounds of our simulation of social structures, is what we read as a more 'human' and 'complex' narrative, a psychological verisimilitude or a more lifelike conception of other minds. Although all simulation is a reductive abstraction to comprehensible formulae, what matters then is *how* reductive our abstraction is: how many causal factors our simulation takes into account.

Although story is possible without intentional causality, it is rare to encounter, as narrative quickly becomes tiresome (perhaps obsolete and robbed of purpose) when the intrigue of motivation is extracted. In Bruner's account of the difference between logical debate and narrative, which he positions as different cognitive modes (a distinction defining the 'narrative turn' of the 1980s, echoed by Donald E. Polkinghorne in the similarly influential *Narrative Knowing and the Human Sciences* [1988: 35]), the former 'leads to a search for universal truth conditions, the other for likely particular connections between two events' (Bruner 1986: 12). This account splits human causal thinking into two categories that we could equally call the cerebral and the procedural, although clearly they are interdependent and each can inspire the other. A strict contradistinction of this nature is problematised in ensuing chapters. However, Bruner also makes a case that, within narrative cognition, 'good' and 'gripping' and 'believable' stories will deal in 'human or human-like intention and action and the vicissitudes and consequences that mark their course' (13). In fact, for Bruner, instead of causality, exploring the vicissitudes of intention is the one true condition for stories to be stories (17).

We are always looking for intentions as they provoke us to wonder *how to act*; this suggests that ethics are the crux of narrative interest. However, we also tend to apply such readings of intention beyond the human. Bruner's analysis points to research, from Fritz Heider and Marianne Simmel in 1944 to Judith Ann Stewart in 1982, demonstrating that we read motivation and intention in abstract animated figures (Bruner 1986: 18). We thus find ourselves mapping human intentionality onto things that may not be similarly motivated (including other living things, the inhuman and posthuman, as well as nature, the cosmic, and the physical world, the origin of theistic and teleological thinking as explored by Pascal Boyer in *Religion Explained*). This meta-ethical challenge to a narrative humanism will be addressed in the following chapter, in an introduction to the philosophy of humanism.

For now, I work with the assumption that at base level, stories offer causalities, and thereafter may apply intention and motivation to causalities, which leads us to ethical pondering.

On first reflection, it almost goes without saying that offering stories – perspectives on series of causalities and intentional mapping – is adaptive, foundationally aiding survival goals including hunting prey and resisting predation, for example, or promoting group bonding and coordination, but thereafter, as immersion in a mediated environment became more extensive, our storytelling instinct splintered into countless other utilities connected to survival and thriving in the increasingly mutable social world. Story provides such a boggling array of uses, both obvious and undiscovered, that it is daunting to consider its totality. It is part of our job as analysts in the humanities to exhume far-reaching concepts of what story can do, and for some scholars (myself included) to make our own inferences about how stories can serve us better to reduce suffering and promote equality, globally and without prejudice. For the past century has taught us, if nothing else, that such ambitions are realistic and achievable, as Edward Said insists in *Humanism and Democratic Criticism*:

> People all over the world can be and are moved by ideals of justice and equality – the South African victory in the liberation struggle is a perfect case in point – and the affiliated notion that humanistic ideals of liberty and learning still supply most disadvantaged people with the energy to resist unjust war and military occupation, for instance, and to try to overturn despotism and tyranny, both strike me as ideas that are alive and well. And despite the (in my opinion) shallow but influential ideas of a certain facile type of radical antifoundationalism, with its insistence that real events are at most linguistic effects, and its close relative, the end-of-history thesis, these are so contradicted by the historical impact of human agency and labor as to make a detailed refutation of them here unnecessary. Change is human history, and human history as made by human action and understood accordingly is the very ground of the humanities. (2004: 10)

There is indeed evidence that real positive change has been made over the years in which we have been engaged with humanist thinking, redeeming belief in human autonomy and progress toward a vast mutual benefit. According to Charles R. Varela, the last century's history of emergent social sciences is also the history of reclaiming faith in a human agency for positive change (2009: ix). I start from the assumption that storytelling entails responsibility, and that improvements can be made to the narratives we distribute (as well as our theories of narrative purpose) that will promote mutual care and prosociality – thence a focus on narrative ethics. Humanism is a kind of hope, and hope presupposes agency to make positive changes in the world, even if the blueprint is elusive, even if we fight about what that blueprint should be. As such, this book presupposes *analysable* human agency. Further, it requests specificity about the conditions of change in lieu of totalising answers to unresolvable questions of free will, or insistence on intellectual attendance to its limitations.[5] With theory we have the power to imagine new ways of living; some of these imaginings will come to fruition.

Not long ago I became aware that a lot of the narratives I enjoyed were consistently nominated by analysts as human or humanistic dramas, however when perusing the literature on humanism's philosophical lineage, the two appeared to have little in common. I became intrigued by the space between the humanisms I had read about, and the potential for a narrative humanism – what was the relationship between the two? This work is in part an attempt to shine a light on that space, but it is also both a descriptive and demonstrative argument for narrative humanism's utility today. The book comes in four parts: the first two comprise a theoretical description of narrative-based humanism and its associated ethics, while the latter two are an application, demonstrating narrative humanism's use in a particular case study.

In Part I of this book, I expand on histories of narrative theory and humanism to locate and detail a humanist hermeneutics, its reasoning and methodology. Part II provides a social narratology – a list, as comprehensive as possible, of narrative's social usages, highlighting the ways in which these functions of narrative may be of interest to a humanist narrative theorist. The theories developed in the first two parts are then put into practice in the latter half of the book. I apply an emergent humanist narratological paradigm to my primary case study in Part III: the American suburban ensemble dramedy film after the turn of the millennium, historicising this cinematic mode, tracing its development, and extrapolating some of the concerns this cinema raises, before moving closer into a reading of an early exemplary film, *Parenthood* (Ron Howard, 1989), in Part IV. I use 'social narratology' to describe inquiry into the social functions of narrative, and 'humanist hermeneutics' to describe the means for reading and evaluating specific works. Together, I abbreviate this discourse to 'narrative humanism', connoting the range of humanist examinations available in the storytelling arts.

In this way I am attempting a demonstrative application of narrative humanism by magnifying it to ever closer readings, suggestive of its scope: humanist hermeneutics are applied to storytelling at large, then a specific genre often described as 'humanistic', offering analytic readings of films within that genre, and finally a close reading of a prototypical film. I hope to communicate narrative humanism's use in capturing detail at many levels of the study of human interaction, and craft the present book into an exciting narrative itself, magnifying its detail as I progress through broad theoretical understandings to situated close study. The latter half primarily concerns film analysis as an example of humanistic story reading. I agree with Murray Smith that 'film theory has, throughout its history, overstated the significance of the specificity of film as a medium and consequently underplayed the extent to which fiction films perform the same imaginative functions as fictions in other media' (1995b: 113–14), and so I will regularly draw from fields outside of film theory in analysing film. Classical narratology has changed shape in the age of media convergence (Jenkins 2006: 2) and a new field has opened up, seeking to integrate awareness of a changing media landscape into narrative theory, as in volumes like *Storyworlds Across Media* in 2014 (Ryan and Thon). I believe that it is best to analyse narratives *as they are used* by their creators and consumers in order to determine their social meaning. This means respecting the ways people choose to work with, negotiate through, and relate to each other using stories – narrative function – even while we emphasise medium specificity and question differences in meaning across media.

Finally, the humanism I refer to must be swiftly severed from universalising, essentialist or exceptionalist claims enshrining a truer humanity. We must be careful not to universalise a particular storied language use, as various languages contain different causal emphases: sentence construction in the native west Canadian Nuu-chah-nulth (Nootka) language, for example, is uniquely dependent on articulation of the cause of an action, event or property, where in English we can construct sentences without referring to causes. It is, in many cases, impossible to translate directly between these languages. For now, where I refer to humanism, I could briefly summarise the perspective as the presumption that we *can have* a more complex or deeper understanding of human otherness, the conviction that in striving to complicate our concept of others we are able to improve our social and political relations, and in my case, in narrative humanism, the notion that we use storytelling as a primary means for facilitating this more realistically complicated view of others, which in turn allows for more inclusive and specific ethical considerations. As

I believe it is misguided to attempt narrative or textual readings without first asking what the stories are used for, and equally misguided to speak of narrative's function without recourse to specific examples, the following chapter is dedicated to unpacking and clarifying humanist hermeneutics, and thereby providing a foundation from which to begin the taxonomic work of social narratology.

Notes

1. Perhaps this is why, in Marie-Laure Ryan's view, the meaning of 'narrative' has been diluted into concepts including 'belief', 'value', 'experience', 'interpretation', or simply 'content' (2006: 6); because all of these things rely on a mental causality that narrative does not quite copy, but simply *is*.
2. This is not to deny that we have thoughts, dispositions and convictions that are acausal; causality is simply our provision of meaning, how we develop and justify those thoughts, dispositions and convictions.
3. Cf. Fivush's 2006 work with Catherine A. Haden and Elaine Reese 'Elaborating on Elaborations'.
4. Note that many of these discussions are centred on American cultural contingencies. Where Nelson assumes a societal trend in American 'personalisation of culture' (2003: 133), variously labelled the individualist or narcissistic trend in popular debate, McAdams contends, 'All societies have their share of generative adults. Americans are likely to be no more or less generative than any other people' (2006: 96) although the manifestation of self-narratives will differ between cultures.
5. Fundamentally, this is a difference of focus: humanism focuses on locating and describing the conditions of human change rather than stasis. Writers after a Foucauldian constructivist tradition have complicated notions of agency, instead preferring to emphasise how our identities are inherited or governed. Problem identification alone yields no template for living, however – humanism demands that after the complexity of a cultural problem is identified, we extend ourselves to look for ethical solutions. Failure to search for such an agency permits theory to self-sustain in tandem with the circumstances it describes. I refer to John Dewey's 'first-rate test' of value in any philosophy: 'does it end in conclusions which, when they are referred back to ordinary life-experiences and their predicaments, render them more significant, more luminous to us, and make our dealings with them more fruitful?' (1958: 7). We cannot end with problem description alone.

PART I
HUMANIST HERMENEUTICS

CHAPTER 1

Reading the Human Drama in Film and Fiction

If I mention the study of humanism, what am I talking about? As a reader, it would be hard to say; too often we read of humanism without any clarifying annotations. We could be discussing Renaissance pedagogy, or deliberating on the intercession of divinity and 'man'; we might be wondering if there are essential or stable properties one could nominate as human nature, perhaps a higher order to the human extending beyond pure materialism, or an agency particular to humans; we could even refer to humanism's precursors in pre-Christian concepts of reason, in Plato, Aristotle and the Stoics, in Greek *paideia* and Roman *studium* (Torrance 2001: 164). In these early philosophies we witness the precursors to Friedrich Immanuel Niethammer's foundational humanist pedagogy – a promotion of the study of humanities sustaining long after its vivication during the Renaissance, and retaining its key place in universities today, often summarised as 'humanistic inquiry'. As Said points out, the purist canonical protectionism of eminent literary scholars such as Harold Bloom takes this usage of the term to its absolutist extreme in expressing the idea that there is one true corpus of classics, which should be studied to enrich the human (Said 2004: 27). No matter what we think of canonical humanism and Bloom's work, however, the question of human value in art, and thus relativist trends in assessing the worth of art, is part of humanist dialogue.

Then again, increasingly in popular usage now, humanism appears spuriously distinct from atheism. Robert M. Torrance positions this extrapolation from secular humanism as a kind of shibboleth, along with its contemporary connotations to a 'vague humanness or humanitarianism' (2001: 165) which ignores Christian humanism and the substantial role the church played in developing a humanist pedagogy in the Renaissance. In light of recent popular usage, though, the project of unifying humanist philosophy with the sciences appears complete. In fact the popular secular affinity with human sciences makes sense when working from the conception of humanism as the ethical imperative to defer to human complexity, as science is never complete – each question uncovers new possible deeper understandings to be accessed by further inquiry, where fideism offers a holistic explanation that is an end in itself. Faith can lock us off from further inquiry and thereby complication of our understanding of others, hence the hostility toward religion displayed by humanist rationalists. And then again, it is possible when I say humanism that I mean something entirely less Euronormative. Scholars such as Lenn E. Goodman in *Islamic Humanism* (2003), Hamid Dabashi in *The World of Persian Literary Humanism* (2012) and María Rosa Menocal in *The Arabic Role in Medieval Literary History* (1987) make the point that there are plenty of examples of humanist thought outside of Europe even before Renaissance humanism. Ken Seigneurie's work clearly identifies a progression to what he calls Arab humanism in contemporary literature (2005: 109), while conversely Ziauddin Sardar and Merryl Wyn Davies (2010) characterise the early humanist movement as 'a reaction against Muslim learning'. Emily Apter's reading of a new Saidian Welt-humanism moots 'that humanism itself be rezoned to avoid misleading cartographic divisions between European and non-European' (2004: 52). While it is not hard to locate instances of Niethammer's *Humanismus*, Francesco Petrarch's epochal Renaissance Catholic pedagogy in *Secretum*, or even the explicit educational liberalism of Wilhelm von Humboldt – humanism's antecedents – used as tools of oppression, this 'flattening [of] the term "humanism" and backdating it uncritically to the Renaissance' (Mousley 2007: 19) wilfully ignores diversity and inconsistency in early modern concepts of human essentialism, sovereignty and individualism, as well as 'original humanism's disruption of the institution- and elite-centred middle ages' (Holland 2013: 6). It also overlooks the new humanism of scholars including Said, Seigneurie and Goodman emergent today, motivating the concept in projects of inclusion and social equity.

I prefer to begin from Murray Bookchin's defence of humanist conviction in *Re-Enchanting Humanity*: 'the serious thinker must look beyond the "real" to speculate *what should be* rather than validate *what is*' (1995: 258). If this is a pragmatic ethic to start from in encouraging progressive thought, it should also be true of the language we use to describe that thought. In this case, it would be important to define how humanism might be discursively useful, looking forward, rather than assert one true Humanism of yore.

In both popular and scholarly film discourse, the descriptor 'humanistic drama' appears to signify something else again. It is my intention in this book to locate a contemporary humanist narrative theory that draws from these philosophies in order to sketch the parameters of an on-screen humanism, and suggest a hermeneutic sensibility that may result. It is also my intent to use humanist theory more common in the history of literary studies and apply it to film theory. In cinema the humanistic drama – or 'human drama' – connotes an attempt to replicate the complexity of human sociality in fiction. Yet this gives rise to certain questions: whose complexity is represented, and how do we decide what complexity is? There is also the problem of fabricated complexity, in that complex explanations do not always reach more truthful or verifiable conclusions. For example, we may have a complex reason to explain a social phenomenon, but we can still be verifiably wrong about its causes; or we may have a complex explanation for another's behaviour, but again, we can still be wrong about their motivation. Complexity does not equal truth, and we can construct complexity anew rather than finding it in the world. Noël Carroll objected to a confounding assembly of semiotics, psychoanalysis and Marxism in 1988's *Mystifying Movies*, for example, and Karl Popper called into question the unfalsifiability of Marx, Freud and Adler in 1963's *Conjectures and Refutations* (1963: 34–5), yet suppositions drawn from their works sustain as the leading mode of evaluation in film theory. Assessing whether or not a complex portrayal of human sociality, in theory or in fictional representation, is fabricated mystification or truly reveals reliable human detail is the trickiest component in humanist hermeneutics. Once again, recourse to human sciences helps us to achieve such assessments, but more on science later.

Humanising the Other

If humanism has a significant challenge in scholarly thought at the moment, it is less an antihumanist attack on human autonomy for positive, progressive or even transhuman change – it is the idea of the posthuman. We cannot say with certainty that we know the parameters of the human; we cannot any longer agree on what a human actually is, suggesting it may be an inadequate concept to start from in understanding the workings of the world. In his book *The Posthuman Condition* Robert Pepperell suggests that we cannot pretend the mind is synonymous with human identity. Neuron activity defines the mind, yet we also have neurons in our stomach – in this case we must consider our stomach a human entity (Pepperell 2003: 93–7, for a more sensitive analysis of what we might call the 'mind-tummy' problem). As we discover more parasites, pathogens and other microbes that have significant effects on our behaviour, often co-adaptive behavioural influences (Moalem and Satonick 2007), concepts of human selfhood again come under scrutiny.[1] Also, if we use machines as ambassadors for our thought – recording our ideas on a computer, for instance, which will go on to represent a version of our thoughts – we are already in a position whereby we cannot easily separate our mind and the machine (and so the extended mind becomes a posthumanism). This conceptualisation of cultural symbol as akin to life, however, is similar to memetics, which has been contradicted by geneticists including Eva Jablonka and Marion J. Lamb, as memes do not contain information of themselves: 'In each case the organism (or group) actively reconstructs the pattern of behaviour, or the pattern of emotions and ideas, through learning. And learning is not blind copying – it is a function- or meaning-sensitive developmental process' (2005: 209), so 'the copying mechanism is not independent of what is copied' (210). Thus it remains problematic to assume non-living ambassadors for our thought have life akin to our own.

Nor have we ever been able to pinpoint exactly where life begins or ends. Japanese researchers have recently announced the creation of the first artificial copper sulphide synapse with little fanfare (Nayak et al. 2012), perhaps making the posthumanist discussion all the more urgent. David Boyle rejects notions of human–machine indivisibility, however: 'The truth is that only if you define humanity as a simple matter of data processing can you ever believe that human beings and machines are alike' (2003: 200). He goes on to critique the cybernetic totalism of Donna Haraway's 'Manifesto for Cyborgs':

> There is fatalism to this debate – as if those who believe there is no difference between real and virtual, being alive and being 'better than well', and no such thing as irony or intimacy or partiality, are somehow bound to win . . . yet we have retained enough of a sense of ourselves to feel nostalgic about the idea of real relationships, real sex, real passion, real bank managers, face-to-face public services, that we have created an underground backlash in their favour. Artificial intelligence is just that: it's artificial. 'Intelligence' has become just a metaphor – and the prophets of AI are like religious fundamentalists in the way they *mistake their metaphors for real descriptions of the world* . . . people are reacting against this kind of reductionism. The closer the AI people get, the more authenticity becomes the critical concept at the heart of culture. (202, emphasis added)

So despite the excitement of such transhuman idylls, there is an observable movement pulling us back toward some notion of authenticity: a real that recognises something more than just *known* data, an unreachable complexity that posthuman daydreamers – resurrecting a Galilean mechanistic theism[2] – deign to conquer with a comforting reduction of human ambiguities to the consistent machine.

As intriguing and urgent as the posthuman ethical debate may be, I would like to suggest a way of looking at the human that makes it possible to move beyond the ontology and semantics of the human entity. We can embrace the *fluidity* of the human mind and form at the same time as acknowledging that the human is *what we have to work with*, even if its parameters cannot be known or subject to essentialist certainty. We cannot sample another reality beyond that dictated by the recurring, evolving natural pattern of the human form and the perspective (obviously limited, as Pepperell stresses) it allows. The fact that the human is fluid should not dismiss our striving to understand this perspective and how it works – we must still be able to discuss concepts and entities without reference to essential properties, or all argument devolves to the same ontological impasse.[3] Humanism is, instead, a kind of methodological naturalism: we proceed with the understanding of the unknowable nature of reality, but it behoves us to accept these limitations and make decisions based on our experience of what is real. At the same time we understand our phenomenal perspective will always be bound to our experience as a human. In deeply understanding other things, thus, we 'humanise' them. In effect, anthropomorphising is all that we can do to understand the experience of a life not our own. 'Humanising the other' involves a projection of what it might be like to be another entity; we need the imaginative process, this kind of anthropomorphising, in order to incorporate other living things into any system of personal moral accountability, including fellow humans, nonhuman entities and indistinct entities like animals and, for some, machines – we consistently need to imagine what it is like to be them in order to accept them as worthy of ethical inclusion. Normative ethics and this variety of humanism can, then, begin to look like the same thing – the indivisibility of ethical culture and humanism is acknowledged by one of the largest international bodies representing the movement, the International Humanist and Ethical Union. It is perhaps useful to look at humanism as the philosophy around the reasons for foregrounding ethical discussions; the emphasis on ethics results from a humanist position.

While it is fallacious to suggest we also have a science that can reliably summarise the mysteries of empathic modelling and projection, we should at least acknowledge that we are referring to a cognitive process. This is why humanism inquires into the experience of empathy with an emphasis on the social sciences rather than metaphysics or speculative ontology. We can have 'humanism without the human' and an 'ethics without metaphysics' (Sheehan 2002: 64).

So our process of understanding other things has to involve some amount of projection. Our imaginative capacities cannot exist in a vacuum:

they are ordered by our own experience – that is, human experience. To comprehend a narrative, we immediately try to connect its events with our own recollected experiences; in this way empathy is an act that innately works from introspection. This is an insurmountable position, and no amount of lip service to the erroneous centrality of the imagined panhuman, Umwelt or qualia, can shift us into seeing wholly as another sees. In Erica Fudge's notion of inevitable anthropocentrism, Francis Bacon's 'false mirror, which, receiving rays irregularly, distorts and discolours the nature of things by mingling its own nature with it' (Bacon [1620] 1996: 54) is 'natural to the human mind and therefore impossible to dismiss' (Fudge 2002: 5). The human is central because for all of us bar none, the human perspective is what we have to work with, and what we then must study to comprehend the moral behaviours and quandaries we foreground as cultural theorists. Or, as Adam Smith put it, 'I judge of your sight by my sight, of your ear by my ear, of your reason by my reason, of your resentment by my resentment, of your love by my love. I never have, nor can have, any other way of judging about them' ([1759] 2002: 23).

As in Fudge's work on early modern English drama, attention to the values of Renaissance humanists reveals disapproval levelled at the killing of both people, in a militaristic sense, and animals, in the crown hunt. See in particular Michel de Montaigne's essay *Of Cruelty*, which by its radically personal nature demonstrates a humanistic departure in opinion writing: the essay form elevates a nascent phenomenological description and resultant empathy into philosophy. Here, analogising human and animal suffering does not necessarily promote the human above other living things, as in much religious doctrine prior to the Renaissance, but instead is a necessary condition of liberalising compassion. In Shakespeare's *As You Like It*, for example, Jacques is reported to lament a deer killed during a pastoral hunt. However, he first imagines himself as *like* the deer, their melancholy and outrage at human incivility being one and the same, and makes elegiac use of metaphors linking the deer's situation to various contexts in human cultures. Despite the deer clearly not possessing these human qualities, the imaginative leap permits Jacques access to an empathy he could not otherwise entertain, as human culture is his only framework for understanding any suffering, and in turn such imagination translates to (extremely performative) compassion. This language 'shows that [Jacques and Duke Senior] can only feel animal suffering when it is imagined as human suffering, a response that might be said to deny the reality and authenticity of animal experience' (Berry 2001: 176). Yet what is the alternative? Is it direct access to a real or authentic animal experience? As this is impossible, Shakespeare instead explores problems with our attempts at human–animal and civility–nature delineation. Even in early humanist thinking, compassion begins from imaginatively and speculatively connecting our experience to the experience of other things – our own (human) vantage is the only tool we have for reaching compassion, with respect to its limitations. Thereafter we can attempt to push against these limitations by learning more about the context, the ecology and biology of the other, but this will still in turn be unpacked by human pattern-seeking perception.

Consequently, if this is all we can do, it is better to have more complex modelling and projection of others, which should lead to better decision-making in collective matters. So we come to ask what it is that storytelling and the storytelling arts offer in this process. The simple answer is that story can complicate our conception of others in revealing ways. Imagining the experience of another entity, be it another person in a remote location or circumstance, or an animal to be slaughtered for consumption, is going to lead to superior ethical judgments about our engagement with them the more nuanced and realistic our understanding of their circumstance – this is, for example, what social realism has sought to provide for the underprivileged. As Brian Boyd puts it:

> Narrative especially helps coordinate groups, by informing their members of one another's actions. It spreads prosocial values, the likeliest to appeal to both tellers and listeners. It develops our capacity to see from different perspectives, and this capacity in turn both arises from and aids the evolution of cooperation and the growth of human mental flexibility. (2009: 176)[4]

Although his analysis foregrounds the role of gossip in social accountability structures, he does go on to suggest, 'But maximum flexibility, in humans as in others, depends on play' (176). In cinema ethics, this process puts to practical work Stanley Cavell's cinema-as-quotidian-philosophising reclaimed from rarefied establishments: 'the latest of the great arts, [showing] philosophy to be the often invisible accompaniment of the ordinary lives that film is so apt to capture' (2004: 6). If we are to evaluate responses to ethical problems beyond those presented by direct interaction with others in our immediate community, we need hypothetical characters: fiction. Writers such as Alex Neill consider empathy for actual persons and fictional characters as one and the same, as projection of the feelings of another is, in essence, always an imaginative act (2006: 257). Hypothetical empathic subjects do not represent the totality of storytelling's place in our lives, of course – stories are much more powerful than that – but these are the functions of storytelling a humanist may be interested in.

Much storytelling that fosters group cohesion equally defines that cohesion in relation to outgroup members, in some cases by vilifying them; think of *Jud Süß* (Veit Harlan, 1940), or political and religious quasi-historical narratives that nominate a 'chosen people'. Humanistic narrative, on the other hand, adopts plural perspectives without needing to concoct an inferior opposite which they will be judged against. So if the type of story matters, then it makes sense to focus on how we might achieve kinder stories – the conditions of storytelling responsibility – and evaluative claims are available to be made. Thence the humanistic focus on human kindness. If humanistic scholars omit the study of such storied kindnesses in favour of hermeneutic admonishments levelled at narrativised bigotry and the cultures that produce it, then we will never learn the conditions under which kinder narratives flourish.[5] This points to a politics of emphasis that circulates philosophical discussions around humanism and antihumanism. Kwame Anthony Appiah refers to the negotiation of 'value terms, meant to shape our responses to the movie. And if the story it tells is truly representative, our discussion of it will help us decide not only what we feel about the characters but how we should act in the world' (2006: 29). Thus, he says of film, 'It keeps our vocabulary of evaluation honed, ready to do its work in our lives. And that work, as I say, is first to help us act together' (30). After grappling with the way cosmopolitanism might deal with the antihumanist charge of normalising humanity and disregarding human difference – with regard to the problems in Jacques Derrida's 'decentred subject' (Schwartz 1990: 33) – Appiah settles for the fact that this 'acting together' after discussion cannot be a reprehensible moral aim, despite its imperfectability.[6] We can locate complex understanding of both similarities and differences in the experience of the other without needing to refer to human exceptionalism or requiring differences to be quelled; indeed, wonder at difference and similarity alike is an important part of comprehension.

There is a lack of vulnerability and humility in much poststructural and antihumanist theory that humanism may seek to recover. A humanist alternative might proffer vulnerability as a necessary condition of discovery, and attempts to reach between people to forge connections, which may then avoid the worst of intrahuman cynicism (bigotry, violence, objectification, oppression). Humility, in this case, is the attribute by which we might access vulnerability, and learn of the new. As Said put it, the 'possibility of a critical understanding that may never be completed but can certainly be provisionally affirmed . . . there can be heroic first readings that enable many others after them' (2004: 67–8). All of these alternatives require imaginative empathic effort, flawed and culturally contingent as these processes may be. Recognising this imperfection, we begin to emphasise the *effort* people put into complex comprehension. To extend this to an ethic: we try to connect our experiences to complex otherness despite barriers or boundaries – we do the best we can.

Similar values can be seen put to use in anthropology. As in mainstream anthropological method, we empathise with disparate people and cultures, not to adopt their perspective (which is impossible), but to learn the complexities and nuances of their being, which allows us to work together from an enhanced intersubjective comprehension. But crucially, this does not invalidate any ethical debate. In other words, *suspending* moral judgment in order to listen and learn – what Edmund Husserl called the 'phenomenological epoché' (1962: 91–100) and is now referred to as 'bracketing' – does not preclude later resolution on moral issues. In participant observation, or the fieldwork prior to an ethnography, a kind of methodological relativism is employed to learn from other peoples: 'a commitment to suspending moral judgment until an attempt can be made to understand another culture's beliefs and practices in their full cultural, material, and historical contexts' (Turner 1997: 275). This method appears to me equally applicable to narrative theory, as stories are culturally produced. We can apply this listening method to distant peoples whose lives are affected by our decisions, niche communities within one's own vicinity, and even one's immediate family members and peers, as all people have their own distinctive experiential heritage to consider, which they tell of in storied communication. In fact, it is a central tenet of narrative humanism that this empathic work can be performed not just in understanding distant others, but proximate others, too; the latter half of this volume interrogates attempts to understand the otherness of those closest to us in Western domestic settings, and takes as a case study the methods filmmakers have developed to represent conflicts and their resolution across a diversity of personhood in American suburbia. The case study of the suburban ensemble dramedy elaborates on humanism in its propinquitous iterations.

The self-reflection and introspection required in such an anthropological method can form an integral part of textual readings. C. Jason Throop expresses the concept thus:

> It is by means of just such a vulnerable, passive and open orientation to another that we are able to confront some of our most deeply ingrained assumptions about ourselves, our world, and those others with whom we interact. In so doing we are able to envision new horizons of experience. To be compelled by another to interrupt our tendency to assimilate experience to the self-sameness of our being, we thus become opened to possibilities for seeing other ways of being that are not, and yet may never be, our own. (2010: 281–2)

Anthropology is, like the storytelling arts and debates around stories, just one kind of humanism in practice. Its heritage of progressively overcoming descriptions that minimise another's humanity, like the notion of the 'primitive', speaks to the self-correcting function of the anthropological method, in that striving for close listening to others can only lead to a more generously complex understanding of their being and their context.

Close attendance to another's perspective is the same as a good story: we risk losing ourselves in its liminal space, we allow ourselves to forget a little of our own lives and concerns, and when we emerge we reconstruct a sense of self to include the disturbances we found so rattling in the implications of the narrative. This pleasure of deep listening involves risk, as we have to allow ourselves to become unbound, no longer whole, to truly admit new knowledge and perspectives. The pleasure is curtailed the less we can admit the inherent self-doubt of coming unbound – we have less to re-evaluate, and so less to gain. Thus all close listening, all real attendance to what others are doing and saying, entails considerable existential risk (Ingold 2014: 389), the vulnerability and humility of assuming doubt rather than projecting it.[7] However, we can never truly let go of our values or our sense of self; we just attempt to take one another seriously by undoing our expectations inasmuch as possible, a courtesy of mutual intersubjective benefit, of learning and allowing others the space to express what they know without the restriction of our preconvictions. So again, we value the attempt, or the work put in, rather than the ideal.

In a sense, humanism always fails. Its project can never be complete as we are never able to be completely inclusive of all human otherness at once, just as we can never completely comprehend another human. Christine Gardner commented in *Anthropology and Humanism* that humanistic ethnography 'lays bare the possibility of partial understanding . . . by allowing discord in the record, by resisting closure for closure's sake, by forsaking completeness for clarity's sake' (1994: 166–7). No narrative will be able to contain due consideration of all relevant humanness. For example, we always have the opportunity to focus on those symbolically omitted from any given narrative, and we tend to use this as an evaluative shortcut: does the narrative represent a true spectrum of sexualities, ethnicities, economic statuses? As the ideal of representing an entire spectrum of human difference is impossible, we place emphasis on *efforts* to comprehend otherness, not the goal of pure comprehension of otherness. This resignation to constant failure and refinement, the relinquishing of ideals in favour of the utility of the attempt, is another source of vulnerability and humility in humanism – it is a narratival kindness.

Character Complexity and Elaboration on the Attempt

When answering a question such as 'why do we tell stories?' we often run the risk of totalising, offering monocausal or telic accounts to serve a thesis. My purpose here is to offer one small corner of the myriad utilities performed through story in human evolution, and in our daily lives. Identifying complexity in our interactions, allowing some awe in the immensity of human systems we cannot totalise, and yoking such an awe to discover more about ourselves, are substantial components in the contemporary humanist project. Often this has been summarised as engaging 'wonder' (Bookchin 1995) in our fellow human.

As such, when addressing questions regarding what character complexity is made up of and why it matters so much, I offer the following response: perhaps there is a place we can reach which both strives to uncover ever more complex human detail (narrativised social and psychological causalities) and derives self-sustaining, generous wonderment from the interminability and incompleteness of this project. We might call this 'human excess'. Clearly there are many kinds of effortful cognition that creative fictions inspire in attempts to complexify our thinking on a variety of concerns, and in this section I turn to elucidate some of their differences. Yet as human excess is foundational to humanistic narrative concerns, I begin by identifying its dispositional humility of unknowing – that in any attempt to represent a complex human system it is still not possible to conceive of all its relevant causal detail together – from which most human dramas themselves begin. The anthropologist Michael D. Jackson marries Theodor Adorno's untruth of identity in *Negative Dialectics* (1973) with John Berger's observations on ineffability and story: 'If every event which occurred could be given a name, there would be no need for stories. As things are here, life outstrips our vocabulary' (1992: 64). From these underpinnings he draws his own existential-humanist concept of human excess in the story arts:

> Concepts represent experience at the cost of leaving a lot unsaid. So long as we use concepts to cut up experience, giving value to some things at the expense of others, we inhibit our sense of the plenitude of Being. We gain some purchase on the world, to be sure, but claiming that our concepts contain all that can be usefully said about experience, we close off the possibility of critique ... writers approach the world so tortuously and obliquely, using 'inept metaphors and obvious paraphrases' to draw attention to a subject they are unwilling to name. It is their way of recognizing that life eludes our grasp and remains at large, always fugitive. (Jackson 1995: 5)[8]

Beyond such a literary surrender to the ineffability of experience lies an affective and intellectual zone reachable by fiction, which does not forfeit knowledge collation but the very unfinished business of it all excites its pursuit: a seeking to represent ever more accurately, through the consilience of new sciences, observation and experience, as much as we are able to truthfully express about life.

Here, multi-causality becomes key in explaining character complexity. No one can claim to have such knowledge of people that they can create a character that is like a human, rather than a constellation of ideas about a human. Characters are, after all, constellations of ideas. But once this is acknowledged, what we can do is offer ideas about the human multitudinous and multi-causal enough that they simultaneously offer insightful perspectives to discuss, and yet also allow us to keep in mind human excess, engaging the aforementioned wonder at our unreachable complexity. The same is true of our peers: we comprehend them as constellations of attributes to which we have emotional responses, but if we are honest, we never quite trust our necessary reductions to discrete explainable details (of motivation, of personality and so on) as truly representing the sum of their identity. This openness is a humanist disposition – we can retain such a generosity of thought even as we construct internal models to imaginatively map their individual and social complexities. If complex understanding of peers corresponds with interest in complex fictive characters, however, is the reverse necessarily also true, and is our engagement with complex fiction transferrable in some way to our conception of others in the real world? Various researchers have attempted to measure the complexity of our understanding of peers against the complexity of comprehension of fictional characters. One such researcher, Susan D. Hynds, found that:

> curiosity about and understanding of people in everyday life is a strong component in the understanding and enjoyment of literature. Further, since developmental studies have established that construct repertoires can indeed be expanded throughout a lifetime, literature provides a vehicle for enlarging students' understanding of the people they are likely to encounter in the social world ... The reading of literature, then, demands a flexibility, an openness, and a willingness to perceive strange people and novel events in all of their multiplicity and dimensionality. (1985: 399)

Given the limitations of such studies, we still employ some conjecture about the nature of this generalizability, but surely there is an observable transfer as we use story to discuss life, and these discussions should be more detailed, more specific, the more detail and specificity is provided to discuss.

The focus on character complexity in film theory is quite different, with a tendency to be more procedural in nature, clarifying narrative techniques more than overall effects. Michael Z. Newman attempted to delineate the differences between narrative and character complexity in comparing the puzzle film *21 Grams* (Alejandro González Iñárritu, 2003) with human drama *Passion Fish* (John Sayles, 1992), concluding on a difference in the focus of our problem-solving cognition:

> unlike *21 Grams*, *Passion Fish* is not the kind of film that makes its audience puzzle out its story moment by moment. The spectator watching the opening scenes of *21 Grams* asks, What is going on? The spectator watching the opening scenes of *Passion Fish* is shown much of what is going on and is free to think about the characters, settings, and themes in more detail and with more intensity. (2006: 93)

After exploring some of the means for developing character complexity in *Passion Fish* (which point to the social multi-causality of ensemble casts), such as loading information about primary characters, reversing our assumptions of their 'types,' and the introduction of minor characters (103), Newman goes on to make a value judgement that elevates the human drama: 'The contrast with *21 Grams* should be clear. A narrative that starts out in confusion is most likely to become clearer, less problematic. But a narrative that starts out simple has the opportunity of developing in the direction of intensified interest, of accumulating sophistication' (104). There may be many kinds of narrative complexity, all of worth in different ways, but we can be engaged with cognitive puzzles which matter internally to narrative comprehension, or illuminate character points which make us think differently about people. Finally, Newman makes a claim that due to their trajectory from clarity to questioning, human dramas provoke a more substantially thoughtful afterlife: '*21 Grams* makes unusual cognitive demands as it unfolds, as it makes itself difficult to understand initially. But *Passion Fish* makes you think when it ends' (105). Such 'character points' might not lead to obvious or ethically unconditional conclusions about how to behave – a straightforward moral. However, if sufficiently complexified, character considerations do fill out a background to our ethical lives by reminding us of the enormity of variation in circumstance and personality implicated in our daily decisions.

This state of openness to otherness should not be viewed as an attainable, conscious permanency; it might only be reachable every now and again. It does not make cognitive sense to sit suspended in a state of expansive acceptance of human complexity, without action or application, without the usual cognitive strains of going about one's day – again, we must be careful to avoid chimeric ideals. Perhaps narrative can simply act as a reminder that such openness to human detail should be called upon when making decisions that affect others. If we are to make the distinction between narrative and character complexity as Newman has done, this may also be what we refer to as narrative complexity: too many concepts conveyed for us to get our head around all together and at once, the excitement of ineffability, intellectual striving and the capacity for new knowledge it brings (clearly accessible by narrative modes outside the human drama, too). So perhaps a final humanistic function of story is not just to suggest human excess epistemologically, but in the limitations of our cognition too. Perhaps we need both social simulation to discuss ethical particularities, and reminders that our simulations will always be inadequate to explain the complex multi-causality that is life.

The Use of Science in Analysis

If we are to continue referring to a 'realistic' complexity, we need to check the veracity of our claims to realism before proceeding. As mentioned above, it is a fallacy to assume an explanation is correct simply because it is complex, so we cannot conclude the project of humanism merely in complexifying our visions of human otherness – we still must ask who gets to decide what is 'realistically complex'? This is the arbitrating purpose of scientific method. Not because all methods calling themselves science are unimpeachable (pseudoscience uses the language of science without the method), but because attempts at the impartial gathering of empirical evidence are the best means we have for ascertaining the validity of a claim – and so this should be equally applicable to claims made by philosophers within the humanities. Many of us use (limited) social science in arts evaluation without even acknowledging that we are doing it: pointing out how American filmmaking fails to include certain demographically relevant groups, for example, relies on impartially gathered data on such demographics. Advances in the natural sciences are gradually subsumed into a general conception of the world philosophers describe. But we can do more. Regressing to a purist notion of realism or the real is precisely what bothers most antihumanists, as it allegedly offers opportunities to invalidate the subjective experience of others, but some notion of reality from which to work is unavoidable. This often means referring to experimental science, a deferring to the expertise of well-researched others to mediate one's view of humans and their sociality; it seems to me that such a practice conversely opens us up to further intersubjective potentialities rather than limiting them. This is not the kind of positivism or scientism philosophers like Popper object to (in *The Logic of Scientific Discovery*, *The Poverty of Historicism* and *Conjectures and Refutations*), whereby the natural sciences can be extended to moral blueprints, teleological certitude and prognostication, or represent the sum of meaningful human thought, but merely the assertion that evidence gathered by others should be a backdrop to our conception and evaluation of human activities, including narrative production. Sometimes we put ourselves above this process, and the humanities and hermeneutics become a pseudoscience – again, the language of complexity without the method of evaluating its veracity.

Clearly there are some observations that cannot be referred to empirical evidence, and measurable data does not represent all that is worthwhile approaching in narrative – but these facts should not excuse narrative theorists from building familiarity with the science around their subject. (Nor can demarcation problems in the social sciences – sometimes called 'pre-science' as opposed to 'hard' science, drawing from Wilhelm Dilthey's initial problem of methodological difference in *Geisteswissenschaft* and *Naturwissenschaft* – permit us to dismiss the knowledge and expertise of researchers working outside of the natural sciences; for example, we cannot ignore evidence in psychology simply because of a knowledge categorisation problem.) At worst, these two truisms – the ineffable and the unquantifiable – are given as excuses to dismiss any evidence contradicting a favoured theory. While 'life outstrips our vocabulary' (Berger 1992: 64), perhaps providing the need for stories, it simply is not true that the narrative arts exclusively explore the space that science cannot reach. Much of the social detail that can be broached in narrative has been equally studied outside of creative practice. To suggest otherwise smacks of poorly conducted research, or willing oversight. Nor does it reduce the impact of arts, but rather the extra richness of detail gleaned in attention to the expertise of others matches a richer experience of narrative engagement, evaluation, and creation.

In cinema studies in particular, after Bordwell and Carroll we have seen a blossoming of cognitivist approaches, with a few, such as Joseph D. Anderson in *The Reality of Illusion* (1996), attempting a union of cognitive and evolutionary approaches to explain film perception. Following contentions around the discovery and relevance of mirror neurons, it seemed to some cognitivists 'preposterous to claim that our capacity to reflect on the intentions, beliefs and desires determining the behaviour of others is *all there is* in social cognition' (Gallese 2007: 659), which put 'the Grand Theory rooted in semiotics and psychoanalysis in a difficult position, foreseeing the advent of a biocultural approach to cinema' (Gallese and Guerra 2012: 188). It also may be time for cinema studies to put the sociality back into social cognition, exploring the mental space between people involved with cinema rather than the isolated neurological studies of individual mental states we have relied on in the past. Thus I propose to look further afield, integrating social research around issues such as, for example, prejudice, ostracism and group dynamics into understanding the storytelling act, and the film experience. An attendance to the communal features of cinema and story does not allow us to ignore the substantial contribution fields like social psychology and evolutionary anthropology can make to the discipline.[9]

Popper contemporary Jarvie wonders why his fellow cognitive film theorists and analytic philosophers, for all their love of science, 'study and cite philosophers, not scientists' (1999: 436). Theorists can be released from *some* of the demand to directly cite scientists when dealing with questions that can have no definitive or falsifiable answer – questions of purpose, for example, or ethics – but Jarvie's imperative to reference scientists, not science in general (437), could be a helpful one in descriptive or evaluative work, or in our application of hermeneutics. However, I am primarily making a case here for a scientific backgrounding (especially in the social sciences) from which to work, not pure scientism. Such a backgrounding merely helps us avoid, inasmuch as possible, saying things that are untrue, and helps us grapple with the truth claims of others, including storytellers.

The nominal problems of science and analysis remain important. While I believe it is remiss to neglect what social sciences may tell us about story culture, I also believe it is important to recognise that our own practice – theory without testing – cannot and should not have pretence to a scientific legitimacy. When theory applies science, we cherry-pick studies to make a point, which is fine as long as the theorising is not conflated with science merely by using it as a reference. The legitimacy theory can claim is in imaginative agitation and uplift, which may be, at least in a humanistic paradigm, of equal importance in finding our way forward (ethically determining *what to do*) as the descriptive and diagnostic potentials of hard science.

Since at least 1931, figures including George Sarton and Cassius Jackson Keyser were publishing monographs in an attempt to unify humanism and science (see *The History of Science and the New Humanism* and *Humanism and Science* respectively). Humanism and science appear to me to have a natural home together as they both start from a place of unknowing rather than top-down theoretical explication – they search for knowledge rather than defend pre-existing knowledge – and they both pursue ever more complex detail and explanations for our selves and the world around us. Indeed, sometimes humanism and scientific rationalism are taken to be synonymous: the Rationalist Association, for example, publishes the *New Humanist* quarterly. As in Edward O. Wilson's version of complexity theory, the complexity of social systems is akin to the complexity of biological systems, or any other process of interaction making up the physical world, and thus emerges the possibility for a non-reductive physicalism:

> To recite one of the mantras of science, the explanations of the physical sciences are necessary but not sufficient. There is too much idiosyncrasy in the arrangement of a particular cell's nucleus and other organelles as well as the molecules composing them, and too much complexity in the cell's constantly shifting chemical exchanges with the environment, to accomplish such a conceptual traverse. And beyond these particularities awaits the still-hidden history of the prescriptive DNA, stretched across countless generations. (1999: 74)

So again, as in the diverse sciences Wilson cites, social narratologists and humanist hermeneuticians might strive for ever-greater descriptions of complex interaction with respect to our limitations (the absence of holistic causal explanation), preventing us from presuming or imposing any totalised conception of human identity, and keeping discovery alive.

Despite monistic physicalist fantasies of the explanatory powers of a oneness of sciences and associated dogma, a humanist epistemology holds that it may be dangerous to believe that our cognitive capacities can hold all meaningful information about the human together at once – from this reductive position, we will always miss deference to an infinite complexity, the acceptance of which mediates our morality and behaviour. In this case, as we will never be able to descriptively and meaningfully totalise human experience into a singular conception, we need theorists to suggest and simulate the excess beyond the sciences we already have awareness of, make imaginative connections between sciences, observe theoretical convergences and concoct hypotheses with such imagination: like story itself, imaginatively providing 'the ability to see possible formal connections before one is able to prove them in any formal way' (Bruner 1986: 13). The theorist can then challenge holistic myths by which we may act on a fallacious assumption that what we already know explains everything, or could explain everything if we just found the right data: 'knowledge is not built from facts that are simply there, waiting to be discovered and organized in terms of concepts and categories . . . it rather grows and is grown in the forge of our relations with others' (Ingold 2014: 391). Fields like film theory, in this case, can move past the necessary specialist study of minutiae to connect a macro perspective between scientific knowledges (an epistemic consilience) and allow us to imagine what to do with the diverse information received. Bruner's 'paradigmatic mode' of abstracted logic, to which science belongs, thereby forfeits its particularity in application, which imaginative and storied modes can recover. Story applies directly to our lives in a way descriptions of the world cannot – it provides the link between abstract knowledge and our lived procedures by playing out knowledge and ideas in realised scenarios. It is our abstract information applied, which subsequently generates new abstractions and new theories of life. In turn, I believe we must pay attention to those who go to test resultant theories, or we are not part of the human epistemological journey; we are obscuring it.

Antihumanism and Alternatives to Humanist Hermeneutics

So far, we have established that we must 'humanise' things to ethically include them; that this process should involve some complication of our understanding of others; that any such resultant complex understanding should be evaluated against available empirical evidence where possible, so that we know whether or not we are empathising with something complex and real rather than a fabricated or misconstrued complexity; further, that we must acknowledge any such project as always incomplete, thereby valuing the attempt to understand above total comprehension; and that storytelling, along with the evaluative work we do around stories, is a primary method for achieving these goals. I have also begun to make the case that film is well positioned to provide an experience whereby we can exercise our complex empathy for the other. This is what humanistic narratives seek to do, and what a humanist hermeneutics can evaluate.

While it is beyond the scope of this book to respond to all of the claims of the various antihumanisms, it is necessary for any narrative-based humanism to approach some of the common objections raised against a humanist hermeneutics in particular. I must reiterate that there is good reason to be sceptical of humanism, in that the term has a history of use in appeals to a universally dominant humanity, and these appeals are in turn used to deny outsiders sovereignty of cultural self-determination and identity:

The single normative foundation of humanism can be used to disqualify some human beings as less qualified to self-governance than others, based on culturally specific criteria for virtuous human behaviour. For example, the development of liberal humanism in European political discourses during the seventeenth, eighteenth and nineteenth centuries can be linked to the popular notion of the 'civilizing mission' used to legitimate colonial expansion. (Laurie 2015: 143-144)

Andy Mousley counters: 'the Renaissance has been located if not as the unprecedented source of individualism, then as a key agent in its development' (2007: 16), and yet a literary or narrative humanism drawn from early modern hope and textual inquiry, he argues, 'has little to do with the humanism which was attacked on various grounds by anti-humanists in the 1970s and 1980s, but ever since then the humanism of the anti-humanists has been routinely invoked as though it encompassed the whole of the humanist tradition' (14). He disrupts the humanist/antihumanist binary by suggesting that ideas of authenticity and ethics, what the human being is and the conditions of its flourishing or compromise,

> are present, for example, in the hope of Marxists that class exploitation and the commodification of human life might one day end. They are also implicated in post-colonialism's critique of dehumanising ideologies of race, even when or especially when such ideologies are perpetrated in the name of humanity. And they are also evident in the feminist commitment to terminate the subjugation of women by men. (11)

While some may hold that imperialism is the inevitable conclusion of all humanist philosophy, a humanism that entertains any notion of a locus for a truer humanity is not the humanism I speak of – in fact, it is a perversion of humanist discourse, if humanist discourse principally comprises, as I am proposing here, learning from others through empathy. 'The humanism of antihumanists' (Soper 1986: 18, 128; Davies 1997: 48–9) is a straw man, attributing traditionalist hubris to humanists whose principles are far removed from the ills described.

Ousting imperial attitudes from the academy appears to have come at a price: a contemporaneous conflation of reasonable (and necessary) cultural relativism (suggested even in use of the term hermeneutics) with vague and generalised disrespect for the insurmountably intrinsic human act of publically discussing ethics. Today, we remain sceptical of the prescriptive values of humanistic texts, and any associated methodology of evaluation. In short, constructivism compels disavowal of moral arguments as such arguments can only reflect the status of the moraliser, ergo moral conclusions made through art may, after all, be mere statements of taste, the kind of status symbol Pierre Bourdieu criticised as symbolic class violence in *La Distinction* ([1979] 1984). However, moral resolution – even after attempts at a suspension of judgement – must be permissible in any humanist reading method. Perhaps pragmatist Jarvie put it best: 'Methods are not true or false, but adequate or inadequate, fruitful or barren . . . but they can be moral or immoral, above all in the investigation of humans' (2007: 582). We should still analyse our ability to harm or aid through narrative texts. It may be time now to find a way to reintegrate morality into narrative theory, while retaining respect for the different contextual challenges, power relations and identities in flux across the globe. These values need not be in conflict: we can ask an ethical question and understand the political context in which ethical decisions will be made. Otherwise, we forfeit the use of moral language to those powerful interests that continue to harness moral discourse as a mechanism for hegemonic social control.

Said's 'nontotalizing, nonessentializing humanism that admits fallibility, limitations in understanding and difference' (Holland 2013: 6) suggested one such way forward while exploring the bounds between secular and theological humanisms:

> One might say that Saidian secular criticism sublimates a repressed politics of transcendence while unmasking organized religion's pose of impartiality. But one might also venture that Said's attentiveness to theological exegesis in the preface to *Mimesis* attests to an intellectual curiosity toward cultures of belief, a willingness to engage 'religiously' with the matter of how philosophies of transcendence have shaped revolutionary ethical militance and subjective freedom. (Apter 2004: 47)

This is, if anything, a Saidian humanism. Said was instrumental in exhuming a secular, emancipatory, optimistically leftist spiritualism from humanism's theological underpinnings, one that located wonderment in identifying commonalities across the depth and detail of texts and languages. It is hopeful in a human agency at once apparent – the evidence is found in stirring literature from all places, all times – and unknowable, hence the presence of a necessary spiritualism in Said's work. If humanism has been, as Apter says, 'a tradition shaped and structured historically by tensions between religion and secular culture' (2004: 46), then after Said's sublimation of humanism beyond national, ethnic or theological fealties to reflect a world of increasingly unbound identities, associated languages and texts, we can ask what is salvageable from the old humanism. For literary Darwinist Joseph Carroll, it is reaffirmation of 'three core ideas in traditional humanism: individual identity, authorial intentions, and reference to a real world' (2011: x). This reintroduces the humility and utility of *listening to others*, yet moreover for Said, in philological close study (or what one might call a close listening through sympathetic study, in an anthropological-hermeneutic sense, to human development and movement), we are able to reveal and honour an untotalisable humanity, and in so doing 'intuit' (Said 1979: 258) a human excess, an unknowable something-more that is our agency, our sympathy toward complex otherness, and thus our will to progress together. In a way, by listening closely to the uplift transmitted through human-produced texts, we access a great relief in not knowing a human essence. We are relieved from the pretence to totally know the variability of human identity and activity which is beyond our ken, a hubristic reductionism that, especially working from the cues of grand theory, it can seem we must accept simply to make an ethical or political argument; at the same time, we also appreciate the human labouring to communicate through narrative which is the fruit of our unified complexity. Thus, to argue against universalising notions of the human misses the point: we do not need to naturalise hierarchical views of superior humanness to engage any of these humanistic pursuits.

For many of the aforementioned antihumanist critics, the fact that some have more access to sympathetic narrative distribution than others invalidates the process; for example, older white male dominance in the demography of the Hollywood Academy of Arts and Science unquestionably dictates the kind of people their mass-produced stories will ask us to sympathise with. A humanist might counter that these empathic processes remain the only means (however imperfect) by which we will overcome such disparity. The production and direction of sympathy is undeniably political, but such critics have put us in a lose-lose situation: extension of group identification is both the goal and the problem. The positioning of sympathiser and sympathised, speaker and spoken for, is an inevitability as long as we have global imbalanced powers, yet the alternative – not listening to, imaginatively connecting with and facilitating stories told of the oppressed – is far worse. When we attack attempts at liberal empathy, we sterilise the means to seriously address power imbalance: the ability of stories to turn grander structural abstractions and observations into applied narratives, through which the relevance of personal detail provides a reason for political action. Nonattendance to the emotional lives of others bars identification and thereby the search for self-sacrificing answers or generative cosmopolitanism in practice, prolonging inequity, which should lead us to a simple maxim: humanism seeks to cosmopolitanise sympathy, but not generalise ethical action. A liberal sympathy grounded in complex understanding of local contingencies has a superior chance of locating actions with genuine mutual benefit.

One could call this an eclectic humanism, then, drawing as it does from profoundly diverse perspectives to upset and extend visions of a panhuman, sometimes called a 'critical humanism' as opposed to a more universalising 'high humanism' (Noonan 2003). However all humanisms might contain this egalitarian imperative where they have fealty to the accumulative pursuit of comprehending human complexity. If the human is understood as sociobiologically adapted to environments they live in and create, never good or evil and yet never able to be removed from cultural-ethical intercourse, there is perhaps something we can learn not only about ourselves, but also the fascinating and unfathomable complexity of all life, from listening deeply to a multiplicity of perspectives and knowledge (cf. Wilson's *Consilience* 1999). From this position, we do not have to take sides or adhere to monocausal accounts of arts adaptation, cultural variations, alleged superior ethical frameworks or truths. We make sense of the world by thinking more generously about people, epistemology and sociality in order to, hopefully, ambitiously, find new answers to old problems.

This egalitarian respect for others' knowledge does not hold that all information is equal. A principle is still applied, as I continue to insist that we ask: does this information *realistically complicate* our understanding of humans and human activity, even where the question cannot be conclusively answered. Identifying patterns of discrimination and normalised prejudice in cultural narratives should not be seen as opposed to this humanism in practice. Humanism just asks what we can do instead, or what the possibilities may be for replacing and moving past discriminatory narratives, instead of concluding with their documentation.

Perhaps another reason humanist readings have fallen out of repute in academe is that the question at its heart is too obvious: how do we be nicer to one another? The answers, however, are complex, and if we are honest, it is the question behind all the rest of our questions, such as 'what is a human?' or 'is the human an adequate ethical subject?' Humanism in the storytelling arts is, foremost, a reminder that when we transmit and discuss story and its theory, we should do so to serve, equally, living things. It is the way in which we go about this act of disturbing ourselves into ethical inclusivity that is of interest, especially in humanist hermeneutics and narratology.

Conclusions and Future Directions

Narrative humanism (for example, the cinematic human drama) and humanist hermeneutics share a common goal – attempts to comprehend a realistically complex human otherness – yet differ in their means, and we might more readily ascertain how we attempt this through storytelling than through scholarship around storytelling. Here, then, is a summary of the hermeneutic method I am proposing: that we begin by listening to others with generosity, which means approaching storied communication from a position of potential unknowing, as we may have something to learn from the storyteller; that thereafter, as evaluation needs a backbone in some sense of the real, we ought to elevate science over unbridled intuition, or the specialised knowledge of others beyond ourselves; and that we can then evaluate how well a text, a cluster of texts, a cultural movement or phenomenon opens us up to complex human otherness, which includes both its imaginative and potentially illuminating simulation of sociality and psychology, as well as how it might represent causal plurality and the vastness of the human unknown. As nothing is finalised in human studies, we value the utility of the attempt at comprehending others above a chimeric completion of human knowledge projects. Finally, if we realistically complicate our comprehension of others through narrative and evaluative discourse in this way, we might access more truly inclusive, more generous, and more apt ethical debates regarding the complex situations confronting others, and ourselves.

This is clearly something of a rescue act that I've been engaged with, a recovery of wonderment (cf. Bookchin 1995) in an age of academic professionalisation that impresses upon us the need to have and defend a presupposed answer to everything human, in the tradition of much grand theory. Adopting such summary approaches to a diversity of lives in turn means that we must resist the grand – and I think exciting – *unknowing* of humanism. It is akin to the productive fretfulness of anthropology, always willing to have core assumptions upset by new communities presenting new knowledge, to admit and work with failures in comprehending others. I also sense that, after the cognitive turn, film theory still needs to catch up not so much with the debate on the nature of empathy, but with integrating new work such as literary Darwinism, as a few philosophers, including Anderson and Torben Grodal, are now engaged with. One nice thing about being a humanist is that in defending our field, we do not have to merely defend an immovable existing framework or paradigmatic reading mechanism – although we may cherish such applications, there is no portentous answer to 'how culture works'. Foremost we defend our right to be excited by new knowledge that we can integrate into our attempts to deeply comprehend others.

The following chapters in Part II present a social narratology. As well as providing a demonstration of the broadest possible kind of humanist analysis – at the level of taxonomic narrative theory – this section of the book also performs groundwork in establishing the many uses of narrative that we should have in mind when we consider, and offer detailed readings of, individual texts. Before we can assume the mantle of ethical scrutiny, we should first be conversant with the ways people are actively using the narratives we critique; this is the work of narratological detail.

As I have continually suggested throughout this introduction, I will be keeping in mind story's adaptive functions, and drawing on literary Darwinism as well as evolutionary anthropology and social psychology to present a catalogue of the vast uses and purposes of narrative formulation and distribution. Before proceeding, however, it seems important to convey the limitations of such an endeavour, and especially to offer a few notes on the explanatory work of Darwinism. I have already qualified that I am not claiming that biological imperatives explain everything, or that any humanities theory using social science makes that theory a science. I also must make it clear *that any action that is good for a majority, utilitarian or cosmopolitan, is not necessarily adaptive.* Understanding human adaptation might help us uncover realistic solutions to encouraging a better-naturedness (for example, demilitarisation) amongst a global populace; however we must remain careful in our use of the term 'adaptive.' Traits are adaptive if they help a species (interspecific adaptation) or individual's genetic material (intraspecific adaptation) sustain and survive, not necessarily if they help people get on better (although in interspecific competition the two outcomes regularly coincide) or reduce suffering (painful self-sacrifice is written into the social structures of many species, such as worker ant autothysis or suicidal altruism). In much of the popularly employed language around evolution – language regarding human progress in particular – we appear to attribute intentionality to selection and other natural processes. Fallacies such as these should be avoided.

Beyond this general disclaimer, however – that our purpose is not nature's purpose – there are a handful of other objections raised against the use of Darwinian considerations in arts evaluation that require abatement. The first is a perceived primacy attributed to biological over cultural explanations of human behaviour when we admit evolutionary theory into the humanities. In *On the Origin of Stories*, Boyd dismisses the circular logic of arguments about the construction of human as culturally determined or otherwise (2009: 23), and goes on to present a discussion of some of the possible human functions of storytelling from an evolutionary perspective. Boyd points out – and I agree – that the apparent opposition between cultural constructivist and sociobiological explanations of human behaviour is a mirage. Although much theory rests on this presumption, there is no naturalist or biologically determinist consensus among evolutionary theorists, and many now work from the conviction that our biology and our culture are synergetic and react to one another. How this happens is the subject of debate. Genetics can be conceived as a series of switches reacting to an environment: as such, nature or nurture is almost always the wrong question to ask. Phenotypic plasticity (how our genes are expressed within an environment, which can change throughout our lifetime) must clearly inform any such analysis; this process begins from the time we are conceived, as we receive information about the environment we will be born into from the gametes of both partners, and from within the womb. This perspective on evolutionary synthesis, then, is compatibilist, often described as a 'gene-culture coevolution' (Wilson 1999: 139), which makes possible a Lamarckian study of acquired characteristics within constructed niches (cultural variance, in this case), admitting that human niche construction in turn changes which traits will be adaptive in the new environment, and ergo selected for.[10] We do not just inherit genes from our ancestors – we also inherit the environment those genes will react to.

For example, a reductive or ad hoc evolutionary theory might look at sexual activities as stemming solely from biological imperatives to reproduce, but as we are highly socially adapted animals, a post-Mendelian evolutionary synthesis provides the understanding that our sexuality and sexual behaviour are equally driven by complex socio-cultural conditions extending beyond direct individual fitness and reproductive goals. The plasticity of psychological mechanisms and malleability of their function to vast unplanned environmental variation and contingencies (Joyce 2006: 6–7) means the relationship between our biology and the environments we create cannot be considered reducible to a simple argument of cultural or innate primacy. Evolution does not equate to biological determinism. The polarity of grand nature versus nurture theories misses a breadth of possibilities in uncovering the way we interact with environments we create, and exaptation in manipulated environments. Extending this perspective to the pancultural occurrence of human morality, one could say that while the framework is hardwired, our programming is flexible – and this is a culturally dynamic phenomenon, so does not invalidate cultural analytical theories.

If we are scared of the prospect of sociobiological determinism not allowing for the ethical sovereignty of cultural exchange, we should remind ourselves too that there is agency in mate selection – and its subsequent genetic reformulations – as well as in cultural negotiation. We may choose a mate based equally on matching ideology (Buston and Emlen 2003) as we do on other complementary factors. Presuming this process as deterministic is revealed merely as a desire to *witness* the long-term effects of a direct agency within our lifetime, but change often happens much more slowly and indirectly, hence a constructivist philosophical focus on cultural negotiation as the totality of human agency. It is indeed a convenient position for the cultural theorist to be in if culture has primacy over all human behaviour and cognition, and happens to dictate all other outcomes. The conscious interactivity of culture is simply more visible, more observable, and therefore makes the case for human agency and change easier to put forward.

Sometimes in cultural criticism too, it seems that the biological is aligned with conservative interests, as they have been misused in the past. However this is far from the truth. Peter Singer has argued for a new Darwinian progressive politics in *A Darwinian Left: Politics, Evolution and Cooperation* (1999), and in so doing, made the point that Darwinism is not so much a blow to human agency as it is to leftist utopianism – a changing of the goal posts. Accepting and striving to understand the nature of the human form leads us to more modest goals than the elimination of competitiveness, power relations and general human strife, so the call to a scientific realism concerning human capabilities renders the ambition of *reducing* the harms of inequity more attainable. Asking for us to analyse how we are sociobiologically ushered to mutually beneficial cooperation takes the place of a former idealism which mystifies the act and places it out of reach. Singer summarises all of this in a brief list of projected features for a Darwinian left distinct from the prophetic past (1999: 60–3). Others, such as Robert H. Frank in *The Darwin Economy: Liberty, Competition, and the Common Good* (2011), have used Darwinian insight to argue convincingly for progressive economics, and writers such as Barbara Creed, who described a 'Darwinian gaze' (2009: 102–26), Elizabeth Grosz (2005: 13–33) and Rebecca J. Hannagan in articles including 'Gendered Political Behavior: A Darwinian Feminist Approach' (2008) have admitted the utility of the Darwinian perspective in the project of equalising gender inequity.

So finally, if we are indeed driven to fasten ourselves to storied causalities, we should make certain we are not misrepresenting what we do know about human altruistic capabilities in order to moralise about what others should do. In extrapolating Darwinism directly to an ethic (rather than using evolutionary studies as an epistemic background to our ethics), we may concoct something akin to social Darwinism or eugenics.[11] How do we avoid this? Literary Darwinism should heed Darwin's own counsel, a maxim he repeated more than once, frustrated by distortion of his claims:

> As my conclusions have lately been much misrepresented, and it has been stated that I attribute the modification of species exclusively to natural selection, I may be permitted to remark that in the first edition of this work, and subsequently, I placed in a most conspicuous position – namely at the close of the Introduction – the following words: 'I am convinced that natural selection has been the main but not the exclusive means of modification.' This has been of no avail. Great is the power of steady misrepresentation. ([1859] 2003: 451)

Our comprehension of natural selection cannot explain all of life. This means, however, that if we resist natural fallacies in approaching Darwinism (of deservedness, or of unilineal progress), attention to its profound elucidatory potentials can – perhaps counterintuitively – temper the claims of theory rather than rendering theory conclusive.

Storytellers, yarn-spinners and producers of narrative art continue to conduct the natural storytelling of the conscious mind, making sense of our lives in an internal dramatic narrative, into intersubjective experience. This begets a moral issue: how ought we attempt to shape one another's internal narrative?[12] Just as humanist storytelling must permit complex multi-causality to offer any workable or realistic view of human operations, so must humanist media studies and hermeneutics permit complex social multi-causality in their readings of narrative function and textual analysis alike. So statements on the true function of fiction, portrayals of the origins of storytelling to explain current circumstances, and doctrinaire readings from a single-purpose paradigm are not enough. When we ask these questions of art, we keep in mind how little we can keep in mind in order to think more generously about one another, and the humility of wonder retained creates new opportunities for knowledge rather than intellectual turf protectionism and paradigmatic warfare. In this ambitious project, I hope to both demonstrate such a capability and establish for my reader a position of openness to complex humanness that we could go on to apply to all our practices of cultural analysis

Notes

1. Recent focus on toxoplasmosis's relationship with intermittent explosive disorder (dubbed 'crazy cat lady syndrome' in the news media) provides a good example.

2. As in Pierre Bourdieu's 'Scholastic Point of View' (1990), scholarly analytical methods mechanise the social world even where our complex relations cannot be so rigidly determined, simply because such systemisation is convenient for theories that seek to master human interactivity; the neatness of this process in explaining the importance of our work as social theorists should not overwhelm our acknowledgement of the limitations of our models, simulations and metaphors (Bono 1990). This gives rise to all sorts of terms expressing excess, unknowables and ineffables (cf. terms like the 'really real' and 'the-rest-of-what-is' in works of existential anthropology such as Mattijs van de Port's *Ecstatic Encounters* 2011).
3. This pragmatism is, perhaps, what Jean-Paul Sartre sought to achieve in exploring the conditions of human agency within an experimental existential humanism (1946); such a perspective need not entertain high humanism's assumptions of individual personhood as unitary and consistent over time, or the human subject as anthropocentrically fixed, unchanging, 'centred' in the universe.
4. A story's effectiveness in this regard would naturally depend on the story being told. Although Boyd is correct to identify the broad appeal of prosocial morals in popular narrative, not all stories will perform the same work, even if we are to nominate the adoption of plural perspectives and attendant group coordination as foundational functions in the genesis of human storytelling. This will be elaborated in the following chapter.
5. Scholarly interest in the conditions of kindness between people – including acts of care across borders and between collectives – is political insofar as it intervenes against a reiterative documentation of abuse, power and exploitation after Foucault, and analyses the relation of the political and personal with an emphasis on emergences of human altruism; this is what I am calling the 'politics of kindness' within narrative theory.
6. All communication, including cinema, might be flawed and imperfect transmission, but this should not lead us to devalue the efficacy of all communicative intent. Mary K. Holland describes recent opposition to these poststructural cues: 'contemporary calls for humanism characterize exactly the baby that antihumanism discarded: literature and theory's ability to be about something, to matter, to communicate meaning, *to foster the sense that language connects us more than it estranges us*, so that we can come together in ways that build relationship and community rather than the alienation and solipsism of antihumanistic postmodern literature' (2013: 6, emphasis added).
7. Of course, self-doubt can be paralysing too, and should not be thought of as a catch-all exhortation for all of our interactions. There is a kindness to assuming doubt, but some experience doubt chronically, and internal balance must be sought between reasonable self-dubiety, confidence and conviction. This is no small task. I clarify that I am describing a method for close listening to others, not a general prescription for all thinking and social interaction.

8. The paradox of metaphor is that the more an expression can mean, the less it *does* mean. One can be aware that properly descriptive acts suppress lingual alterity in a way that cannot match the world's depth, as with science's less proscriptive use of metaphor (Bono 1990: 81), and yet still see that restraining conceptive possibilities has utility. This is because at the same time, eliminating possibilities makes way for new possibilities – at the moment of scientific breakthrough, the avenues for understanding the world that are closed are more often replaced by many more avenues for new knowledge. The same is true of cogent language. In summarising one part of the world, lucidity opens new possibilities for observation and articulation from the groundwork of its condensation. The world becomes bigger, not smaller, in articulation. Jackson's quote demonstrates the kindness it extends to its subjects: writing can be poetic and specific at the same time. Similarly, science and scientific description can obliterate possibilities and remain open to the human unknown. Our descriptions of the world become more negotiable when we can be sure we are negotiating the same concept – so again, conceptual precision's invitation to negotiation is, paradoxically, an opening rather than a closing of possibility.
9. This is in addition to the thorough cognitivist perception studies and mysticising psychoanalytic pseudoscience now so familiar in film theory. While psychoanalysis could be seen as having poetic value in its circuitous ambiguity, when it is used to colonise other people's experiences with static, universally applicable metaphors that do not admit cultural variation, it should be put into question. If only an elite community possesses access to acquisition of such a language, which is then used to summarise the experience of others with a pretence to empirical truth or science without contact, psychoanalysis could be seen as a kind of class violence (and another example of fallacious proof by verbose intimidation).
10. We might note too that vice versa, our genes predispose us to choose and manipulate certain environments that then affect the expression of those genes, a process known as 'gene-environment correlation'.
11. Anxieties like these, and the 'biologisation' of political rhetoric, are historicised by Virginia Richter in *Literature After Darwin* (2011).
12. I intend for these normative 'ought' questions, with their emphasis on a prescriptive rather than a descriptive ethics of narrative, to augment recent meta-ethical works in media and cognition (such as Carl Plantinga's *Screen Stories*, describing the emotional underpinnings of character engagement and spectatorship), and in literary studies (such as Hanna Meretoja's *The Ethics of Storytelling*, elaborating ethical 'possibilities' implicit within the framework of cultural studies scholarship). In a way, narrative humanism is interested not only in exploring the space between these two disciplines, the sociocultural and the biocultural, but also in asking a further question: given this information, how ought we act? What stories ought we tell each other, and what ought we then do with those stories?

PART II
SOCIAL NARRATOLOGY

CHAPTER 2

Foundational Functions of Fiction

Introduction to Social Narratology: A Catalogue of Storytelling Social Functions from a Humanist Perspective

> There was not enough time for human heredity to cope with the vastness of new contingent possibilities revealed by high intelligence ... The arts filled the gap. Early humans invited them in an attempt to express and control through magic the abundance of the environment, the power of solidarity, and other forces in their lives that mattered most to survival and reproduction. (Wilson 1999: 255)

I begin with Edward O. Wilson's much-quoted passage, as in respecting a multiplicity of the uses of art it reminds us that communication itself has evolutionary causes. Story, he suggests, helped manage the confusions arising as a result of the processing power of incomparable neurological development. As such, it is also a good place to start in mapping out just some of the functions of narrative in our daily lives. These early developments introduced complex internal worlds that more direct communication could not fully represent the dynamism of. Projections, including imagined future events, the existential terror and anxieties made possible in reflexive rumination on those projections, simulations of another's internal state, metacognition, social cognition, and complex, blended affect may not be fully conveyed without using the drama and refracted interior conflicts of storytelling. Fiction introduces new resources to represent complex internal states, in some cases mirroring the inherent speculation, imprecision and boundlessness of everyday imaginative capacities. Heeding Wilson's own advice, we should recall, however, that the evolutionary perspective can only take us so far: the origins of a human activity do not necessarily account for our appropriation of the activity for different purposes across millennia, any more than we could claim that our hands developed to facilitate typing on a keyboard. We find new uses for old adaptations, which cannot necessarily be traced to a clear and direct survival goal. We refract instincts and goals through complex culture, which is multi-purposeful. Human systems – epistemological, sociocultural, historical – are gestalt. This is a core principle of social narratology.

Much of what we call narratology appears to me to be concerned with cataloguing, in particular making lists of story mechanics and functions: from Mieke Bal's structuralist or Algirdas Julien Greimas's semiotic narratology to Mar and Oatley's psychological narratology, and from Gerald Prince's *Dictionary of Narratology* to Peter Hühn et al.'s 'Living Handbook of Narratology' at the University of Hamburg, narratology has always been taxonomic. Social narratology is, along with previous works in the narratological field, a kind of complexivism, in that it seeks to describe a complex system. However, the complex system it seeks to describe is social – it is the space between people that is facilitated by stories. Where cognitive narratology has been particularly good at describing the psychological relationship between a reader and a text, social narratology refocuses the science of storytelling to the relationship between two or more people engaged with a text.

To put it another way, although many cognitive theorists have been at pains to point out the non-exclusive nature of the applications of cognitive studies (Herman 2013), much of the current research leans toward perception studies precisely because the cognitive sciences are good at investigating the *moment of engagement* with narrative.[1] Social narratology, on the other hand, extends from our knowledge of textual responses to ask questions regarding the social use these relationships with narrative are then put to – how a story facilitates or mediates relations between people, for instance. It might be regarded as a particular application of cognitive theory rather than a difference of kind (it draws on many of the same sources), or simply a shifting of the focus of cognitive studies. Social narratology reintegrates some of cognitive science's formative disciplines, and as such engages more extensively with anthropological and evolutionary biological research, and turns to the explanatory powers of social psychology more so than neuroscience (although again, they are not in any way exclusive, but rather complementary fields of inquiry).[2] In the conclusion to his work on cognitive film theory and emotion, *Moving Viewers*, Carl Plantinga suggests room for further direction on social cognition: 'Popular narratives have a communal function, the significance of which can easily be undervalued. In embodying virtual solutions to traumatic problems, they play a role in the development of what might be called distributed or social cognition' (2009: 225–6). I intend to pick up where these works leave off, and I hope that this will in turn inspire a broadening of the epistemic palette cognitivists might draw from.

The purpose of this part of the book is both to lay a foundational comprehension of this extraordinary human behaviour that we might retain when offering closer textual readings, and to suggest a human excess by the very span, multiplicity and challenge of this list. The ineffable untotalisability of any life is always subject to the limits of reliable human science – limits we must acknowledge in order to remain realistic about any claims of a 'human nature' or our moral capabilities. This honesty in turn, I hope, should stimulate wonder and deepen understanding at the same time. I will extend each description of a storied behaviour and its social purpose to speculate on humanist-ethical approaches to the responsibilities of narrative. The point, too, is not just to list pre-existing narrative theories, but also to explore new ground that might be less familiar in narrative theory, to develop and interrogate new insights into the social functions of fiction. In keeping with the explorative values of humanism and wonderment, this narratology should provide expansion, not stagnation.

Although the latter half of this book uses filmic genre study as a primary example of humanist analysis, I am determined not to pretend that humanism or the human drama *belongs* to any one expression or art. This is why, in the following narratology, I analyse a broad range of story media, and join a growing number of theorists in calling for a media-conscious narratology (Ryan and Thon 2014). This means that while we can remain aware of each medium's distinctive characteristics, possible affects, and devices for carrying a story, we can also look beyond medium specificity to stress the foundational narrative functions that unite various storied acts. Working as a film scholar, there can be a pressure to specialise in that which is unique to the medium rather than how films are received and used as narrative, much like any other art. Film, then, should not be discussed in isolation from other media as comparison generates a broader understanding of how stories function in different contexts, yet while we remain aware of media differences, it is important not to overstate their value. To an extent, social narratology equalises media forms by treating them on the same level – as acts of storytelling.[3]

What ensues is a social narratology (emphasising the relationship between individuals as facilitated by narrative), working from a cinematic Darwinism, cognitivism and anthropology (privileging examples from the cinema), resulting in a humanist ethics (speculation on what to do with this information) and ultimately, a refinement of humanist hermeneutics, which I will later apply to closer readings of specific examples from the cinema. I thereby unite social narratology and humanistic hermeneutics into what I am calling 'narrative humanism.'

This narratology demonstrates four key points: that it is in their social expression that the cognitive sciences we apply to film and narrative theory find their meaning; that we can use the findings of such sciences to help us answer questions of narrative ethics and responsibility; that it is not possible to summate all human motives for engaging in narrative behind one unitary function; and hopefully, to demonstrate that when investigating and cataloguing a multiplicity of narrative functions, a tandem story of human complexity emerges that opens further avenues for narratological description and knowledge, and ultimately understanding the people we live with through their storied behaviours. Finally, the positively ambitious nature of the following is a vulnerability that is open to human complexity, and thus social narratology is a narrative humanism, an explorative story of our interactivity that invites discovery, complication and extension. The five chapters in this second part of the book make up its most substantial component. I intend for these chapters to be read together as a single project, a continuous essay – the development of a humanistically motivated social narratology. The division of this project into five chapters denotes the taxonomic work that is a component of this narratology: the chapters suggest some catgegorisations which might help make sense of the breadth of this list, while subheadings branch those categories into further relational groups.

Foundational Functions of Fiction

Foremost, **we use stories as part of a discussion about what we can mutually hold to be real**, the different ways we can understand and experience what is real, as well as what is important for us to pay attention to. Michelle Scalise Sugiyama (2001: 237) describes how non-fictive causal communication per se may have developed to overcome the constraints in energy cost, risk and time spent on personal information-gathering across local environmental variation; so we learned to receive causal information second-hand. It is clear how this may be attempted through nonfiction (news stories, for example), however fiction also provides a trigger or even a facilitator for discussion about the actual. Whether the story is realist, allegorical, abstract, nonlinear or somewhere inbetween, we ask what the story wanted to infer about our world. The question, then, is how the utility of complex information-sharing translated into an appetite for fiction. Malcolm Turvey (2014: 56) doubts that we evolved a taste for fiction in order to convey environmental information germane to our survival, as the information imparted in fiction appears remarkably unreliable. All evolutionary theory can really tell us, he argues, is that stories betray our taste for information in general, not reliable information. But the claim here is not that stories tell us what is real, rather that stories provide a compelling space for discussing what is real. We still need to explain, though, why fiction is a particularly apt place for these discussions to occur, rather than direct communication.

The argument for fiction as adaptation often hinges upon the memorability of emotionally contrived information: 'The didactic purpose of storytelling is diminished in literate cultures, but by providing a vivid and memorable way of communicating information, it likely had actual survival benefits in the Pleistocene' (Dutton 2009: 110). The causality of narrative is crucial to this explanation. Because storied communication links information causally, it allows us to 'live' through a narrative. Imagining complex causalities between sensations, stories activate parts of the brain not only used for language processing, but also the sensory, motor and frontal cortices, and areas associated with emotions and social memory, the co-stimulation of which may help us remember the narrative substance by causal association to the narrative's sensation (as in the mnemonic link system). Fiction has the potential to exaggerate conflict and produce a more memorable simulation. We see selective fitness and survival-related goals playing out in all manner of narratives, however the transmission of knowledge becomes more complicated the further it is extended into complex narrativity, where survival goals are displaced and truth claims are more abstracted and conceptual.

For many this is a crude way of thinking epistemically about the meaning of the storytelling arts and their production. Disciples of popular film theoreticians such as Gilles Deleuze, for example, may be openly hostile to the idea that a primary function of cinema is to open an intersubjective dialogue and refine our perspectives on a mutual ontic externality (rather than endlessly producing experiential novelties). Yet even when we accept our inability to experience, know or rationalise an externality or perfectly access another's perception, the emphasis on perceptual frailty explains nothing: 'If there were no common human experience and no common cognitive means of representing and responding to that experience, storytelling would be futile' (Sugiyama 2001: 245). Various epistemological scepticisms present platitudes at best, and describe little about the world beyond reasserting our undeniable subjectivity. As Noël Carroll (1988) argues convincingly in *Mystifying Movies*, these concepts inhibit comprehension of processes readily understandable by reference to available and verifiable knowledge and sciences. When Deleuze uses 'brain biology' to bolster his claims, he favours obscurant analogy over clarification, 'making sometimes difficult to understand the real meaning of [neuroscientific] terms' (Gallese and Guerra 2012: 187). These metaphysical alternatives effectively ask us to solve an unsolvable, speculative ontological question before we get to the work of discussing human interaction, a hierarchical positioning of philosophical thought which obscures our ability to talk specifically of the needs of living things; in this case we might read such positioning as antihumanist. Story is an intrinsic part of human sociality – we need to share information, and we use causal narratives to do so.

It is evident not just that we can, but that we do use fiction as an inroad to discuss not only truth claims about fundamental workings of the world around us, but also some of the more complex, conceptual and obscured workings of the world. When an audience exits a film arguing about the way women have been represented, for example, they use the film as groundwork to discuss what is and is not real about the fictional world, and gauge how the filmmakers' perspective may or may not match up with their own experience. The same may be true of representations of physics in fiction, for example we may be annoyed that a film fails to reflect basic physical properties.[4] Abstract stories, too, are often thought to express an internal, emotional or conceptual 'higher' truth. Finally, we might use, for instance, a biopic as a pedagogical device, not to accept its version of events, but to craft interest in those events and generate a number of talking points from which we might debate what is and is not real about their representation. Hence, we use story as a springboard into articulation of what we can mutually hold to be real; we do not need to solve an epistemological materialist dilemma to do this.

American Splendor (Shari Springer and Berman Robert Pulcini, 2003) is a good example of a film that calls attention to an audience's implicit search for truth claims. The film begins as a biopic. Actors play characters from a series of autobiographical comics by author Harvey Pekar. Initially, the affected performances of characters like Toby Radloff (Judah Friedlander) might seem far-fetched, but eventually the film begins to include interviews with the real-life figures being represented in both film and comic. Toby's demeanour and self-presentation is surprisingly even more affected than Friedlander's performance. The dissonant moment gives us pause to reflect upon our presumptions of what is real and what is not – an important component in the film's radical mix of the fictive and non-fictive. The search for a foundational reality to rely upon remains with us, often implicitly and tacitly as we move through a narrative. The actor is always a site of doubt, scepticism and interrogation, or as Huw

Griffiths puts it, 'the body of the actor is revealed as a site in which faith cannot readily be located' (2013: 94). We wonder what they intend to tell us through their performance, what parts of their performance constitute their intention, how this connects with the intentions of the other storytellers involved in a performance, and thereby what, if any, 'real' we can draw from the actor. Even in these more abstract spaces within narrative, beyond its plot or procedure, we can search for a mutual real – and crucially, we can become *aware* of our search for a mutual real, and its problems.

These attentional politics lead us to a related function of narrative. As well as inciting non-fictive discussions about what is real, **stories can make a claim about what is important for us to pay attention to**, and we often conflate the two. As story theorists, we can make the mistake of assuming that the claim someone makes when they put together a narrative is: 'this is the way things are, or the way people are'. Yet the primary claim made by a storyteller might be more attentional than ontological. That is, it might have more to do with what kind of causality is worthy of our attention – after all, we attend a narrative to have our attention diverted from our daily concerns, which is a powerful commandeering of another's time. Consider the discourse of public relations practitioners, often casting themselves as expert storytellers: this does not mean that they attempt to accurately represent our lives; it means that they use story to pull our attention toward their product, service, public figure or other interest, and our attention is the prized commodity more so than any of the meanings that might be imparted by the narratives they use to snag our time and consideration. In fact, narrative itself is sometimes characterised as a conducting of attentional cues to produce coherence (Mar and Oatley 2008: 176). As story theorists, we tend to study the ways in which narrative imparts or transmits meaning, often at the expense of attentional politics (that which tells us what is important rather than what is). The point I would like to make is that we can never assume allegorical readings are the most apt to explain narrative's influence; it can be fairer and more clarifying to start from a question of why a particular story has been chosen above all others. Our attention is ethical and political because stories constitute claims of relative importance. This makes subject choice ethically evaluable. We should remain aware of how our attention is manipulated by all manner of storytelling.[5]

These two foundational concepts – of representation and attention – become more complex when we take historiographical considerations into account: **how we use stories in attempts to record and understand our history** and events we will never be present for but that we could learn from. Without contesting the subjectivity of storytelling historicity, we can say we attempt an understanding and recording of human history through chains of cause and event. This is, as Donald E. Polkinghorne has it, the way we connect identified events into 'synoptic judgment', a narrative coherence or plot (1988: 63); only in this case, that synopsised plot is human history. The selective and summary nature of history is crucial to its coherence. Any practice of retelling our past is a string of distillations of causality, and as events can rarely be considered monocausal, we make claims about the most important causes that are most worthy of our attention, which then become history, told and redistributed such that we might make better choices in future – or sometimes, of course, we distort such reportage for political gains. Yet it remains that we are able to use our distillation of the most important causes and events to engage advanced predictive faculties, which inform our decision-making, both at an individual and organisational level. Aristotle in *Poetics* suggests that fiction in particular can locate universals between past, present and projected future events to predict the probability of what may happen; again, this aids decision-making ([330 BCE] 1987: 13). After Karl Popper's *The Poverty of Historicism*, though, this can be no science of prognostication or historical determinism, attempting to reduce human movements to mathematically quantifiable repeating and isolated systems they will never conform to – but like the test subject receiving electric shocks on reaching for a reward, we do need to be able to read probability into past events to make informed decisions for our future.

Stories can also contain inadvertent traces of our history. Comparative mythology studies looks at information regarding environmental locality and human migration contained in extant myths across the globe (Witzel 2012). Versions of the same myth can reference different flora, fauna and places, telling its own story of human movement and our shared history. In fact, much of the project of literary Darwinism has been a search for elements of our shared past within narrative structures. So we use stories to understand our history even where they were not explicitly crafted to impart reliable historical details.

The accounts of storytelling above all refer to telic sequential narratives, as well as outlining some of their limitations. Yet there is another kind of thought available to us in fiction when we resist or refuse to recognise causality or patterns: we can also **upset narratives of causality** with nonlinear structures and, generally, not making immediate causal sense. In Bruner's construction: 'While it is true that the world of a story (to achieve verisimilitude) must conform to canons of logical consistency, it can use violations of such consistency as a basis of drama' (1986: 12). Narratives employing such techniques can conduct our attention to reflect on our paucity of ontic certainties, how little we know about our lives, meaning, why and how the universe operates. To an audience member fixated upon our existential condition, absurdism, for instance, might come across as gratifyingly honest – even profound. The therapeutic benefits of absurdity have been recognised by artists across many fields: songwriter Robert Wyatt uses nonsensical verse alongside pained internal monologues and political outcries in *Rock Bottom* and cartoon blogger Allie Brosh combats depression with the pictorial non sequitur in *Hyperbole and a Half*; their strategies are backed up by humour research in psychology (Brooks et al. 2009; Crawford and Caltabiano 2011; Long and Greenwood 2013). We upset narratives of causality, predictable spatiality and temporality, to draw attention to our perceptual limitations, experiential limitations, tendency to monocausality and empiricism; in sum, how little we know. These are the reasons a figure such as David Lynch has come to support reams of scholarly writing, as this version of cognitive dissonance in cinema retains critical favour as a metaphysical 'profundity' (Moss-Wellington 2017), a scholarly narrative and aesthetic interest sustained since late modernity: rejection of the perceived telic imposition wrought by linear narrative conventions.

Problematic distinctions between the causally suggestive and causally disruptive have followed us throughout the history of narrative theory, and they are bound with a host of other attempts at erecting related binaries: theories versus narratives; causal events versus causal ideas; narrative immersion versus reflexive thought; and higher versus lower art. When Jean Cocteau, for example, indicates that his 'primary concern in a film is to prevent the images from flowing, to oppose them to each other, to anchor them and join them without destroying their relief' (Fraigneau 1967: 151), his distinction between cinema as entertainment and the cinematograph as a 'vehicle for thought' mirrors Bruner's conceptions of logical debate and narrative as different cognitive modes. By inhibiting our ability to read causal *events* in a film, we are theoretically drawn into consideration of a different and more cerebral causality: that of an author's ideas and the discussions they might inspire. Whether or not these two attentional causalities are so clearly separable is in dispute. Throughout this social narratology, I make an implicit case that immersion in (more-or-less linear or discernably causal) narrative should not be conceived as negating intellectual or political concern, or indeed any other reflexivity in spectatorship.[6] There is scant evidence, in practice or in theory, that focussing our pattern-recognition causal cognition upon narrative events will preclude the subsequent use of these same faculties to ruminate on their moral implications, or develop structured, theoretical accounts of those events, a story's 'meaning'; narratives that upset linear causality simply foreground the inherent unreliability of these cognitions.

Having explored some of the broadest possible functions of story, I now turn to some of their correlate, yet often more covert, functions. Principally, what does the emotional content of narrative provide for us?

Notes

1. Some, such as Malcolm Turvey, have questioned the ability of perception studies to tell us much at all about film. He argues that the mantra of many cinematic Darwinists from Joseph D. Anderson onward – that the language of film developed to appeal to perceptual faculties originating in the Pleistocene – is hardly surprising, and a claim that does little to illuminate anything about cinema in particular (2014: 50–1).
2. As in much of the work within cognitive film studies, these accounts sit alongside insights from literary theory, philosophy and experimental media research to see what can be gleaned from their comparison. I am calling upon much more wide-ranging sources in addition to those noted here, presenting an attempt at interdisciplinary consilience, or a humanistic unifying of knowledge from various backgrounds in the humanities and sciences; in Murray Smith's (2017) terms, an attempt at a 'third culture.'
3. It should be noted too that the following narratology errs toward English-language texts, simply because these are the texts I am most intimately acquainted with and best equipped to offer studies of. Examples for many of the following points could be found in a breadth of storytelling contexts. Some of the following functions will speak specifically to Western contexts and some comparatively observe cultural variation, while other functions speak more broadly to story in general. In a chapter on 'The Geography of Film Viewing', Daniel Barratt (2014) points out that some cognitive processes are found to be universal while others are culturally influenced; in a social narratology, both are interesting. The following stresses the importance of niche cultures within communities that are sometimes assumed to be homogeneous. Above all, films are expensive to produce, and in a globalised era they have become, like innumerable other commodities, economic balancing acts, the funding of which rarely defers to cartographic boundaries, and this has implications for the cross-cultural distribution and consumption of narrative.
4. This somewhat depends on the context of the film. When protagonists survive a tornado while tied to flimsy pipes with leather straps in the climax of *Twister* (Jan de Bont, 1996), we may feel let down that the film did not try

harder to craft excitement from a plausible physical scenario, limiting our investment. However in a film like *Sharknado* (Thunder Levin, 2013), we might take pleasure in a complete flouting of physical properties when the protagonists use bombs to eradicate tornados. Stories are able to disavow truth claims to focus us on other spectatorial experiences.
5. By the same token, media users, readers and viewers are not passive, and still have some agency to choose subjects they will engage with. When we overemphasise the influence of storytellers, we disavow the dialogical relationship underpinning all narrative practices.
6. As Rita Felski has it, literary enchantment can coexist with 'a phenomenology of self-scrutiny' (2008: 35) and its broader political implications, so she calls for literary theory to 'face up to the limits of demystification as a critical method and a theoretical ideal . . . the modern dogma that our lives should become thoroughly disenchanted' (76).

CHAPTER 3

Affective Functions of Fiction

Drawing Meaning from Emotion

In story, we can **safely exercise emotional responses and mortality/need threats not required in day-to-day life**. Different varieties of emotional arousal, adrenaline release and suspense, focused on variations in the subject causing the arousal – from terrifying monsters to romantic anxieties – translate to pleasure, gratification and enjoyment for different audiences. When we use terms such as 'feeling alive' or 'having our buttons pushed' in relation to audience experience, this is the experience we are talking about: 'the quest for excitement in unexciting societies' (Elias and Dunning 1970: 31). However, first of all, the existential components in this process need to be unpacked and understood. There are now multiple contexts across the developed world in which humans encounter very few direct threats to mortality on a daily basis, yet we still seem to seek the feeling of that threat, a safe activation of the flight-or-fight response, or we may well ask 'what are we doing here, then?' Working from a Darwinian approach to story, in which there is no tropologically objective higher ordering of our motivation, all we are really compelled to do in our lives is procreate, survive and help kin survive, so that we (or our genes) keep surviving, even if this is a gestalt and culturally refracted process – if the immediacy of this process is gone, perhaps we displace the impulse elsewhere, as in narrative.

Survival offers meaning even when distantly or vicariously related to our mortality or fitness, and many have posited that other attempts at creating meaning (acquisitional culture, relationships, humour and political conviction, for example) stem from a desire to create distance between oblivion and our sense of selfhood. Throughout her 1987 work *Beyond Fear*, Dorothy Rowe describes the many ways in which we are driven to displace existential anxieties to corporeal goals.[1] Drama relies on conflict; we can create dramatic conflicts as a safe way to achieve these feelings, conquer them by making it out of the other end of the story alive, and recover mortal meaning without adding similar conflict to our actual lives or the lives of those around us.

This hypothesis must be carefully distinguished from relief theory or the argument from catharsis (from Aristotle to popular psychology). In these models, there is a negative affect inside us that we have the opportunity to jettison by simulating the emotion in narrative. There is scant evidence that via 'exploration' or mere re-experience of a problematic emotion, we curtail it (Gerbner et al. 1994; Bushman et al. 1999). It is not merely proximity to the affect that releases it, although recognition of that affect (via personal expression or narrative engagement) can lead to reflective listening, problem-solving and reappraisal, which may reduce distress (Littrell 1998; Littrell 2009). So an emotion is not necessarily abated when addressed through narrative, and as narrative creators and consumers we cannot assume merely airing an emotion will do the job for us – but we still must confront the phenomenon that people overwhelmingly pursue the opportunity to feel closer to problematic affect, and derive pleasure from experiencing affect that would, outside of narrative contexts, be something we choose to avoid.

Clearly the dynamism of human identities means we all have different appetites for emotional manipulation through story – for those who like a lot of push and pull, it remains a safe place to exercise and explore one's affective extremities. Consider that those scoring high on sensation-seeking personality traits are likely to attend more horror movies than their peers, for example (Oliver and Sanders 2004: 244–5; we will return to the specific offerings of the horror genre shortly). Emotions elicited by fiction can even reinforce a sense of identity: if we identify as a 'deep feeling' person, we might enjoy rehearsing these responses by watching tearjerker films (Oliver 1993), as the emotion itself reinscribes a grander autobiographical narrative about our own appropriate responses to the world's ills. In other words, emotions form part of our procedural scripts, rehearsed through fiction. These scripts connect to feelings of purpose and meaning (this is largely a function of the amygdala: to register the emotional significance of events). Moreover, as Ellen Dissanayake puts it: 'I suspect that most people hunger for a more profound life. The arts – ours and those of others – are *ways of treating the inner life seriously*' (2000: 192). She connects this lack of a sense of purpose to the political devaluation of arts within affluent nations in particular. Perhaps too, as religion has long been a primary site of narrative distribution, the decline of social contact through religious institutions could help explain our contemporary demand for fiction.

A symptom of a shrunken hippocampus, one function of which is to correlate action with mood, is depression (Schmaal et al. 2016). There is clearly an interaction here between the amygdala (crafting meaning from emotion) and the hippocampus (suggesting courses of action based upon our mood) that is being worked through narrative arts to generate meaning and derive purpose. This is why theorists who suggest that emotional appeal depletes intellectual engagement should resist disparaging those who find meaning through emotive art: it could be helping to stave off purposelessness. Mary Beth Oliver and Arthur Raney's (2011) research also goes some way toward explaining media engagement motivations as more than just hedonic, but also 'eudaimonic', in that we craft meaning directly from our emotional experiences in narrative rather than just feeling their excitations. Tenderness, for example, is not just something we experience for its own sake, but because it can then spur us to think about and discuss human purpose. Eudaimonic responses involve distributed connections between regions of the brain separate to the reward circuit. For a species so aware of its imminent passing, the effect of stories has existential value. Oliver and Raney's study shows that this is exactly how many film viewers conceive of their own motivation for engaging in dramatic narratives: the emotions are a platform to work from in thinking through a film's insights and meaning. We can go through an emotional experience, and then discuss its outcome.[2] The eudaimonic can operate 'as an additional (but not opposite) motivation for individuals' entertainment selections' (989). Oliver and Raney remind us not to look at hedonic motivations in isolation from other social and meaning-making motivations in media selection, as focusing on hedonic gratification alone misconstrues us all as solely pleasure-seeking machines rather than complex pleasure- and meaning-seeking entities. A cognitive fixation on the hedonic aspects of media engagement can fail to extricate sensation-seeking motivations and dispositions from their attendant meaning-seeking motivations; as they are so intimately tied, they can often look like the same thing. No doubt as neuroscience develops, this picture will become ever more complex.

Accounting for the development of human emotion in lieu of a pure reason has occupied many evolutionary theorists. Dylan Evans (2001) describes an 'evolutionary rationality' in which our emotions enable swifter responses to familiar situations and environments than reason alone could provide (without which the active possibilities available with pure reason would be paralysingly multitudinous). As Martin L. Hoffman puts it, 'humans must be equipped biologically to function effectively in many social situations without undue reliance on cognitive processes' (1981: 79); this is a popular explanation for the evolution of emotion. As we have established, reason and rationality are to an extent subject to emotional cues: cues ordering what we *expect to achieve* through reason. This can take the form of an affective projection or simulation, and narrative can harness this capacity for autobiographical projection or 'future thinking.' When we picture the death of a loved one, we use an emotional imagination to access the pain we project we may feel, in order that we may avoid behaviours that could result in such a scenario. If we were not able to imaginatively feel this pain, it might not make rational sense to avoid actions that could result in their death – it would not matter unless their life served another non-emotional goal for us. One wonders, then, with what purpose in mind we would act without emotion, if we would need to locate life's purpose for every decision we made, and be thwarted by our own rationality which defeats even the very idea of a purpose. That is, perhaps we would need to solve the puzzle of the reason for caring about our survival and procreation at every instance of decision-making. Indeed, many of the psychopathologies that are characterised by a lack of feeling are correlated with depression, such as anhedonic depression, and studies have found that 'psychopathy was negatively correlated with positive affect, happiness, and life satisfaction, and positively correlated with negative affect and depression' (Love and Holder 2014: 114–15). As emotions give us impetus that we cannot have in rational thought alone, humanist narrative permits emotive appeal and may even rely upon emotional imagination, the description and discovery of far-reaching nuances in emotional experience. Emotion lays a foundation for the empathic functions of narrative. The rational mind also, we cannot forget, never has access to perfect information to work with, so in many cases may be liable to lead us astray when making decisions from environmentally contingent information, and without the innate memory of emotions. Thus, emotions may be a way to keep in contact with lessons learned throughout our past, and even our collective past stored in the human epigenome – lessons which may be fatally bypassed by a purely rational mind.

Reaching back to figures such as Bertholt Brecht, there has long been a theoretical imperative to dismiss emotional responses to narrative, emotional absorption or emotive appeals in narrative as antithetical to our application of reason and ergo political action, but this could not be further from the truth:

> The dominant tradition in Western thought has regarded emotion as a burden to human existence, an impediment to reason – a view manifest in thinkers as varied as Descartes, Kant and the playwright Bertolt Brecht. And if anything, this is a view of emotion even more entrenched in popular culture than it is in the realms of philosophy and art theory – think of those models of supreme intelligence, the emotion-free Spock and Data from *Star Trek*. (Smith 2010: 259)[3]

David Boyle also notes this fantasy of human as mere data processor (the computational theory of mind) as a driving supposition behind many post- and transhuman aspirations (2003: 197–201). The limbic system, associated with mood regulation and emotions, is one of the most primordial networks in the brain and has a much more complex relationship with other regions than could be described as merely 'computational'. When interrogated, the suggestion of the emotional automaton – that we would be better off or more computationally rational if we could supress emotive responses, or at least not validate these responses as authenticity – also starts to look suspiciously like a normalisation of a culture of psychopathy, characterised by emotional response deficiency (Herpertz and Sass 2000), resistant responses to emotionally provocative stimuli (Patrick 1994) as opposed to operational appraisal of emotional cues (Lorenz and Newman 2002) or 'cognitive empathy', and problems with early emotional development and learning (see *The Psychopath: Emotion and the Brain* by James Blair, Derek Mitchell and Karina Blair 2005). Although this is a contentious claim, it is one that needs to be made: successive literary and dramatic theorists in the Brechtian tradition have advanced notions impelling us to avoid emotional absorption in narrative to further political ends, or what director Michael Haneke describes as 'clarifying distance in place of violating closeness' (1992: 89), yet empathic concern relies on emotional responses that should then inform our political reasoning, without which we may approach something akin to a cultural psychopathy.[4] As Jesse Prinz points out, 'emotional deficits result in moral blindness' (2008: 369) and politics without moral ends in mind is precisely what we should look to avoid.[5]

Some evolutionary theorists come to a similarly trivialising conclusion about the emotive values of art, totalising all of its functions as mere supernormal stimuli. Writers such as Steven Pinker, echoing Stephen Jay Gould, dismiss this matrix of functions the arts serve as exaptive neural 'cheesecake, pack[ing] a sensual wallop unlike anything in the natural world because it is a brew of megadoses of agreeable stimuli' which potentially evolved to serve other adaptive functions (1997: 524–5). He goes on to single out music in particular as 'a pure pleasure technology, a cocktail of recreational drugs that we ingest through the ear to stimulate a mass of pleasure circuits at once' (528). He positions music and art as spandrels, or phenotypic byproducts of other qualities that were selected for. Spandrels are not necessarily adaptive – they 'piggyback' on other adaptations. This is the argument from mere superstimulus, and Pinker is correct that we seek activations of a dopamine system developed in earlier humans that music harnesses (along with much storytelling art, and activities ranging in direct fitness utility from purposeful exercise to the mere thrill-seeking of a rollercoaster ride).⁶ Yet surely superstimuli can still be reappropriated into other productive and purposeful behaviours, as we adapt to a world with cheesecake in it, working it into peripheral advantage (such as everything social that happens around such a stimulus)? Darwin himself thought that music offered early humans a way to exhibit passion, a demonstration of feeling that might be assumed by potential mates to be a sign of strength (even if this was not the case), conferring survival advantage that was thereby selected for (1989: 872). This function may have changed over time, especially as music and storytelling formalised and professionalised. The memorability of a melody that may remind us of the person who performed it, leading to predisposition toward them as a mating partner (Levitin 2006: 261), might be less important now than an extended display of dedication to a music group, and what the allegiance broadcasts about our social aptitudes. Music tells a story of affective causality (at a very basic level, for example, the push and pull of movement between major and minor chords), and one thing that both music and stories can provide is **a demonstration of affective aptitude or emotional intelligence**: our propensity to navigate the social world of emotions, and sometimes allegiance to a particular emotion (from Goths to Emos). Consider also the display of affective unity that is dance, which is inseparable from music.

So a superstimulus is rarely 'mere' superstimulus where more than one human is involved. Likewise many recreational drugs are considered superstimuli, but can be used socially or antisocially in a variety of ways. The interesting part of the story is not their status as superstimuli or spandrels, but the use such superstimuli are then put to. Exaptation continues; it does not halt at the generation of a superstimulus. In Joseph Carroll's summary of the 'cheesecake' perspective, art is 'a nonadaptive exploitation of adaptive sources of pleasure' (2004: 64). Carroll goes on to object to this view, as art and literature can provoke fitness by allowing us to imagine better ways of living (66–8). His view connotes a kind of fulfilling emotional imagination, which encourages us not only to foresee possibilities for living that may help us circumnavigate environmental challenges, but also to attach to, craft meaning and purpose from, and desire these changes. This would also be foundational to ethical conceptions of narrative's use, such as Charles Taylor's notion of storied projection as a means to imagine possible future moral identities ([1989] 2006: 48). Again, emotional projection provides the reason for change, and we will often demonstrate our emotional projections to others while engaged in narrative to broadcast these capacities.

There are further academic attenuations of the sensation-seeking function of narrative art. One politico-cultural argument proposes mainstream consumer culture's politically sedating excesses as motivationally centred on seeking affective commodities (Hardt and Negri 2008: 62) and affective newness (Bauman 2004: 26). Consumers seek affective stimulation; ergo emotive arts are bound in a study of commodity cultures. Pointing out the concurrence of consumer culture and our need for emotional stimulation, however, myopically ignores a rich history of similar use for story and art spanning millennia. Seeking such emotional stimulation is an ancient pancultural human behaviour, which we have consistently used our free time to engage in. If it has burgeoned today, we need to ask why that may be – it may turn out to be an abundance of non-work time which we have traditionally used to engage in emotion-seeking or -mediating activities, in which case fiction's proliferation is not the culprit so much as a symptom of post-producer and post-religious cultures.

The above rationalisations of narrative emotion-stoking in contemporary Western cultures may all be unfair characterisations of our emotional needs, as without emotional cues, our rational thought struggles to locate pivotal purpose (as in anhedonia), and where removed entirely can veer toward the psychopathic (of which a defining characteristic, in pathology, is an inhibited response to emotive stimuli).

It is also likely that we may be using story for different purposes now than those that presumably propelled its origins in the Pleistocene, thus the position of Carroll, Dissanayake and myself that we should presume in audiences some manner of 'fulfilment' motive: that we now use story to mediate our mood in a way that may keep us mentally fit, or that we assume may make us feel better, as in uses and gratifications theory. The **use of media to regulate our mood or shift affect** has been recognised by numerous researchers. For example, Greenwood and Long (2009a) ask what media we are most likely to turn to in differing affective states, while Edgar C. O'Neal and S. Levi Taylor (1989) look at how we might choose media to sustain an existing mood for an ulterior purpose, such as the choice of violent media when angered subjects perceive the opportunity to retaliate against a low-status provocateur. Shifting, sustaining or otherwise moderating affect through emotive storytelling can also distract us from our own daily concerns, and perhaps provide welcome relief from negative affect we have difficulty self-regulating. Consider going to a film when in the doldrums – the experience can quite seriously and lastingly change one's mood by transferring thought from our own tribulations to sympathy for others. We can even use narrative media simply to relax for long enough to get to sleep, a mood regulation that offers displacement of habitual thought processes, and the possibility of entering trance-like states. And we cannot forget that storytellers as well as audiences work to regulate their own emotional states. As Kay Redfield Jamison puts it: 'creative work can act as a way of structuring chaotic emotions and thoughts, numbing pain through abstraction and the rigours of disciplined thought, and creating a distance from the source of despair' ([1993] 1996: 123). So mood regulation provides not only another impetus to formulate and distribute stories, but it also allows us to explain emotional shifts to ourselves, and through narrativised causality feel in control of our own negatively valenced emotions – structuring them, displacing them, or otherwise taming them.

Although David Hume dismissed the 'excitation' explanation for fictive negative affect in his essay 'Of Tragedy', it is clear that most audiences exhibit sensation-seeking motivation that relies in some way on negative affect, even if it is balanced with correlate positive affect, or what Plantinga calls a 'working through' of negative emotions, leveraging them against positive affect to make our enjoyment of those emotions stronger (2009: 178–9). He postulates: 'If strong negative emotions are accompanied by physiological arousal, this arousal may contribute to the strength of the positive emotions' provoked later in the narrative (187); this is a version of excitation-transfer theory. Each narrative contains a roadmap of causal mood shifts that we might find pleasurable, perhaps as a rehearsal of methods for dealing with negative affect.[7] However, Hume also points out another motive for enjoying a narrative's particular suspense and sadness: they are turned into pleasure upon reflection of the artistry or eloquence of the author's expression of those emotions. We do clearly like to have pain expressed in narrative, as it is an acknowledgment of common feeling. When a sad story impresses us in its telling, we respond to how well it matches our own lived experience of sorrow. As in other non-narrative arts, we are taken by a kind of affective verisimilitude, if not a stylistically accurate representation of the world then indeed an emotional one. Once articulated and shared, a common emotion often seems easier to manage. This reaches behind the sensation-seeking to its social underpinnings: we feel these emotions in fiction to discuss their influence on us, perhaps gain a mastery over negative affect, and perhaps to shift our mood through socially distributed recognition of those feelings.

Of course, different media have different regulatory capacities, with Greenwood and Long finding:

> that individuals may derive more emotional satisfaction from music, which they can tailor to fit or uplift various positive and negative mood states. However, when feeling disengaged from their immediate social or emotional environment, television may offer viewers relaxation, structure and diversion. It is also possible that increased television viewing inhibits the development of alternative and perhaps

more successful solutions to boredom. In support of this idea, research has documented a 'passive spillover effect' in which viewers may continue to watch television even as the emotional gratifications of viewing have receded. (2009a: 620)

So various media will affect mood states in divergent ways, perhaps some more lastingly or effectively than others. Some media, for example, may have a greater capacity to orchestrate parallel neural responses across a range of viewers (Hasson et al. 2008), or activate mirror neurons, or be more effective in achieving emotional contagion, described by Elaine Hatfield et al. as 'the tendency to automatically mimic and synchronise facial expressions, vocalisations, postures, movements with those of another person, and, consequently, to converge emotionally' (1993: 96). Emotional contagion is just one of the many contagions a storyteller might attempt to affect in their audience, however. We also tell stories **to stimulate all manner of contagions in addition to the emotional**, from ideas and ideologies to ways of life and states of being. In *Connected*, Nicholas A. Christakis and James H. Fowler (2010) make a strong argument for the far-reaching influence of contagions (emotional, ideological, medical, dispositional, to name a few) across social networks, extending to people we have never met (our friend's friend's friend); thus the need for human studies to commit to social rather than individual psychological analysis. Stories are resolutely part of this process, and we will return to more specific uses of various contagions throughout the remainder of this narratology.

Exploring emotions has another side, too: we can use the narrative act to **achieve proximity to extreme emotion or a trauma that is hard to process, in order to replace mystification with causal attributions.** Melanie A. Greenberg et al. (1996) demonstrated that, beyond the established benefits of disclosure in recovering from personal trauma (not necessarily in a therapeutic setting), sharing narratives of both real and imagined traumas amongst fellow victims resulted in fewer illness visits, perhaps representing recovery or mental health gains. In their abstract, the researchers summarised possible attributions for their findings, which 'could reflect catharsis, emotional regulation, or construction of resilient possible selves' (1996: 588). James W. Pennebaker and Anna Graybeal contend of written narratives in trauma recovery, however:

> There is now sufficient evidence to suggest that the power of writing is not due to mere emotional expression in the sense of cathartic venting, or 'blowing off steam.' For example, participants who wrote only about their emotions about their most traumatic experience, without a description of the event itself, did not reap the benefits seen by those who both described the event and expressed their feelings about it (Pennebaker & Beall, 1986). Also, those who reported that writing served a cathartic function invariably had poorer health than other writers. (2001: 91)

Jessica McDermott Sales et al. also found, in 2003, that parents naturally tend to more causal prompting rather than emotional elaboration in discussing traumatic events with their children. It should be noted, however, that storytelling as therapy cannot be liberally applied to all situations. Camilla Asplund Ingemark outlines some Swedish studies questioning the 'cultural imperative to narrate' (2013: 12–13). Perhaps there are times when linear causal retelling of trauma becomes a re-living of that trauma, and needs to be put aside as a therapeutic method.

Whether or not the process could be called catharsis or a kind of purging, whether it allows for identity reconstruction or the means for control over one's emotions, it appears that simulating a proximity to extreme events and emotions via storytelling acts is a beneficial means to at least approach difficult psychological processes, and cope with them by application of a causal narrative structure. I would also stress that this process could be fictive (an abstraction from real-life experience) or non-fictive. Following Jill Littrell's 'Expression of Emotion: When It Causes Trauma and When It Helps' (2009), the exploration and reappraisal is what matters, and perhaps fictional displacement could help avoid re-ignition of trauma through retelling. Littrell's process of reflective 'listening, paraphrasing and acknowledging' followed by the question 'where to next?' and its inherent attendance to problem-solving cognition in trauma-recovery social work, the imperative to 'reframe, refocus and rework' (314), is similar to that attempted in much dramatic and humanistic fiction working in a realist mode: listening to and representing problems in a populace, and then directing attention to the agency of socio-ethical problem-solving. It could also apply to a humanist hermeneutics: listening to an author, reframing and refocusing their perspective through reading and debate, and then actively *working* with the results to ask where we ought to go next. I hope this discussion has demonstrated that the emotional functions of narrative reach far beyond the purely hedonic. I now turn to some more specific emotions bound in genre fictions.

Fear and Anger in Fiction

Affect studies – and particularly of that contradictory experience we seek out between the very controllability of our engagement in self-selected fiction and our involuntary emotional-state-matching – leads us naturally to the experience of horror in fiction. I have addressed appetites for negative affect such as sadness and tragedy in fiction; however we cannot address all aversive emotions as one, and it should be noted that horror provides a very different set of experiences deserved of their own scrutiny.[8] We use horror **in attempts to test our fears for validity and deflate fears**

that are not needed, and contrariwise to indulge and generate fears in others. This is just one dimension in the functions horror can serve, of course, as people of differing personalities will have different motivations for pursuing horror narrative (for example gore-watching, thrill-watching, independent watching and problem watching as identified by Deirdre D. Johnston in 'Adolescents' motivations for viewing graphic horror' 1995) and thus such narratives may produce different affects according to motivation. Aside from the pleasure of adrenaline (horror provides excesses of adrenaline) and existential meanings we attribute in proximity to extreme affect (covered above), we have long established that successive simulated exposure can be used to combat phobia, following Watson and Marks's findings in 1971 ('Relevant and Irrelevant Fear'). The same may be true of broaching irrational fears in narrative. Take the child, for example, afraid of the monster in the closet, growing up on a diet of monster movies, surviving, and effectively bringing themselves to the realisation that monsters are not much of an issue. Spectators who watch horror cinema consistently report desensitisation to its manipulations as they become more familiar with its cues (although we will investigate shortly how generalisable this desensitisation is to fears in the world). This phenomenon could be explained by 'the developmental shift from perceptual to conceptual processing' (Cantor and Oliver 2004: 232): the change in children's threat appraisal as they learn that things that look scary are not always the most pertinent dangers. Many writers, especially in the substantial tradition of psychoanalytic horror studies (including, surprisingly, psychoanalysis sceptic Noël Carroll [1990], albeit from an incongruity theory perspective), have focused on the repulsion felt toward human or bodily deviation and otherness, but this is just half the story.[9]

While fears of threatening animal otherness might not be innate (Thrasher and LoBue 2016), it makes sense that attention to the signs of danger – readable malice, the neuroaesthetic call of the colour red, and so on – would be prominently hereditary. Nonhuman monster designs can dole out these properties to a level of extreme superstimulus as can, for example, hyper-aestheticised cinematography of a crime scene. This may generate in some a self-sustaining feedback loop of fascination and repulsion; when we resolve the cognitive dissonance of these conflicting spectatorial urges by elevating the value of one response, the other reasserts itself, perhaps creating an internal puzzle over whether or not to engage (Moss-Wellington 2017: 48). Although the heredity of fascination with violence appears self-evident, as genes without sensitivity to the potential for others (including nonhuman others) to cause us mortal harm might not have lasted, perhaps various facets of these fears must be discarded through our experience when we find they are not needed, for example when we do not encounter seriously threatening animal otherness in our daily lives. Humans have the unique ability to *attempt* to use cognitive control (what we often call 'executive function') to ignore fear responses. Johnston also found a level of fear-mastery motivation in attendance to graphic horror (slasher films with human antagonists) was applicable across a number of personality traits, including differing levels of empathy:

> Although there is a subset of adolescents who view graphic horror for gore-watching motivations and who hold disturbing beliefs and responses to the viewing of graphic horror [such as female victims 'getting what they deserve'] . . . It is also comforting that independent watchers – who seek mastery over their fears, are characterized by low empathy, and report positive affective responses – tend to identify with the victim rather than the killer in these movies. (1995: 548)

It has also been suggested that the long-term effects of filmic fright (anxiety specific to horrific scenes can even last for years, unlike most other emotions media elicits) may be explained by the extremity of empathic engagement the genre requires (Cantor 2004: 297). But none of this is to suggest that our fear-mastery is necessarily successful – the important point is that we *attempt* to deflate fears through this kind of narrative, but perhaps when we minimise them in narrative, we in turn indulge or enlarge them elsewhere.

Dolf Zillman is a staunch sceptic of the fear-relief hypothesis (1998: 183–7), although the research he cites reveals that we have no serious longitudinal studies to ascertain prolonged exposure in young people to supernatural horror and recovery from its terrors, and it remains that, success or not, horror attendees report fear-mastery as one of their motivators (Johnston 1995). Zillman also postulates that humans share primal aggressive tendencies and fight-or-flight responses with other mammals, the usefulness of which is blunted or counterproductive in contemporary societies, and that we address this through violent media:

> Today's humans rarely can act on their fears and their anger by destroying the agents of circumstances that instigate these emotions. Feeling threatened by air pollution or global warming, for example, is unlikely to be remedied by any physical assault or by literally running away from it . . . It is this lack of evolutionary adjustment by the brain, then, that can be held accountable for a continuing, not entirely appropriate sensitivity to danger. (1998: 194)

However, he remains sceptical of another, more speculative Darwinian hypothesis 'that for millennia blood and gore were linked to the gratifications of food intake, to well-being, and to survival . . . a trace [from the selected paleomammalian brain] that manifests itself in a continuing interest in blood and gore and kills made by others' (192). Perhaps we need a more sensitive theory than emotional catharsis, then – a kind of fear regulation rather than expulsion, like the mood regulation outlined above – to properly analyse how horror attendees use the experience.[10]

Stories can alert us to dangers, and horror alerts us to the intent of others that mean us harm, but potentially not with the greatest success in directing our attention to the most relevant or preventable dangers: we are much more likely to be killed in a car accident than by another living thing with ill intent, yet we are less attuned to this in narrative (Grodal 2009: 108). Many have analysed fear as a political tool, however some, including George Gerbner and Larry Gross, see the stoking of fears specifically through media violence as a control mechanism with primacy above all others, or 'the established religion of the industrial order, relating to governance as the church did in earlier times' (1976: 194). These reminders of the generalisability and misattribution of fears explain why horror film may not always be viewed seriously, rated comparatively 'more predictable, silly, and low quality' (Oliver and Sanders 2004: 255) compared to other suspenseful media, and why horror comedy sits at an intriguing point in our psyche: through humour, we are questioning what may be a legitimate threat.

Cognitive anthropologist Pascal Boyer (2001) would hold the view that, as we have developed instinctual cognitive assets for both predator and prey detection, and it has benefited our ancestors to be hyper-alert to the mere possibility of danger, we are prone to a kind of pareidolia of agency, a cognitive inference over-detecting agency in natural phenomena which can play out as religious and supernatural belief – dispositional characteristics styled by Justin Barrett as 'hyperactive agency detection devices' in his book *Why Would Anyone Believe in God?* (2004). However, it is not just irrational fears that we deal with in horror narrative. We also observe people who live with violence in their everyday lives attending more horror films, leading back to the hypothesis of a coping method (see Boyanowski et al. 1974; Goldstein 1975; and Williams 1989). In any case, it seems that horror is used in attempts to process, test and potentially move past oppressive fears of aggression and victimisation, and that this impulse can equally be exploited through narrative, possibly to produce the reverse effect.

Sometimes we engage with narrative specifically to feel angry, or for a space to feel that our anger, despair and confusion in the face of a bafflingly cruel world is shared. So **we also use horror to experience existential oneness and shared anger**. Horror demographics, while not exclusively, still retain a spike of younger people in their audience (Val Morgan Cinema Network), and it may be an important developmental activity to bond through the particular anger of discovering the extent of injustices we face in the world we are being inducted into; this bonding can last later into life. Following Harvey Whitehouse's hypothesis that dysphoric rituals promote not just group identification, but also identity fusion, especially where routinised and activating an assumed collective memory (2013: 284–5), horror may also be a way to relate to and feel closer to peers, as well as others undergoing the experience simultaneously, through a simulation of shared traumatic experience. This could equally apply to sad stories and other genre film, and can actively be seen in our desire to be together while we witness dramatic storytelling, from the darkened theatre full of bodies to the pyjama party movie night, from the campfire singalong to the intimate folk gig. However, well-orchestrated terror holds a special place in the simulation of shared dysphoric experience. Neurocinematic researchers found that Hitchcock's *Bang! You're Dead* 'was able to orchestrate the responses of so many different brain regions . . . turning them on and off at the same time across all viewers' (Hasson et al. 2008: 16), much more so than other (non-frightening) media studied. This would also seem to give credence to the notion that horror is reliant on an intensified level of empathetic response, if we define affective empathy as feeling what another feels (feeling with as opposed to feeling for). However, if we value subtlety, subjective viewer agency, moral and political attention and questioning, or the capacity of films to inspire a range of different reactions and thought, such manipulations via screen could prove problematic. Social research also shows us that films offering extreme arousal, such as horror cinema, can have the effect of generating increases in attraction and behaviours such as talking and touching (Cohen et al. 1989). This could explain the enduring convention of horror movies used as date movies (Oliver and Sanders 2004: 248), perhaps even generating unity through the emotional contagion of alarm pheromones (Mujica-Parodi et al. 2009). This feeling of oneness – a presumption of shared experience that binds us, the sense of a kind of social monism – amounts to a storied method of social bonding. In social psychology, this is also referred to as 'self-other overlap'. Social psychologists have identified the emergence of this sensation in varying contexts, from the intimate 'feeling of "oneness" or merged identity with relationship partners' (Clark and Lemay 2010: 920) to feelings of oneness with strangers (Maner et al. 2002), both of which are predictors of prosocial and helping behaviours toward those we feel 'at one' with.

As an example, consider the recent popular zombie fad, emergent about half a century after *Night of the Living Dead* (George A. Romero, 1968) established the contemporary zombie's lasting iteration. Perhaps, as many popular horror creators including Stephen King have suggested (Tamborini and Stiff 1987: 433), horror provides a safe outlet for anger at our fellows, and the kind of human-on-human graphic violence which is the hallmark of the zombie genre would seem to support this (of course, another component of the zombie genre's endurance is the application of its central metaphor of contagious human malignancy across social and political contexts). This could provide an explanation for Tamborini and Stiff's finding that 'the graphic portrayal of destruction' is yet another motivation for viewing horror movies (432–3). By way of personal anecdote, not long ago I asked a friend how he feels at the end of a story in which zombies have obliterated the living world, and he replied, 'calm and cleansed'.[11] The increase in morbid conclusions of the apocalyptic variety across the zombie genre, and the spectator's pleasure in such ends, presents a challenge to Zillman's insistence on moral monitoring and the euphoric deliverance of justice as the primary motivator for audiences of violent fiction, contingent upon a built-up excitation transfer over the period of a narrative. This destruction delivers no justice (although it may for those totalising misanthropes among us), but in fact obliterates the need for justice. Perhaps if we dispositionally (or have reason to) experience generalised anger at humans but cannot express our misanthropy another way, apocalyptic horror is a harmless way to bond and experience oneness through such a frustration, recover some faith in fellows who share our ire and know that someone else also fantasises about total destruction. Perhaps this is sharing a kind of totalised justice *acknowledged* as a fantasy. Like voicing one's innermost anxieties to a trusted friend, we might begin knowing that our anxieties are overwrought and are not reliable reflections on the world, but still have trouble minimising them; after vocalising and externalising them, the feelings seem to have less dominance over us through their mutuality – the mystery and potential shame of these feelings is expelled. This is not quite the individual catharsis envisaged by King, but rather a social catharsis of implied affective mutuality. The theory points again to Wayne C. Booth's (1988) thesis of fiction as friendship. However, perhaps providing friendship is not so much the function of narrative here (as a real-life corporeal companion entails many other qualities not accessible by fiction); the feelings of relationality in our shared destructive horror fantasies might again distance us from our oblivion, or the weight of our daily worries, or the shame of feeling defective in one's negative effect, merely by having these things voiced.

Notes

1. These earlier treatises eventually gave way to the dominant terror-management theory (TMT) in which existential terror is alleviated by absorption in cultural narratives of progress or longevity, offering symbolic displacement of our mortality (for example, personal achievement, career progress, or the success of groups that will last after our death such as the family or nation state). Narratives of progress undergird such goals, and so threats to these goals in story are proxies: an indirect yet existentially felt impingement upon our survival (Maxfield et al. 2014).
2. Meaningfulness is more than just another pleasurable affect: Corey L. M. Keyes, Dov Shmotkin and Carol D. Ryff (2002) distinguish between subjective wellbeing (largely hedonic) and psychological wellbeing (largely attitudinal). Meaning and insight may have emotions attached, but they describe more than just an affective experience – they also describe ideas.
3. Although Smith rightly calls attention to the emotion–intellect binary, Spock and Data are actually interesting examples of characters envisioned as a challenge to this presumption. Characters such as these are regularly used in the *Star Trek* universe to examine logic's inability to account for an inconsistent world (for which we have incomplete knowledge) or for the social utility of emotion.
4. As Frans de Waal indicates regarding the kind of moral perspective-taking we find in narrative: 'Without emotional engagement induced by state-matching, perspective-taking would be a cold phenomenon that could just as easily lead to torture as to helping' (2008: 287). He describes this as, 'the beauty of the empathy-altruism connection: the mechanism works so well because it gives individuals an emotional stake in the welfare of others' (292). As Douglas Allchin explained in 2009's 'The Evolution of Morality', specific comprehension of the social conditions of reciprocity is not evolutionarily essential to allow for selection of cooperative and selfless traits – so other impulses beyond a conscious, rational, calculated or self-interested altruistic motivation can still influence moral behaviours.
5. In effect, these admonishments of audience emotion are an ethical overreach, in that they police abstract thoughts rather than actions.
6. One impetus for enjoying the negative affect of art could simply be that the biochemical stimulation triggers homeostatic mechanisms to produce pleasure. Just as crying at a tragedy in one's life might trigger an increase in levels of the prolactin hormone, consoling us with sweeter and more comforting feelings afterward, so might a sad song produce the same endocrine response (Huron 2011).
7. This can even have a much more direct survival benefit: we are more likely to procreate when in a good mood!
8. Happiness, sadness and mood regulation only take us halfway. Horror is unique as it combines the four other so-called 'basic emotions' (cf. Ekman 1992) – fear, anger, disgust and surprise.

9. Horror psychoanalysts have also, unsurprisingly, emphasised repressed violent desires, although fascination and obsession with violence may in fact be borne of our fear of committing immoral acts rather than a foundational, internalised and restrained desire to harm, or see others harm (Miller and Spiegel 2015). This would be similar to a 'high place effect' or *l'appel du vide* (Hames et al. 2012), as it does not express a desire but a fear. Desires and fears should not be so easily conflated. The fact that we imagine ourselves performing an action does not mean we have a repressed desire to do it. We just tend to fixate upon that which irks us, as in horror cinema that depicts the infliction of violence upon others: the notion of causing as much as receiving pain could be one of our deepest fears.
10. One example of fear regulation might be located in the post-atomic horror cinema of Japan, through which notions of complicity and victimhood are thrashed out and extricated, but not necessarily expelled.
11. Death metal fans experience a similar response, with 'peace and wonder' among the emotions they derive from violent and aggressive music (Thompson et al. 2018).

CHAPTER 4

Connectedness and Character

The Connectedness of Fiction

Experiencing oneness or closeness to others is not restricted to horror or other violent narrative, of course. We also **explore multiple affects and avenues for achieving a sense of connectedness through narrative, as stories facilitate foundational intimacy.** The following chapter explores uses of fiction related to our connectedness. Dissanayake (2000: 29) has pointed out that stories do not merely encourage intimacy; they can also be our means for *learning* how to be intimate with our family members and peers. She uses the complexities of baby talk and protoconversations as a primary example. Dissanayake identifies love as the experience of mutuality, and the arts as its elaboration (11), which is a pancultural phenomenon (cf. Murdock 1945); again, she sees these qualities as fundamental to our selective fitness, yet our understanding of these narratival utilities and our societal integration of their benefits can fluctuate. Even disagreements around narrative can bring people closer: consider the prevalence of book clubs in which we come together to air conflicting readings, or the way that when we discuss favourite songs and bands we really discuss minutiae and differences of opinion that we take pleasure in, and that often feel binding despite their disparities, simultaneously representing that which makes us different and the same. Greenwood and Long found that individuals high in the 'need to belong' (NTB) personality trait scale:

> may be particularly likely to feel lonely when not in the presence of others and/or use their time alone to reflect on missed or lost loved ones. Engaging more intensely with media may be one way that individuals high in social inclusion needs attempt to cope with loneliness. Media programs are after all, inherently social (indeed, even nature programs feature compelling narrators or experts), and may offer individuals with increased belongingness needs a soothing if temporary replacement for genuine social interaction. Moreover, recent research

> finds that individuals high in the NTB are also more empathically attuned to and accurate at interpreting others' emotions . . . This social and emotional vigilance may enhance the gratifications associated with transporting into media narratives, as well as identifying with and feeling imagined kinship with media characters. (2009b: 640)

So NTB is a predictor of cognitive and affective empathy, which might predispose some toward the gratifications of narrative transportation. The intimacy of the storytelling act – whether we call it connection, love or empathy – challenges boundaries in a globalised context, in which stories may travel at the lightning speed of a social media feed. Story's potential for intimacy at a distance is, therefore, an integral tool in the cosmopolitanisation of our social structures. This should be kept in mind while exploring related functions of fiction.

Intimacy and connectedness lead us again back to the capacity of narrative to provide something akin to friendship, and in Greenwood and Long's case above, **to combat loneliness**. This is hardly a contentious claim, yet what Greenwood and Long suggest is that media programmes may be *effective* in assuaging our loneliness in some circumstances. Clearly there are select cases when media practices such as television use, online social gaming, cinephilia or celebrity obsession come to replace more effective means to fulfil social needs, but we can use media to temporarily replace such activities. Often there is good reason why we cannot be closer to other people (including geographic isolation), and so we use absent or imagined others in narrative instead; not just parasocial relationships with fictive characters, but we also might imagine a connection to fellow audience members, narrative producers, or use more interactive modes of engagement (talking to a screen, gaming or role-playing) that rely less upon a notion of any precise other behind the narrative. We can again consider the shared attention that is part of narrative (Boyd 2009: 101), such as consuming media together or the particular pleasure of being read to. Sometimes we need to simulate this sense of unity when more direct options are not available.

The desire to feel closer to one another via narrative can be identified widely: through common knowledge of television characters and celebrities we can potentially discuss even with strangers, the common experience of being in a theatre and reacting as one, affinity with the ontic assumptions or insights a story presents or relies on, our familiarity with the conventions and culture around an arts practice or storytelling community, and so on. These experiences help us feel closer to others and build communities, and in some cases can reinforce pack mentality or **establish ingroups through common language**. Common language and discursive shorthand are necessary of course. A plumber, for example, has a list of terms she will not need to explain to others who are not plumbers – the language necessarily establishes a community for ease of communication. But sometimes the process isn't merely about facilitating ease of communication, rather it is also about demonstrating closeness to others through shared communicative codes, or challenging thoughts and ideas of outgroups using lingual exclusion. Consider that this happens in literary and media theory too: we erect boundaries of acceptable language use (and in hermeneutics, acceptable readings, often opposed to a disfavoured group's methodologies). A good example can be found in Terry Eagleton's inductive instruction for aspiring academics in *Literary Theory*:

> Nobody is especially concerned about what you say, with what extreme, moderate, radical or conservative positions you adopt, provided they are compatible with, and can be articulated within, a specific form of discourse ... Those employed to teach you this discourse will remember whether or not you were able to speak it proficiently long after they have forgotten what you said. Literary theorists, critics and teachers, then, are not so much purveyors of doctrine as custodians of a discourse. Their task is to preserve this discourse, extend and elaborate it as necessary, defend it from other forms of discourse, initiate newcomers into it and determine whether or not they have successfully mastered it. (1983: 175)

This dismally nihilistic example is apt as it robs scholarly communication of all other purpose than its use in defining an ingroup.

The phenomenon can readily be explained by communication accommodation theory: the way we adjust all manner of language, including 'pronunciation, pause and utterance lengths, vocal intensities, non verbal behaviors, and intimacy of self disclosures' (Giles and Smith 1979: 46), depending on whom we are speaking to. Communication accommodation extends to language selection (Giles and Smith also study how people select which language to use in bilingual encounters), as well as more abstract language use, such as mediated storytelling. Thus stories can establish ingroups through a common language as can everyday conversation and jargon use. When a film diverges from classic Hollywood formula, for example, and calls into question the conventions of a film language we have absorbed in order to comprehend these stories, we may become excited because it is marked *for us*, for intellectuals and cinephiles.

The languages used to achieve a narratival ingroup can be auditory as well as visual. Consider Michel Chion's (1994) concept of 'emanation speech', dismissed by Sarah Kozloff on humanistic grounds:

> Chion regrets the dominance of intelligibility; he prefers what he calls 'emanation speech' (what I term 'verbal wallpaper') – speech that may be inaudible, decentred, and that serves no narrative function. I find his argument misanthropic. (2000: 120)

In effect, Chion and many others in his wake have told us that our fascination with fellow humans is somehow intellectually inferior. The idea that unintelligibility of voices would more truthfully represent the 'cacophony' of 'the sounds of the world reproduced naturalistically in cinema' (Tarkovsky 1989: 159) is also wildly inaccurate – the human ear has, in part, co-developed with the larynx and vocal folds to privilege the frequencies on which the human voice projects its vibrations, and single them out for special attention. Once sounds are recorded (via the artifice of microphone selection), there is no ideal or more 'natural' amplification of those sounds. Differences in mixing decisions may speak to different audiences and in some cases mark themselves as being *for* certain audiences, as is the case with Chion's emanation speech. Substantial numbers of filmgoers enjoy and find much value in words and dialogue as a primary means to comprehend film; they are not wrong to enjoy this, and no one inroad into film appreciation is superior. Film theory, unfortunately, is littered with these false lingual binaries and battle lines, which are ready to be revealed as ingroup establishments. While ingroups are necessary, they need not be generated in such direct opposition to others (they can be practical more so than punitive), and where this is the case, we must be careful we are not engaging in bigotry.

Ingroup establishment and pack loyalty must be seen as evolutionarily purposeful human behaviours without diminishing our ability to problematise them, and we must acknowledge that these behaviours carry a lot of meaning for participants: most of us have familial loyalty, for example, offering clear survival and fitness benefits, which are pleasurably reinforced through storytelling and language codes specific to the family (Barnier and Van Bergen 2014; Fivush et al. 2011), although like any fealty it is contestable on cosmopolitan grounds. Yet extending the inclusivity of lingual group formation can be problematic too. Marketers of popular commercial narratives can attempt to offer the experience of being inducted into a community, a 'family' of fans or a world of related stories connected to a pivotal narrative experience, which serve as socially gratifying acceptance into a unique discursive space with its own language and social codes. We can consider fandom or alternate reality gaming as different examples of this process.¹ Jargon and specialised language are uniquely powerful in promoting group cohesion – for example, new nurses bond by adopting jargon (Wolf 1989). However, this discursive induction can be wielded as a commercial tool with great potency. Social media marketers can disguise themselves as disinterested members of the public, and moreover mimic the language used by audiences to create a sense of group solidarity. This means that they have an interest in making neophytes feel special when they are granted access to a new vocabulary with which to broadcast their allegiance. Ingroup language facilitates community-generation, but we cannot demonise or romanticise the process, as it is equally an innate component of our sociality, and of our attempts to manipulate social behaviours to exploit others.

Social Elevation and Fiction

Relatedly, stories can also quite clearly **help us to feel intelligent or equipped with special knowledge**, not just by presenting as 'intelligent', as in the puzzle film or smart-wave, but also in our rejection of perceived falsehoods or ineptitudes propagated through other stories. Recently, for example, we have seen the extension of B-film appreciation to vast fan cultures built around inept cinema such as *The Room* (Tommy Wiseau, 2003) and *Troll 2* (Claudio Fragasso, 1990), or 'so bad it's good' or 'badfilm' (Sconce 1995). We construct identities around a self-congratulatory cultural recognition. At times this function of story can take a turn for the haughty or downright degrading. Internet microstory phenomena, including viral Youtube videos, have introduced us to many new ways to scorn others, and can turn psychosis or other mental illness into objects of ridicule. Yet dramatic readings of illiterate missives such as 'How is Babby Formed' or 'Dot Dot Dot' can reveal both a sense of superiority against clear signs of dyslexia, or a developing use of English, and at the same time joy in appreciating its resultant peculiarity of expression and detachment from familiar language use. This particular phenomenon can seem new, but it is far from being unique to contemporary media. In *A Midsummer Night's Dream*, a play acutely concerned with our responses to outwardly bad, tasteless or inappropriate storytelling, Theseus requests his fellow audience members receive The Mechanicals' play with a particular kind of generosity:

> The kinder we, to give them thanks for nothing.
> Our sport shall be to take what they mistake:
> And what poor duty cannot do, noble respect
> Takes it in might, not merit. (5.1.89–92)

Theseus appeals not only for his fellow audience members to acknowledge the effort put into work that is not one's proficiency, effectively claiming that value can be found in processes and gestures rather than the merit of a finished product,[2] but he also models a method for enjoying the creativity of those who misunderstand social cues and language that we may find instinctive: in observing misunderstandings, savvy audiences have to explain to themselves precisely what was misunderstood. There exists a re-evaluative tension when we must reconcile a potential violation in the compromise of meaning (similarly to puns) and erosion of social norms, benign as they are refracted through the safe interposition of fiction. In our attempts to explain lingual or narratival norms, how they operate and how they have been mishandled, they become no longer instinctual and reveal their tacitly assumed codes. This too is 'our sport' when we watch *The Room* or 'How is Babby Formed', and a new kind of attentiveness is produced. What this makes an audience do is question *what exactly* we were laughing at, as per the ensuing interferences of Theseus and the lovers (with Hippolyta in turn questioning their response).

We have historically used all manner of narrative acts to single out the ways in which we are different, and sometimes intellectually superior, to others. By the same token, we also use narrative to consolidate or reify opinions – which may well be prosocial – by mere virtue of their collective production. When a product is formalised in the marketplace, such as the collective effort of a publishing house mass-producing a novel, there is a sense in which it is legitimated by the number of people involved in its production and distribution. This draws from our presumption of the validity of group thinking over individual thinking, which is contradicted by phenomena such as 'group polarisation', whereby groups tend to make more extreme decisions than individuals (Myers and Lamm 1976), collaborative inhibitions, in which working together in certain conditions can produce less favourable results for tasks requiring memory, and groupthink. Legitimation of a narrative in this way hinges on four qualities: more than one worker, using a substantial amount of resources, working through established procedures to reach us, with a greater audience share implying greater validity. Film studios, for example, play on these presumptions with grandiose title sequences. The Universal or 20th Century Fox logos connote the toil of many workers reaching many spectators working from reputably proven traditions at great expense. Narrative formalised through the norms of engagement with a medium can be very powerful in reinforcing the impression that our opinions are shared by important others, and therefore valuable. There can be some self-congratulation involved when we presume our artistic predilection is shared by a vast sum of others.

This can clearly be related to the function of story **to flatter oneself and others, and thereby concoct hierarchies of personal attributes**. Most narratives contain messages of congratulations to their audience for merely engaging with them – in fact some have positioned the inherent flattery of all media, in that it so consistently treats our attention as a prizeworthy goal and is designed to please us, as the primary gauge of a mediated epoch (Zengotita 2007). There are many clear objects of flattery available to a storyteller (for the venerable Baron Munchausen, his own valour, extraordinary undertakings and conquests are prime), but for now I will continue to focus on intelligence, which is one of the primary objects of storied flattery. Media presuming a certain level of audience acumen can become used as an apparatus to determine intelligence hierarchies, which in some cases eclipses other meanings suggested by the content. Thomas Elsaesser, writing on the puzzle movie, points out that some popular film scholars conflate cinema with 'doing philosophy' in order to elevate the gravitas of their concerns when viewing film (2009: 36). Similarly, D. A. Miller describes his concept of 'Too Close Reading' (2010) through the prism of the nested metatextual puzzles in *Strangers on a Train* (Alfred Hitchcock, 1951). While he keeps returning to the seeming 'pointlessness' (125) of the pursuit, and in so doing makes a case for narrative reading as a kind of autotelic fun, he also reveals the self-congratulation that such fun is grounded in. After a fleeting reference to 'our swollen heads', he backhandedly offers the following regarding Hitchcock's appearances in the film: 'One would also suppose that many people in the audience, less clever than ourselves, fail to notice his appearance, even though (barring infants and aliens) such ignorant spectators are hard to come by' (107). Later, he becomes enthralled by measuring his intelligence against the director's: 'We'd thought we were patronizing Hitchcock when all along it was he who was patronizing us; in smugly discerning him, we were only being his dupes' (113). Essentially what this demonstrates is that Hitchcock's works flatter us, and that we respond with expressions of our own self-flattery in re-narrating them, but then if we look closer, good stories can also offer opportunities to dismantle that flattery. Miller, in his facetiously camp style, suggests interpretive, scholarly or hermeneutic one-upmanship as part of the narrative itself; the problem is that he sadly does not push himself to imagine anything beyond the gameplay. For Miller, the appeal of narrative readings and hermeneutics is, at least in part, about separating out who is intelligent, and who is less so. When we posit the hierarchic politics of flattery, cajoling, intelligence and superiority in art as a grander narrative beyond the text, this function of fiction can come to transcend any relevant meaning-making provided by the text itself. In this way, any text can become a redundant cipher for our own smartness, or allow us to order people, real and imagined, into hierarchies of traits including intelligence (or moral hierarchies, or aesthetic hierarchies, given the right narrative). Texts can flatter the reader, the author(s) and the communities they share by virtue of having engaged with the same text, and by distribution of the values associated with that text. Conversely, we should also acknowledge the capacity for mental work performed by audiences following a narrative – from puzzle films to their crime fiction predecessors – as potentially exercising and developing mental feats which have pragmatic use in our daily lives, including social problem-solving. Stories can probably both make us more intelligent, and make us *feel* more intelligent.

Another curious narrative experience that allows us to feel clever is the prediction of correct ways to respond to a given text, often positively reinforced by setups and payoffs. For example, we have probably all experienced being seated in the cinema next to someone who laughs outrageously, forecasts oncoming events from blatant signposts, or names the effect associated with a sequence ('isn't that sad'), demonstrating that they know the correct way to respond to a narrative's cues. This is a version of the mere-exposure effect, first documented by Gustav Fechner in 1876, and comprehensively researched by Robert Zajonc in the 1960s:

> People seem to misattribute their increased perceptual fluency – their improved ability to process the triangle or the picture or the melody – not to the prior experience, but to some quality of the object itself. Instead of thinking: 'I've seen that triangle before, that's why I know it,' they seem to think: 'Gee, I like that triangle. It makes me feel clever.' (Margulis 2014)

Elizabeth Hellmuth Margulis asserts that this is why we enjoy repetition in music, and also that 'repetition serves as a handprint of human intent'. Reacting in the way a narrative elicits – and in some cases demonstrating affect contrary to that which a narrative attempts to invoke – can make us feel intelligent, socially included, comforted by the 'flow' of ingrained readership practices (in the Csíkszentmihályi sense), satisfied with one's own performance as reader or spectator, reassured by the corroboration of recognised rules, traditions and symbols, and perhaps satisfied that we can trust the narrator. Thus we also use story to **engage in ritual**. Story can be seen as having a function like innumerable other rituals performed with others: it can comfort or reinscribe values with procedural scripts and provides social cohesion. It solaces by allowing us not to have to worry about what to do in a given circumstance – we know how to proceed through a narrative, just as we know the expected procedures at a funeral, not necessarily because they have inherent meaning, but because they provide a succouring script which circumnavigates the discomfort of having to manage both one's independent actions and grief simultaneously.

In Whitehouse's (2013) distinction between imagistic and doctrinal modes of group cohesion, ritualised story behaviours may be an imagistic method to make us feel fused with others undergoing the same narrative experience: 'The impression of sharing subtle or hidden meanings of the ritual experience is thought to contribute to high levels of identity fusion among participants. We call this the "imagistic mode" of group cohesion' (284–5). This could apply where we perceive that we share special access to the particulars of a text, from collective knowledge of genre tropes or broadly applied media knowledge (such as cultural references), to identification of small innovations or deviations within a text, and subtle reactive behaviours the reader of the text may exhibit to their fellows during engagement. However, people use ritualised narrative in different ways: one cinemagoer may attend twice a year, another may routinise their participation to a weekly event or an appreciation society. As narrative appreciation involves procedural scripts – ways we are supposed to respond and act – participation, in this case, also involves some doctrinally ritualistic qualities. It is not surprising that the more we participate in a ritual (such as attendance at a regular event, a reading group, a songwriting club, or cheap cinema Tuesdays), the more trust and cooperation will be generated with people we see undergoing the same experience.

However, the ritual aspect of story offers more than a Durkheimian social organisation or reinforcement. In Victor Turner's interpretation, story is a liminoid experience that depicts and mimics liminal experience, and is perhaps proliferating in the post-industrial world (our story addiction again) as a means to make up for a lack of liminal ritual in our lives. He argues that genres in entertainment and theatre can be:

> historically continuous with ritual, and possess something of the sacred seriousness, even the 'rites de passage' structure of their antecedents. Nevertheless, crucial differences separate the structure, function, style, scope, and symbology of the liminal in 'tribal and agrarian ritual and myth' from what we may perhaps call the 'liminoid,' or leisure genres, of symbolic forms and action in complex, industrial societies. (1974: 72)

Turner has analogised ritual at all levels of society with theatre, noting the social drama characterising both: breach, schism, redress and reintegration (1982). Redress is a critical moment of possibility emulating the space before and after a ritualised experience, whereby the individual is put into a kind of crisis, becomes no longer whole, unresolved, and must move through the upheaval to find a new resolved self.[3] Stories are the 'play' or 'leisure' or 'nonserious' version of such a crisis, thus liminoid. Returning to our exemplary loud audience member introduced above, the demonstrative and performative acts within a theatre audience reveal a presumption of communitas at the time of engagement: the supposed equality of spectators during their common experience in proceeding through a narrative together seems to permit acknowledgement of the common experience, and perhaps a desire to resolve its inherent upset (or 'drama') socially. The process of acknowledging an affective-procedural unity chimes with both Whitehouse's cohesive and Turner's antagonising conceptions of ritual. Thereafter, narratives can offer us an apparent way to resolve the crisis, tools to resolve it, or leave us hanging within the liminal emulation – all have their place.

A particular kind of ritual outlined above deserves special recognition: **story as rite of passage introduces a subsequent bartering of control via access to narrative**. Arnold van Gennep's (1909) early musings on the rite of passage ritual inspired Turner to expand on the liminal in broader ritualised settings, yet what is of interest to us here is what happens *around* this particular ritual rather than its actual procedure. Stories, where constructed as rites of passage, are negotiated as maturity markers. For example, parents often withhold certain media from their children until they reach a certain age. This can be regulated at a political level through governmentally recognised ratings systems and enforced by retailers or admissions staff. The rite of passage may then be used as a tool to haggle power and identity formation: some children, for example, will attempt to see films containing content their parents do not want them to witness before permission is granted, thus the story becomes a device for parent, child and state to negotiate the development of the child's agency.

Character and Identity

The relationship between ritual and identity suggests another major inroad to narrative pleasure for a majority of audiences: character identification. We **articulate our identities through character comparisons,** often subliminally throughout a lifetime's absorption of reiterated identity handles across media; and simultaneously we enter the very familiar ground of identity politics. Media theorists such as bell hooks and Douglas Kellner have attempted to demonstrate just how far the pedagogical function of cultural artefacts, such as film, extends. Perhaps, they suggest, identity options gleaned from media narratives are more ingrained than any attempted complication of such narratives in formalised education. Hooks presumes a primacy of media content above other means for identity formation: 'my students learned more about race, sex, and class from movies than from all the theoretical literature I was urging them to read' ([1996] 2009: 3). One question that can be asked about these identity politics, however, is how much an individual film or product is able to tell us about identity formation. That is, close readings of texts can neglect the influence of media saturation or cultivation, and likewise the values that percolate in peer groups and at home, the influence of which could explain more about our lives and behaviour than the content of the texts themselves; this casts some doubt over a more traditional text-based hermeneutics. For now, we should keep these contextual considerations in mind when we approach identity politics.

If, as hooks suggests, we choose to identify with fictional characters before we identify with the moral dialogue the characters spur, then media fictions have powerful ethical agency. But there are other possibilities: audiences can also be more conversant with rather than receptive of identity markers. Theodor Adorno, for instance, sees all forms of identification as reductive constructs and therefore focuses instead on what he calls non-identities in *Negative Dialectics* (1973). Once established, we tend to be drawn to question the efficaciousness and validity of apparent identity reductions such as, for example, our blackness or whiteness, maleness or femaleness; these discussions of validity are subsumed into the ethical dialogue identity handles introduce. This tension is recognised by writers as diverse as Murray Smith, in *Engaging Characters* (1995a), and Jane Stadler, who submits the possibility of a more reflexive 'ethical gaze' (2008: 211, 215) and a film's ethical 'afterlife' (2): the effects of our ethical attention to character may echo in a Riceourian fashion beyond our conscious investment in the story itself at the time of engagement. For Charles Taylor, identity *is* a story about our moral orientation and its mutability, 'similar to orientation in physical space' ([1989] 2006: 48). Constructs, reductions to conceptual scripts, and the ease of ethical determination and action these scripts provide must have some utility to be in such widespread use. Identity may be a helpful reasoning shortcut to avoid decision paralysis if we had to weigh every decision based on ideals of the self and the other constructed in each instance. Martha Nussbaum, in fact, sees the identification process as essential to theory of mind, reason and empathy:

> The narrative imagination is not uncritical: for we always bring ourselves and our own judgments to the encounter with another, and when we identify with a character in a novel, or a distant person whose life story we imagine, we inevitably will not merely identify, we will also judge that story in the light of our own goals and aspirations. But the first step of understanding the world from the point of view of the other is essential to any responsible act of judgment. (2002: 299)

The reductive nature of identity description promotes coherence by which we then have a tangible other to identify and empathise with, but this also means we have to decide when identity handles become too reductive, or 'typified' beyond reason, and when they misinform us about human complexity and otherness. This is a debate reaching all parts of our lives. Its foundational presumptions and complication may occur in our homes and amongst family and peers as much as it does in media. It will have sociobiological and dispositional components. Consumers also talk back to media producers when they foreground certain identity handles at the expense of others. Some scholarship presumes that audiences do not have awareness of the character types our media trades in, but a sexist, for example, may be acutely aware of reductive or essentialised notions of a male and female type, and yet still subscribe to those notions, being less aware of precisely how their thinking about those types produces biases. Humanistic narrative, cultural scholarship (like that of hooks) and narrativised methods for mapping the experience of others (like phenomenological ethnography) are not just an exercise in promoting awareness of the types we use – they also extend to awareness of our biases around those types. A narrative's trajectory can reveal the biases evident in both our view of others and our self-schemas.

As well as ordering and informing our own personality and aspirations, sometimes having characters we identify with onscreen can make us feel like the person we are is okay, as our pre-existing self-concepts are recognised; through representation, we are implicitly accepted by an external party (and in this way, we identify too with a presumed author). When we read a book and identify with the protagonist, for instance, we might feel comforted that the values that make up our self-schema are shared. We might also **broadcast our self-schemas using the stories we like**. For instance, the books on our bookshelf introduce other people to our chosen identities – even books we have not read can sit on our shelves to tell a grander story about our own self-schema.

None of this is to suggest that it does not matter whom we identify with, or that the moral dialogue and cohesion available in character identification should be seen as an ethical end in itself. John H. Lichter and David W. Johnson's seminal 1969 research showing prejudice reduction in children exposed to multiethnic story characters was corroborated by Phyllis A. Katz and Sue R. Zalk in 1978, who went on to show that exposure to a fifteen-minute story featuring African-American characters was possibly more effective at reducing bias than superordinate goals, and the effects were still observable four months after the exposure. If this is what storytellers are capable of, there is, then, an ethical imperative to expand the bounds of representation past those known handles an audience may ordinarily choose to identify with. The humanist storyteller might strive to circumnavigate the demand-driven marketplace for stories already known to the audience, with easy identification handles, and wherever possible represent multiple others their audience is less likely to have contact with (so especially minorities). In summary, identity is a series of reductions by which our moral selves and choices are made comprehensible, electable and governable, yet their inherently reductive nature introduces moral debate and a humanistic imperative not just to complicate types, but also the complex processes by which we attach to biases around those types. This will include representation of a range of characters of varied backgrounds in fiction.

While on the subject of perspective-taking, we also use narrative **to vicariously roleplay**. In addition to character identification, we live through characters' experiences of events that we would never be party to, and observe behaviours we ourselves would never perform. To witness someone else perform an exciting other life is a pleasure that can be different from mere identification, as it does not necessarily rely on us feeling like – or even wanting to *be* like – a protagonist. This principle can be extended to personality traits we do not covet, but enjoy imagining what it might be like to live with: most of us do not want to be as bloodthirsty or ill-tempered as an action hero, for example, but still enjoy the simulation of someone else's experience of these traits. If a function of fiction is to play out alternate realities, courses of action and moral responses, then there may be a particular kind of pleasure in adopting the perspective of a character who leads us somewhere new, simply as they behave in ways we would never condone; such a simulation could reinforce the reasonableness of our own moral actions by showing us the consequences of poorer alternatives, for instance. That this is somewhat a vicarious version of roleplay, without attendant fantasies of real-life imitation, complicates notions of pure identification or mimesis. Any line between observing values in fiction and absorbing those values needs to be very carefully drawn. We also cannot forget the pleasure the actor can take in playing a role, or that a nonactor may take when playfully adopting a storied role among friends (think of a *How to Host a Murder Party* game), or indeed any kind of performative gesture we enjoy with others, however fleeting.

This points to the experience of videogamers, as roleplaying a character or avatar is a convention most games rely upon. Fears of the loss of human identity or posthuman claims of an identity fusion between consumer and medium have followed past media developments, right back to the notion of the camera apparatus stealing one's soul, and Charlie Chaplin becoming one with the machinery of *Modern Times* (Charlie Chaplin, 1936). These qualms continue to shift focus to new media as it arrives, such as videogaming today (see the essays in Jahn-Sudmann and Stockmann *Computer Games as a Sociocultural Phenomenon* 2008), and similar horrors of posthuman identity fusion with machines are played out in films like *eXistenZ* (David Cronenberg, 1999) and television series such as *Black Mirror*. But in order to take seriously these fears of a loss of identity, we need to ignore the vicarious nature of storied roleplay, in that it is still a social storied act, an authored world created for others to consume with parameters that delineate the extent of the possibilities for an avatar's action, and therefore restrain free identification. Histrionics centred on the boundaries of the human under threat prevent us from being specific about the changing nature of cognitive engagement in new media forms, and the narrative relationship between developers and their audiences.

On the other hand, we still seek stories that **affirm ideological positions to justify our own lives and beliefs**. Instead of engaging in narrative to explore different moral identities, attitudes or outcomes, it has long been noted that we seek out stories that flatter or justify pre-existing dispositions (producing effects such as confirmation bias). When we discuss fiction's relative ability to change hearts and minds, this is the question that is often silently addressed: whether or not one's self-schema is able to be touched, and whether or not our purposeful engagement with fiction as self-flattery diminishes its power to reach us. However, surely fiction is capable of both reifying prior beliefs as well as sowing the seeds of doubt, if not subverting our ideologies unhindered? In an observation of Leon Trotsky's *Literature and Revolution* ([1925] 2005: 120), which subsequently became a popular maxim of early documentary filmmaker and theorist John Grierson (quoted in Ellis 2000: 236), art is not a mirror but a hammer. Not only can it be used to 'shape society' as such, but it is also by repetition and reiteration that the values imparted in the narrative arts are absorbed. Especially in experimental media studies, we often run the risk of privileging singular fictional engagement above the longitudinal study of repetition in storied cultures. Perhaps single narratives tell us less than trends. However, I am certain that most can recall a number of powerful moments in narratives that have left them shaken, and opened a liminal space where they were at least able to question their ideologies; some may seek this narrative experience more than others. It remains, however, that much of the time we seek narratives that will complement our prevailing belief systems.

The ability of stories to reinforce self-schemas also points toward **narrative's function as status marker**. For some, engagement with a particular narrative artform – for example opera or ballet – will also be used to broadcast their social standing. This is not to dispute enjoyment of that art, but merely to point out that the narratives we choose can be a status marker like any other accoutrement we use to display our social class, our allegiance to and even solidarity with that class. From Thorstein Veblen's recognition of the wilfully 'conspicuous' or performative nature of consumption in 1899's *Theory of the Leisure Class* to Quentin Bell's *On Human Finery* in 1947, many have noted that fashion tells a story of one's class, and likewise so do story choices. It is not just the medium or form itself that speaks of our status, but particular narratives within a medium too – we might want people to know that we enjoy arthouse movies because they tell of our access to education, or Adam Sandler movies because they tell of our solidarity with another class of presumed audience members. These underlying narrative engagement signifiers introduce a subtextual level of communication that becomes evident when we analyse the symbolism associated with various media. I now turn to address the utility of such symbols.

Proximity and Refraction

Character and identity clearly entail an interpretive push and pull for the audience, the examination of which reveals a close and often overlapping relationship between literal and symbolic representations of humanness; in turn we might ask what function the abstraction of symbolism performs for us in narrative. In symbolic representation, we can **displace discursive candour to a safer allegorical realm** when dealing with sensitive interpersonal matters. Writer/director John Sayles's 1999 film *Limbo* reconsiders all manner of storytelling activities, including his own role as a filmmaker, through a matrix of inconclusive narratives: not only does his own film end in the middle of a survival crisis, the conclusion of which would have told us the correct response to the situation, but the film also features multiple nested stories, many ethically stimulating, which reach no conclusion – a challenge to our need for ethical closure and certitude. Moreover, many of the characters use open-ended stories to talk about their lives analogically, rather than directly. A primary example is the fiction Noelle (Vanessa Martínez) crafts in an attempt to convey her emotional problems to mother Donna (Mary Elizabeth Mastrantonio). Says Sayles: 'Sometimes the storytelling just takes her and sometimes she looks at her mother and just lays it out, especially the angry parts. She could not have those literal conversations with her mother, but she can tell those stories' (West and West 1999: 30). In this realm of vague allegory, it is possible to hurt others, but it is also possible to avoid hurting them too much with directness or candour – and perhaps the ambiguity of the act opens the possibility of finding new answers to our personal problems. Sonya Dal Cin et al., for example, argue in 'Narrative Persuasion and Overcoming Resistance' (2004) that fictional stories may be especially persuasive for those who hold strong countervailing attitudes, not only because the ideas embedded in a story are implied rather than explicitly stated, but also because the simulation demanded by stories leaves few resources for counterarguing.[4] Perhaps this rhetorical technique could be extended to a pedagogical function, too. One might teach fictionalised versions of events in films like *Capote* (Bennett Miller, 2005) or *Frost/Nixon* (Ron Howard, 2008) to journalism or history students, or use the teaching of humanistic literature and cinema to convey prosocial notions without having to state them so directly that students may balk or be otherwise put off (one foundational premise in educational English studies from the nineteenth century onwards). To be told explicitly of these things outside of narrative might be less appealing, and even be received as a kind of condescension. It is also a way to reach those students who are more predisposed toward narrative transportation (Dal Cin et al. 2004: 186) in addition to those who value a more directly discursive learning. In a way, the discursive refraction of narrative can actively hide persuasive and informative intent if an audience is primed against these functions; so stories provide a way to reach people through allegory or other refractive devices, who may not be as receptive to direct communication.

Katz and Zalk's (1978) research suggests that perhaps the psychological distance and sense of control afforded by mediated perspective-taking may in some cases be more beneficial for empathy production than working cooperatively with outgroup members or superordinate goals (Mar and Oatley 2008: 181). So **generating emotional distance by which**

social relationships seem more manageable may be another function of storytelling, which in turn may generate empathy. If this is the case, perhaps through stories **we rehearse care responses to others in a controllable fictive environment**, so rather than relying on a spontaneous direct empathy when encountering another, we may be ready with a procedural empathic script to reach for, based upon identity handles gleaned from media or story. Consider the case of sentimental, sensational or Romantic story modes, as well as Peter Brooks ([1984] 1985) and Ben Singer's (2001) works on the complexities of the melodrama: the emotional excesses on show (and the intended audience's mirroring of characters' internal states) could be a rehearsal of care responses to others. Rehearsing responses, which occur in the safe space of narrative, not only primes empathy, but also its increased familiarity could make us feel more in control of, and less threatened by, our responses to unfamiliar others or the inherent vulnerability required to navigate human differences in a social world.

However, explicatory accounts of a fictive character's psychology and identity allow us to **simulate a direct access to mental states**. The kind of private information we are afforded to a fictive character moves far beyond that which we would have in life. We use such insight into inner worlds to make inferences about how people operate. As emphasised by Mar and Oatley throughout 'The Function of Fiction' (2008), this is story as practical shorthand for describing social fabrics. Proximity to a character's thoughts and the social fabric it describes, however, need not be opposed to allegorical refraction: we can tell an internal narrative with expository prose that both describes a thought process and still entertains symbolist readings (Moss-Wellington 2017: 53–7).

Similarly, stories can offer **a simulated experience of authenticity or direct access to a truth** that is not internal or personal. David Boyle (2003) contradicts writers like Thomas de Zengotita in claiming that, despite the march of pervasive mediation and exposure to artifice across an increasingly virtualised globe, there is a strong, collective and instinctive pull in the opposite direction toward a principle we may feel necessary, even while we cannot quite define its precise nature or its value to ourselves: this is authenticity. He writes, 'Despite the possibilities of cosmetic pharmacology, despite the conveniences of virtual communities or the demands of the market, the possibility of inconveniently human relationships with real people won't somehow slip unnoticed out of our lives' (Boyle 2003: 202–3). The concept of an unmediated real is the site of resistance to conglomerates masquerading as individuals, embedding advertorial narratives in news media, product placement in entertainment media, or even concocting creative fictions of their own that sit unnoticed alongside non-commercially motivated arts, like a Disney mural comingling with the work of a local graffiti or street artist. These paranarratives goad us to think of and respond to their originary institutions as acquaintances and friends, often using social media to blur the lines between friendship and information-exchange on the one hand, and public relations, advertorial, personalised commodification and brand enthrallment on the other. While Boyle focuses on the way in which businesses motivate ideals of purer humanness – and even the symbols of counter-culture and rebellion become owned by a handful of companies (122) – we can also look at story as a linked component: neither stories nor businesses are corporeal entities capable of registering pleasure or pain, but they both attempt to connect with us in a way that feels like real human connection.

So if we do need to assess the authenticity value of narratives, how can this be achieved? In making such assessments we begin with a definitional problem, in that different notions of authenticity are applied to different entities. Take food production, for example. The food that reaches us has gone through a variety of human mediations: planting, tending, harvesting, packaging and transportation, all of which can be subject to analysis of relative artificiality. Evaluating authenticity in food production, then, has more to do with the *number* of processes the food has been through and how synthesised they are (for example, the chemical compounds involved in each process), and in some cases, the newness of these procedures stands in for our evaluation of how artificial they are. This has been the case from the publication of Carlo Petrini's *Slow Food Manifesto* in 1989 right up to today's Palaeolithic Diet. Thus food authenticity standards, and the narratives of purity they rely on, are different from the standards by which we evaluate a business or a story or even an individual. The authenticity of an individual, for example, usually describes how beholden they are to inauthentic culture (divisive claims of this kind have been made by philosophers including Kierkegaard, Heidegger, Sartre and Nietzsche). Contrariwise, the authenticity of a business is often motivated by claims about its size, locality and processes. Following from this conceptualisation of corporate authenticity, the extent of collaboration on a product can, perhaps unfairly, be used to assess its legitimacy – and this is true of stories, too. In film studies, auteur theory bridges the authenticity claims between business and story, as figures such as Andrew Sarris emphasise the quality of directorial 'dominance' (1976: 246). Sarris suggests that in any filmmaking context the authoritative ideas of a singular individual will be more valuable than ideas developed and expressed by an egalitarian group without 'dominance'. The absurdity of the claim is revealed when we apply the same concept to any other field outside of the arts: we may ask whether such a dominance by one figure in the family, in a government, or indeed a business, reduces or expands the quantity and quality – or the authentic legitimacy – of ideas and output. Our notions of authenticity, then, are often contradictory and mutable depending on the object of evaluation, providing uneasy foundations from which to ask how we assess the legitimacy of a given narrative.

That said, the longing for authenticity is completely understandable as the 'strategic responsiveness' (Brants 2012: 24) of tailored content becomes more prevalent (cf. Davies 2008), media becomes redundantly fawning (c.. Zengotita 2007) in order to get to the real business of selling us a product, and media engagement becomes ubiquitous and inescapable across our daily routines. We want to have trust in storytellers, our facilitators of social dialogue, with good reason: not only is higher social trust linked to health outcomes (Barefoot et al. 1998; Subramanian et al. 2002), as Richard Wilkinson and Kate Pickett point out, 'Trust is of course an important ingredient in any society, but it becomes essential in modern developed societies with a high degree of interdependence' (2010: 214). This is why stories can embed a claim on authenticity to comfort an audience, to affect trustworthiness. Yet trust is not uncomplicated, either. Mistrust can be both a healthy and reasoned component in our interactions with the media, and those interests the media selectively represents (Schudson 2012). It is no coincidence that the erosion of perceived trustworthiness in authority figures and their channels of representation (Peters and Broersma 2012: passim) is correlated with an increase in elite wealth-concentration and inequality across the globe (Wilkinson and Pickett 2010: passim); as power is consolidated, we have good reason for a generalised media scepticism. But this does not mean that mistrust will always be directed toward the most harmful storytellers or institutions (the Trump phenomenon is a disastrous case in point). Some see the genesis of prejudice as a historical biological imperative to mistrust strangers and outsiders, a heritable trait that helped our ancestors protect against pathogens and parasites within the village community (Schaller 2006).[5] In a largely urbanised globe, traits once adaptive in the village community are gradually, collectively reassessed through cultural mediation. Perhaps this is an important part of the re-evaluative process we are addressing through narrative: reassessment of the conditions of a reasonable trust in others is part of our cultural evolution. Kees Brants wrote ominously of journalistic media, 'If trust is the glue of social relations and the medicine for restoring or establishing cohesion in a society in a midlife crisis, then we are slightly in trouble. Trust is a necessity for the contribution of politics and media to a well-functioning and legitimate democracy' (2012: 26). In emphasising the value of critical inquiry, perhaps scholars can overlook its complication – scepticism and scrutiny must be balanced with the human need for public trust, a comfort that authenticity narratives provide, in journalism as in fiction.

Despite all this, it is sobering to remember that at times we genuinely need media to represent the real. Our daily choices have international consequences, and we require information sources at least attempting objectivity *and* an enlightened perspective on the information to know how to behave, considering the frightening array of ethical decisions we now confront in the developed world. So we rely on shortcuts of reasoning to assess believability and reliability of sources and information, which is reasonable, as we cannot spend our whole lives researching each source. That is, breeding more critical thought, which might be seen as a key pedagogical goal within the humanities, does not solve the problem of our inherent need for information and stories to trust. Stressing the political efficacy of public trust in media, Stephen Coleman et al. admit, 'we need to be able to rely upon the reputation of the reporter without having to check and recheck every single account that is given to us' (2009: 4). The falsification problem of proliferated informational sources online breeds its own makeshift solutions. Many of the shortcuts we might take to trusting a source are aesthetic, which is a great contemporary dilemma: the creators best at understanding the politics of representing reality need not have a premium on authenticity or truth. For example, as Monroe Lefkowitz et al. (1955) demonstrated, we appear to place greater trust in people wearing suits; perhaps likewise with handheld camerawork, exploiting our recollection of documentary footage, or an internet site with a minimum of design errors (Bierhoff 2004: 49). In fact, it is quite likely the only difference between these creators is that the credible-appearing source could afford the means to affect more expensive representations of truthfulness – that is, they purchased credibility. This is a worry. Increasingly, one of the moral-societal dilemmas of the information revolution appears to be how we will choose to trust representations of reality. Knowledge of this problem is naturally going to make us suspicious of anything that appears to buy our trust by emulating reality. Affecting outsider status through carefully constructed aesthetic 'error' may connote a reaction against this problem, but it does not solve the twin dilemmas of authenticity and the need for public trust.

Any humanist hermeneutics, then, must take into account a human social need for public trust, iterated in authenticity narratives, whenever we stress a generalised benefit to some manner of sceptical or media-critical thought; yet such readings must also acknowledge how these needs are exploitable through narrative. We might even use this understanding to reclaim hermeneutic interest in the functional intent of authors and conglomerates, rather than omit motivation entirely from our readings to elude intentional fallacy.

Manipulation and Power Relations

Authenticity and trust in particular encapsulate some key concerns regarding narrative's use in power relations and governance. So we can use story both **to trade in manipulations, and derive comfort from our trust in storytellers and their manipulations**. I could easily have said that we use story to manipulate others here, but that does not tell the whole story. As we have already covered, there is a certain comfort in merely knowing how to react to a narrative – to respond in the ways the narrative asks us to. We are willing participants in the manipulations endemic to all storytelling, and the security we derive from responding to a story in the manner the story elicits must be recognised. This is a kind of trust, and is closely related to feelings of 'oneness' or closeness to others when we come closer to responding as one. When, as an adult, we watch the latest computer-animated family film from a major studio such as Pixar, we are familiar with the conventions that manipulate us and want to, in some way, give ourselves over to them – a thoughtful family weepy like *Inside Out* (Peter Docter, 2015) would not work without such complicity. When browsing a beauty magazine, one can be aware of the ways in which one is being manipulated, and yet still enjoy the process of responding to manipulative (and photographically manipulated) images with exactly the kind of receptivity prompted by its marketers. Evidence abounds for the cross-cultural absorption of unrealistic body image norms (Yan and Bissell 2014; Jung and Lee 2009) and contradictory messages (Duncan and Klos 2014) in beauty and fashion journalism; these magazines are not without harm, but perhaps we should still comprehend the reader-viewer as an agent that is more conversant with the material. The reader-viewer can either wilfully overlook the manipulation in order to reach a neuroaesthetic relationship with the images unburdened by consumer consciousness, or keep the psychological damage of airbrushed figures always in mind while appreciating a particular fantasy of heavily mediated beauty achievable through advertised products. In any case, fashion and beauty magazines contain aesthetic and storied manipulation that is desired, sought out and paid for.

The uses of story for manipulative purposes are so multifaceted that I cannot cover them all here, and on this much has already been written – dissecting power relations is the purview of countless scholarly disciplines. However I do want to illuminate one important concept for humanist studies, as I believe it is an important concept to remember, and that is debt manipulation. Many manipulative acts depend on erection of a psychical debt (consider the flow of gifts from public relations agencies to media outlets or the bartering of physical and verbal affection between parent and child), and similarly, an unarticulated debt (or enthymematic debt) can be erected through a range of narrative acts. Thus **the inherent antagonism of storytelling – in that it seeks to provoke – is a kind of gift**, and as such involves a fundamental reciprocity (sometimes even a price of admission). In fact, at times we purchase or create stories for one another *as* gifts. Thus the act of storytelling bears striking resemblance to many power dynamics present in gift giving, elaborated in *The Question of the Gift*, a 2002 cross-disciplinary volume edited by Mark Osteen. Barry Schwartz's summary of such power dynamics in 'The Social Psychology of the Gift' (1967) can also be extended to story as gift. He considers the gift as imposing identity on recipients, broadcasting a giver's identity, using this identity mediation as a method to control others, generating the debt of gratitude, establishing group boundaries and social rank, and guilt atonement or abatement for the giver; all of these functions, including the coercive functions, can contribute to tacit social contracts that help us relate, but can also be abused.

Not only are stories and their perspectives gifts in themselves, but stories can also work to create a sense of indebtedness to others within their diegesis. Even when presenting, say, a piece of social realism which encourages us to consider the lives of those less fortunate, the authors and distributors of the work have attempted to provoke the idea that we owe something to another. I call this 'unarticulated' debt, as any exact parameters concerning what is expected of us in correcting the balance sheet of inter-responsibility are not defined within the narrative, and debt manipulation can be much more powerful this way. In some films, too, desired audience actions are clearly articulated, prescribing a moral course of action, as with more directly political cinema. Consider the conclusion of a film like *Fair Game* (Doug Liman, 2010) in which Joseph C. Wilson (Sean Penn) lectures an audience about democratic participation and the responsibility of all citizens to question powerful interests.[6] When we speak of generating care or consideration for the other, we should always keep this idea of debt manipulation in mind in order to understand how stories may operate in shifting our perspective and hopefully our behaviour. I am also using this concept to reveal that there are varieties of manipulation we achieve through story that are socially acceptable, mutually performed, ethically dynamic and even desirable.

Stories are undoubtedly commoditised using such power dynamics, but there may be danger in assuming there is no alternative to the storied gift as coercion and control. Despite popular theorists such as Derrida and Bourdieu advising 'that giving gifts involves bad faith, that we lie to ourselves by choosing to ignore or forget our calculation of self-interest' (Osteen 2002: 16) and imploring us to focus exclusively on their power dynamics, it must be noted that Marcel Mauss himself (author of the inciting 1925 work *The Gift*) conjectured that gifts could also include genuinely altruistic motivation in a matrix of impetuses, calculated and otherwise. As Jonathan Parry put it, 'Mauss repeatedly stresses a combination of interest and disinterest, of freedom and constraint, in the gift' (1986: 456). There is also no reason we cannot see many instances of gifted story within the framework of David Graeber's everyday communism, or the economy of reciprocity underlying many of our most basic transactions, 'small courtesies' transferring particularised skills, knowledge and objects, or even responding to the extreme need of a stranger, to which no debt is attached (2011: 97). So while we remain aware of the ways in which the storied gift is used to generate indebtedness and activate control mechanisms, we can also admit the prospect of those circumstances where one may be motivated to unconditionally 'gift' a story out of care for the recipient or interest in their wellbeing, even where the storyteller experiences secondary benefits such as the pleasure of performativity.

Unarticulated debt and the power dynamics of gift giving point to **story's function as a regulatory tool and a mediator of group behaviours – yet also story's simultaneous ability to demonstrate transgression against mediation.** The development of more complex moral codes seems to coincide with a gradual increase in the size of local and extended communities throughout human history. Larger group sizes required greater social coordination, which meant enforcement of codes and social norms to maintain group cohesion (to borrow the terms from Durkheim's *Division of Labour in Society* [1893], this is a transition from mechanical to organic solidarity). As Prinz puts it, moral 'rules are as varied as the problems' (2008: 405) and so increases in population density produce an increase in social problems to be managed, which in turn produces greater complexity of moral codes for dispute management, whether enforced by custom or governance. By the time of global urbanism, proximate populations are so diverse and interactive that they no longer extensively agree on many of these moral codes.[7] So at first, stories may provide avenues for moral regulation, such as cautionary tales, but they also accumulate use in transgressing against and questioning prevailing moral codes as population density increases. The prevalence of fictive story in contemporary urban routines may be explained by an amplified need for discussion and mediation of mutual morality and governance as social problems change. From the private sermon of yesteryear to the broadcast evangelism of today, stories, then, are often intended to influence the way a group behaves. Many hope for influence or ideological contagion spreading far beyond the initial, listening audience. Along with story's clear utility as a regulator and mediator of group behaviours, other storytellers have found a way to use the same function as a rebellion against such mediation. Trash cinema, such as the work of John Waters, is one such example, along with other avant-gardists and counter-cultural icons across media, from Alfred Jarry to Frank Zappa. At the same time these artists demonstrate another kind of rebellion in the face of serious, moral and proscriptive narrative: story's function as play.

Notes

1. Alternate-reality gaming has been used as a method to create communities in which to sell other products. For example, 42 Entertainment created an alternate reality game to generate a community around *The Dark Knight* (Christopher Nolan, 2008) prior to its release; Warner Bros. subsequently had marketing access to this community.
2. Theseus later references their position as poor labourers to draw attention to theatre as a rare space of direct contact with authority figures.
3. Redress recalls the vulnerability and humility of humanism covered in the first chapter. Another means of communication that might provoke a similar affective openness is the 'deep and meaningful' conversation (colloquially abbreviated as D&M). A film like Richard Linklater's *Before Sunrise* (1995) attempts to demonstrate the similarities between the liminoid space of a story and these exploratory, risk-taking conversations, in which the world seems alive with philosophical possibility while one is unbound. *Before Sunrise* maps the experience of a D&M onto a film narrative.
4. This refraction can obviously be a matter of personal survival as well, in contexts where political dissent is punishable and radical ideas must be concealed in allegory.
5. A meta-analysis of 24 studies examining the association between the behavioural immune system (including an amplified response to stimuli provoking disgust, for some translating as sociomoral disgust) and social conservatism confirmed a correlation (Terrizzi et al. 2013).
6. This kind of polemic in narrative is in disrepute, perhaps unfairly – fiction workers are often chided for telling an audience explicitly what to do or think. Some writers, however, have explicitly lambasted the 'show don't tell' rule espoused by screenwriting gurus like Robert McKee and Syd Field

(Mesce n.d.). Similarly, Claudia Puig's review of *Lions for Lambs* demonstrates the shifting priorities of film journalism, which decrees politics a lesser function to 'entertainment': 'the film feels preachy and falls flat as entertainment' (2007) she says. Perhaps, on occasion, narratives suggesting a course of action can be more helpful than the generation of unarticulated psychical debt, provided the action is reasonable and thought through. Expository dialogue or politicised direct address point to another usage of such narratives: the exegetic work of fiction.
7. Cf. Hans-Peter Müller's disruption of Durkheim's somewhat utopian notions of advanced moral cooperation in 'Social Differentiation and Organic Solidarity' (1994).

CHAPTER 5

Mental Work and Memory

Fantasy, Imagination and Play

Imaginative capacities have thus far been a recurring theme, connecting as they do to our ability to concoct fictions. As imagination appears key to so many other narrative functions, I now turn to the use of story **to flex our imagination, and to play**. The ludic, the autotelic and various forms of serious play are all components in the storytelling act. Murray Smith considers that fiction may have developed as an evolutionary by-product of learning to imagine. He writes:

> to imagine: one thing that sets us apart from other species is our ability to simulate, in our minds, circumstances which we might encounter, or indeed which we have encountered in the past. And in doing so, we are able to rehearse how things might go in circumstances we have not actually experienced. The imagination, in other words, enhances our foresight and supercharges our ability to plan; and it is not hard to see how this improves our fitness in the environment of human action. (2010: 259)

Thus imagination is a pivotal part of the storytelling act from which many other functions may arise. One of these is the intrinsic drive to the cognitive developments afforded by play, as Boyd suggests in *On the Origin of Stories* (2009).[1] Subsequently, there is also a direct application of the imagination to find solutions to environmental challenges. The imaginative expansion offered by play crucially also guides moral development, and is therefore relevant to pedagogical theory. Introducing a narrative-focused edition of the *Journal of Moral Education,* Carol Witherell notes the concomitance of education, imagination, morality and narrative: 'To educate in the moral realm is to enter the world of imagination as well as judgement' (1991: 239). Understanding when developmental imaginative acts should be free and explorative (as in non-interventionist or agentive play) and when they should be guided (as in moral education) relies on a concept of imaginative reciprocity. Sometimes when elders extend themselves into the imaginative openness of the child's world of play, we can see a reciprocal connection that yields surprisingly gratifying results: think of the innovation on themes of childhood development and play in computer-animated films from *Toy Story* (John Lasseter, 1995) to *Shrek* (Andrew Adamson and Vicky Jenson, 2001), and *Despicable Me* (Pierre Coffin and Chris Renaud, 2010) to *Inside Out*. Part of what is affecting about these films is the imaginative 'reaching out' between intergenerational worlds, our concept of the film's workers admitting that imaginative and moral development are never over, and thus they find surprising new ways to tell stories. The construction of digitised characters that feel so well rounded, for example, is a feat of the human imagination – an imagination centred on the recognition of many social components working together.

Moral development's dependence on imagination does not end when we reach a certain age. In the opening lines of his song 'King Strut', metaphysical wordsmith, songwriter and cartoonist Peter Blegvad likens imagination to a muscle, growing as it is used, and the titular character is described as developing their imagination in dreaming and fibbing. The character's capacity for playfully imaginative storytelling eventually leads him to concoct effective political solutions to social ills. One of his many examples of the power of story as play, Blegvad uses both cartoons and songs as metaphysical games, the fun of which can provide stimulating uplift and potentially challenge the boundaries between imaginative acts and their real-life applications. He once said of his incompatibility with more 'serious' songwriters: 'People who take themselves very seriously make me giggle; it's a problem of mine. Of course, if they're pointing a weapon at me or my loved ones, I don't giggle. That's why I giggle when they're not, because I expect that's the sort of person who one day will. So before they're armed, I get my giggle in' (Blegvad n.p.). Even Blegvad's defence of a playful disposition deconstructs itself playfully, and points to a mortal counterpoint his sense of play grapples with. His works are unabashedly metaphysical in theme (akin to puzzle films in songform), yet his singular refusal to take the metaphysical storytelling act too seriously may work to the advantage of imaginative capacities, and its proximity to mortal goals at the same time points to what we call 'the seriousness of play' (Turner *From Ritual to Theatre: The Human Seriousness of Play* 1982; Levell *The Seriousness of Play* 2015).

Imagination's foundational importance in moral development is often linked to the maturation of our empathic competences. As Daniel B. Johnson suggests in 'Altruistic Behavior and the Development of the Self in Infants' (1982), mirror self-recognition and cognitive empathy appear co-emergent in infants and other animals; this complex understanding of the self provides a foundation from which to imagine the experience of another. Early childhood games often incorporate roleplay. The child concocts scenarios in which they imaginatively adopt the experience of others – from ordinary domestic situations to an astronaut in extraordinary circumstances. They may also perform roleplay in conjunction with others, and imaginatively exchange between them a world for those characters to exist within. More formalised versions of this exchange may be employed later in life, for example performing as an actor in a film or play with others, or roleplaying games like Dungeons & Dragons. Play is a place where identities become open and negotiable, which is why it is ripe for regulation by authorities, as with child labour (a play deprivation) and the strict artistic standards enforced by many dictatorial states. Regulated environments produce narratives of resistance that often incorporate elements of playfulness, indicating that imaginative or noninterventionist play (play without guidance) is likely a fundamental human need. This is true of the regulation of women's identities in storytelling media (Lauretis 1985): for example, the playfulness of the young women pranksters in 1966 Czechoslovak New Wave film *Daisies* (Věra Chytilová) outraged authorities, which banned the picture and prevented Chytilová from working in the (centrally controlled) Czech national film industry until 1975. The Czech authorities famously clamped down on its depiction of the 'wanton' or sense of play unbefitting of its leads, and cited food wastage as a reason for the film's suppression.

On the one hand, the physical, cognitive and social developments associated with these activities and their interactive demands should be clear; play deprivation has been linked to the perpetration of violent crime (Frost and Jacobs 1995), for example. On the other hand, maintenance of a play world is complex. Incongruity in the particularities of the imagined world and each player's motivations within and outside of it are in need of constant revision. We could equally consider the very fine line between the seriousness and the frivolity of play: one moment two children are playing happily together, and then for one of them the game's implications become serious. The concern they exhibit (for example, crying) disrupts or potentially dispels the imaginative world between them. Play is fragile, as is agreeing on what constitutes play. The tacitly negotiable overlap between serious and non-serious play remains an important component in our dealings with art and narrative later in life, and it is precisely what makes play in art so difficult to define. We might be able to identify perceived playfulness in the performing arts, but it is much harder to describe what distinguishes it from the non-playful. For example, some playful elements might be motivated in service of a seriously rebellious goal.

Consider Jarry's *Ubu* plays, or Lindsay Anderson's 'Mick Travis' films, in which absurdist elements are playfully motivated to make severe political statements. Much avant cinema employs playful and explorative methods toward serious ends. Hans-Georg Gadamer recognised many of these contradictions in art and play: it is a form of both restraint (in the mutual rules we construct around storied play) and freedom (in our mutual ownership of those rules), and its indivisibility from our lives confirms its highest seriousness at the same time as it flaunts exuberant abandon (1986: 30).

There are other benefits to interactive play. For example, Sayles's interest in places where those who would not usually come into contact interact (Godfrey 2011: 101) such as the American high school, which he calls 'the last bastion of American democracy' (Osborne 1982: 36), recognises the inverse relationship between contact and prejudice (Pettigrew and Tropp 2006). When disparate communities are forced to work together, adopting superordinate goals (Sherif 1966), racism, for example, is inhibited and we extend our field of ethical inclusion. Yet here's the rub: recent studies suggest that merely *imagining* working with the other could have positive results (Crisp and Turner 'Imagining Intergroup Contact Reduces Implicit Prejudice' 2010). I contend that this could point to an imaginative complicity that comes from adopting not only the perspective of a fictive other, but also the goals bound to that perspective. We might have direct contact with others through early play, but we also need imaginatively projected contact with others to extend throughout our lives if we are to continue to expand our field of inclusivity. This is just one of the narrative functions a figure like Sayles intends to provide.

When we talk of the seriousness of play, we do tend to emphasise it as 'working' under-acknowledged cognitive functions. However, in play, **stories can also offer relief from purposeful cognitive work**. Quite simply, engagement with narrative can offer us downtime from the daily strains of achievement, a space for our other tasks and concerns to recede while we are absorbed in an observational practice that has no end in mind. This relief, like the experience of boredom, can 'kill time' (Misek 2010: 779) in ways that can be reflective, like mindfulness, or just a more simple relief, releasing load from the hippocampal translation of mood to actions, and transferring our problem-solving skills to an interpretable object which will require no further action.

As with roleplay, fantasy can be an integral component in play. So we use story to **fantasise, and to separate fantasy from what we can mutually hold to be real, and to escape, by which we can comparatively appreciate the real**. The challenge in a Darwinian account of fantastical storytelling is that the problems faced by its protagonists are far removed from the structural fitness challenges of our actual environment. At the same time, these narratives clearly replicate many familiar challenges from our past and present: evading beasts, identifying and struggling with those who mean us harm, reputation management, and so on. Mar and Oatley maintain that fantasy still 'strives for realism in the most important aspects of human experience: the psychological and the social' (2008: 185). However, we can ask what leads us to entertain fantastical allegory in lieu of attempts at verisimilitude or direct realist representation. Grodal thinks that the appeal of these narratives may have something to do with a cognitive call to attention whenever events unexpectedly deviate from our usual causal pattern recognition, and regarding supernatural or fantastical themes, that this is most evident in our concept of physics and the natural: 'Changes, deviations, and novelty attract our interest. As soon as events are slotted into familiar and well-explained patterns, they lose their salience, unless they prompt us to further action' (2009: 98). He sees film as unique in stoking this particular kind of cognition (100). This concept of genre development appears to fit neatly with Pinker's view of narrative development as superstimulus or spandrel, a pleasurable activation of cognitive processes adapted for other purposes. However, given that disbelief requires more cognitive effort than belief (Gilbert et al. 1990), belief being our initial subconscious position, perhaps we should look to the work of decoupling cognition to explain fantasy's utility. Fantasy in narrative locates negotiable crossovers between the fact and fiction it presents, and as we become attuned to those crossovers, it provides a place to discuss the nature of reality by comparing the simulated world with the real one. Lest this appear absurd, given the conspicuousness of fictions concocted across fantasy genres, we should recall how prominently superstitions and attributions of nature's intent retain a place in political and group decision-making across the globe. Moreover, Grodal points out that superstition and supernature are integral concepts in art cinema – consider Bergman, Tarkovsky, Wenders, Kieslowski, Lynch and Trier (2009: 106). Not only does such cinema point to the very contested nature of objective externalities, reminding us of the breadth of phenomena unchartered by our sciences, but in calling attention to dissonances between our experience of the world and the diegesis described, it may also exercise our ability to locate (and probably *create*) hidden textual meanings, to identify and question the relations between artifice and intention in storied communication. What may be contested is how much more of this discrepancy-identification a fantasy viewer may need, whether it diverts from other mental tasks, and whether the experience of flow in fantastical discrepancy-identification becomes self-fulfilling and hardwired to the specifics of the genre itself. The question remains whether contemporary fantasy-adventure stories reveal more or indulge more of these misconceptions.

There are other clear excitations we undergo specifically in the 'high' or 'heroic' adventure fantasy genre: many have focused on wish fulfilment (reaching back to Freud's *Wunscherfüllung* in *The Interpretation of Dreams* 1900), and especially fantasies of supernatural power, strength, and control. But these worlds are equally filled with near uncontrollable dangers and matches of strength against strength, good against evil, and horrors, so unparalleled power is not a holistic explanation. How, then, would we explain the emotionally moving powerlessness of the characters populating literature such as Mervyn Peake's *Titus* trilogy? Grodal believes that, like religious narratives, 'The fantastic makes life more complicated, more colorful, and more uncertain, because it increases both poison and antidote' (2009: 104). However, more often than not, it seems these worlds provide a kind of gratifyingly idealistic reductionism, as the supernatural laws fantasy worlds introduce make the poison and antidote knowable or known. Good and evil are very often clearly demarked (morality manifests overtly and materially through supernature), as are free will and an 'agency of the spirit' made material (109–11); human power and ability progress in a linear fashion; ordinarily motiveless natural objects, such as trees or weather events, are given comprehensible intention; and a vast world is reduced to an index of important places, events and characters defined by the author. That is, the world is manageably reduced. Think of the title sequence to the television adaptation *Game of Thrones*, the comforting familiarity and self-satisfaction felt when we know the map's most important places. In many stories (especially those featuring ghosts), disembodied mental activity is also provided a material form and objective after death, solving another worrying problem by projecting realisation of an afterlife. At the same time many of these narratives are journeys of discovery, but the conditions of discovery, the reasons for discovery, and the manner in which discovery should happen are all customarily laid out in an initial quest, if not discovered along the way. The fantasy in fantasy genres, therefore, can be seen as reductive: applying a myth of purpose, our great desire to have clear goals and know what to do in life, and to separate clearly ever-confounding artificial constructs like right and wrong.

This all puts fantasy in a unique position: the cognitive excitation of the uncanny or physical dissonance between a diegesis and our own world seems open to possibility, discovery and negotiability, while the fantasies of verifiable purpose, intent and salient, encompassing world-knowledge seem closed. Fantasy can clearly offer both of these experiences, but in any case we witness in these works **the relief stories can offer by reducing our world to an index of its salient properties, and the reprieve we can find in comparing fantasy worlds back to the complexity of life**. Perhaps one reason we enjoy fantasy in narrative so much – and especially its reductive element – is that we can comparatively appreciate the real. This is evident in the counter-relief we might feel on, say, walking out of a cinema even after we enjoyed a film. Although we all have different thresholds for how much story we can take, at some point we always feel a little bit glad to return to real life. Escapism tends to allow us to appreciate the real and the complexity of life by making us think comparatively about our fantasies.

Wonder, sensory stimulation and fantasy coalesce and augment one another when we use story **to ogle at human invention**. Nonverbal storytelling techniques are able to provoke impressions of human achievement and advancement; filmic special effects are an obvious example here. Neuroaesthetics may help explain foundational responses to spectacular stimuli, attention and appreciation, yet we still craft narratives from our initial reaction. We integrate our sensory response into a comprehension of the fiction and its eudaimonic meaning, and we construct for ourselves a story of human achievement to explain the pleasure of engagement. We consistently feel the need to rationalise sensory pleasure using a narrative of technical progression, and our own comprehension of effects innovation. The resounding sentiment is, just as with any spectacle involving skilled manufacture or virtuosic artifice: look what humans are capable of. Special effects and spectacle are, at least in part, a pat on the back for being us.

Tom Gunning's (2000) cinema of attractions fixated on qualities that move beyond diegetic immersion and therefore beyond narratival concerns. I contend that spectacle focuses us on a different kind of story, however: that which we construct for ourselves about our interest in film art and spectacle, or about appreciation of the achievements of artists we admire, and their innovations as representing human potential per se. Writers such as Michele Pierson (2002) have moved forward from Gunning's notions of cinema language development to look at the various narratives of technocentric progression fostered by special-effects connoisseurs (now a mainstream sport). The stimulus that promotes wonderment goes on to be incorporated and understood as part of a narrative of the self – this is human achievement, and recognising technical progress in skilled human actions is another way we imagine ourselves as akin to others. There are innumerable examples: much musical theatre creates a recognisable, delimited spectacle focusing us on the genius of its singers, dancers and technicians that impresses by its very immensity, and the narrative around art games often focuses on the design genius of its creators, appealing to notions of sophisticated medium-specific comprehension in discerning videogamers. Even if our primary concern is how a movie pleased the eye, or how a piece of music moved us through an emotive soundscape, or how it felt to be in the theatre during a particular performance, we are still asking questions about what these experiences mean to us, and so therefore what they say about the experience of being human.

The oeuvre of writer/director Terry Gilliam offers the perfect demonstrative union of all these concepts: artistic playfulness, fantasy and the appreciation of human invention. His more frivolous works explore the boundaries of the fantasy-adventure genre, upset polar nodes of genre comprehension we rely on, question what story means to us, and always suggest excess beyond the knowable by cluttering his frames with all manner of visual detail that cannot be clearly made out. We have to become used to the kind of cognitive-perceptual mess of highly composed visual clutter to enjoy his films; we are always aware we are missing details, and this is key to Gilliam's sense of play. This impulse has been with him from early films like *Jabberwocky* (1977). Gilliam upset laws of physics by making them contingent to superstition, raconteurism, consumerist and religious fantasy in *Time Bandits* (1981) and *The Adventures of Baron Munchausen* (1988); he upset recognisable genre forms in *The Brothers Grimm* (2005), wherein we are as confused as the eponymous brothers whether we are engaged in horror or family adventure, a world of real dangers or a world of make-believe dangers; and he upset the very moral binaries fantasy relies on in *The Imaginarium of Doctor Parnassus* (2009), especially as the Devil (Tom Waits) is robbed of any sense of moral certitude toward the end of the film (he is more interested in the gameplay of 'evil' than its actualisation). As Peter Marks points out in his analysis of the more sombre *12 Monkeys* (1995), Gilliam's most popularly enduring studio picture upsets notions of interpretation and perceptual reliability we find ourselves navigating on the precipice of the information age (2009: 161). The complication of sensory information is a common theme in accounts of film history and technical achievement (see, for example, Fraigneau and Cocteau 1967).[2] *Vertigo* (Alfred Hitchcock, 1958) in particular is a recurrent reference, and one that *12 Monkeys* addresses to call attention to its conversation with film history. Using time travel as a device to challenge telicity, *12 Monkeys* like its predecessor *La Jetée* (Chris Marker, 1962) upsets concepts of cultural chronology and cinema development, too: *12 Monkeys* features the re-purposing of old motion capture and projection technologies to nefarious ends, despotic interrogation and surveillance.

Similarly, technologies like plastic are re-purposed and become unstuck in time – the time travel device is flimsy, unreliable and patched together like all of our technologies, including film effects and their manipulation of perceptive faculties, which we might deploy while never quite wholly understanding their operative principles. Despite being cobbled together and exploitable, these human inventions still inspire wonder, from the filmed image to a time machine made of plastic.

Gilliam's work is also, much of the time, imaginatively comedic – another variety of play. We tell stories **to laugh, to account for, to explore and perhaps deflate our concerns and anxieties in comedy**. The subject of mountains of theory, often asserting one particular cause or effect of humour as foundational, comedy is a substantial component in narrative with human and social functions that may be as multitudinous as those of storytelling itself. It is perhaps not surprising that a breadth of storytelling styles, including those operating outside of strictly comic genres, use humour as a narrative device. Humour has been demonstrated as particularly effective in establishing reciprocally enjoyable connections between strangers (Treger et al. 2013), which may help to develop a bond of trust between storytellers and their audience. Humour also mitigates stress in favour of feelings of wellbeing (Crawford and Caltabiano 2011), which could countervail the agitating influence of the conflicts on which stories rely. A recent theory put forward by Peter McGraw and Caleb Warren (2010), however, has been advanced from Thomas C. Veatch's 1998 work 'A Theory of Humor': benign violation theory (styled as BVT) carries great analytic potential and synthesises a breadth of historic theories of laughter and the comic into a comprehensible phenomenon. A violation is defined as the perception 'when something seems wrong, unsettling or threatening' and it is benign when 'it seems okay, acceptable, or safe' (McGraw and Warner 2014: 10). The website for McGraw's Humor Research Lab offers a succinct elucidation:

> humor occurs when and only when three conditions are satisfied: (1) a situation is a violation, (2) the situation is benign, and (3) both perceptions occur simultaneously. For example, play fighting and tickling, which produce laughter in humans (and other primates), are benign violations because they are physically threatening but harmless attacks. (2014)

I would add that it is possible our swift cognitive *transition through* perception of violation to down-regulated status of an event as benign could also explain such phenomena as laughter *following* a surprise or shock; the perceptions may or may not occur strictly simultaneously, but they are definitely in conflict. This concept of humour chimes with incongruity theory, whereby 'some thing or event we perceive or think about violates our normal mental patterns and normal expectations' (Morreall 2009: 11), but it both identifies the specifics of the incongruity required to produce humour (cognitive dissonance can equally produce discomfort), and suggests a practical social reason for our humour needs.

In fact, BVT specifies the humour value in the three major pillars of humour theory, each of which seem to identify only one aspect of humour: superiority; relief; and incongruity. From the vantage of BVT, many of the hitherto surveyed functions of laughter seem understandable: the conditions of ambiguity and incongruity are specified; Freud's ([1905] 1960) emphasis on repression of unacceptable thoughts and behaviours clearly explores potential social violations (usually benign as they are only thoughts, not actions and so reveal no consequences); our ability to cope with the potential impingements of grotesquery and chaos also lie at the intersection of the threatening and safe; schadenfreude and Aristotelian superiority cover the area where we recognise a threat but it is benign because it is not our own; conflicts in our perceptive faculties may present a threat in surprise and confusion, a brief experience of cognitive dissonance, sensory perplexity or mistaken reasoning, resolved swiftly as we move through a gag or point of humour in narrative, cognitively consigned to the benign; this same principle of brisk dissonance applies to recognition of the unreality of our mechanised regulation of nature and life, apropos Bergson's (1911) famed *Laughter* essay and its precedents in Kant and Schopenhauer, or the deceptive dehumanising of a person represented as a material thing; and the relief offered by relegating mortal violations to a more benign status could be explained by the need for a self-aware mind to navigate the threat of existential terror. The latter explanation of the integral nature of death and attention to impermanence in humour is bolstered by research performed by Long and Greenwood (2013), who found that priming subjects with subliminal thoughts of death aided humour-production, potentially as a defensive mechanism (cf. Vaillant 1992), promoting resilience against existential anxieties, and also possibly allowing for enhanced creativity and open-mindedness. Bergson reminded us that humour is a social phenomenon – often the effects are amplified when experienced alongside others. Following Bergson's defence of a social corrective or moral function of humour, and its synthesis in BVT, we can look to humour as a political tool by which we mediate amongst ourselves what is a threat worthy of our attention and what anxieties are unfounded or unneeded. Exploring these zones in narrative may allow us to be more specific about the aspects of social problems that are genuinely worrying, or that are distracting us from matters of genuine concern. The consequent politics of laughter could inform both humanistic storytellers and a humanist hermeneutics.

Hovering somewhere nearby comedic narrative, forever treading a line between the benign and the violating, is **story's function as titillation**. Much mainstream pornography still constructs a cursory narrative as some kind of anchor to sexual display; arousal appears to depend upon a narrative context, a path into comprehending the action as something more than just body parts on a screen, to merge with a viewer's internal fantasies. Alan McKee's work on the narrativity of pornography finds that adult entertainment fulfills many of the same goals as other narrative entertainment or 'audience-centred' media (2012: 548). One of these goals might concern the nature of pleasure audiences find in the representation of and identification with fictional characters: the characters that populate pornographic media are schematic – quite clearly constructed and typified – yet somehow still produce real longing and real arousal in the viewer (Frow 2012). In 'Generic Pleasures', Linda Williams (2006) notes genres that feature similar extents of affective and stylistic repetition centred on heterosexual unions – in particular Hollywood musicals – and disciplines that similarly construct sex as a 'problem' that needs to be solved with more knowledge and accommodation of desire, and proximity to the gendered other, like sexology. The foundation of a problem that needs solving is ubiquitous in narrative. It should not, then, come as any surprise that titillating media requires some groundwork of narrative structure to develop arousal or viewer interest. That dramatic conflict, in pornography, is an absence of sexual accord, which is 'solved' by an extreme level of sexual accommodation.

Sex and sexuality need not be so cursory, however. Story is also used in **courtship and mateship displays, mate selection, and even friend and acquaintance selection**. This can be a much more extended process, especially in the display of desirable skills and traits associated with narrative construction and artistry. During the height of the feminist sex wars, a range of writers including Gayle Rubin (1984) and Pat Califia (1994) adopted the term 'sex positivity' to connote the philosophy of acceptance of consensual sexuality in all its different and difficult iterations, and a deflation of the shame and stigma around diverse expressions of sexuality, like sadomasochism. In narrative theory, a sex-positive theory could attempt to find ways to portray the difficulties we have in sexual relations in a light that demonstrates the normalcy and ubiquity of interpersonal sexual problems, and thereby makes them easier to deal with. In interviews about her performance in *The Sessions* (Ben Lewin, 2012), actor Helen Hunt, playing a sex surrogate for a disabled man, described how she wanted to be part of a story that demonstrated what she termed 'sex positivity':

> Sex is never perfectly elegant: The light isn't just right, and the underwear doesn't fall on the floor perfectly, and the hands don't clutch, and you don't come at the same time—it's all bullshit, basically . . . And the disability of this character renders all of that impossible, so you're left with something much more like your own experience as a nondisabled person, which is that you're human and that it's good and it's bad and it's weird that it's silly, and it's embarrassing that it's scary, so I think that the disability is just a way to get to what it's actually like. (Zakarin 2012)

The dimensional complexity of sexual and bodily shame in cinema, which Hunt refers to, can be represented as a natural problem to productively work with, or sexual fears can instead be leveraged to heighten the drama of a narrative in a way that amplifies rather than questions sexual stigma, as in films like *Shame* (Steve McQueen, 2011) or *Happiness* (Todd Solondz, 1998). These films conduct the audience's pre-existing sexual fears to an emotionally intense and dramatic rather than a deflating or diagnostic effect, leaving less room between the spectator and their reactive sexual shame, and thereby, I would argue, less room for the kind of reflective analysis prompted by Hunt and Lewin. Other films that attempt a deflating or diagnostic effect include *Bedrooms and Hallways* (Rose Troche, 1998), *Shortbus* (John Cameron Mitchell, 2006), *Women in Trouble* (Sebastian Gutierrez, 2009) and the works of a figure like Pedro Almodóvar. A humanist critic might therefore ask: does this story provoke or question our established sexual stigma?

Of course, we can also create narratives and exhibit story preferences that aid in other kinds of social choice beyond sexual selection – for example, a music scene that generates friendship circles of likeminded people, or communities of niche genre enthusiasts. Chamorro-Premuzic et al. write that, 'movie preferences are an important ingredient of interpersonal etiquette, providing a topic of conversation, as well as a vehicle for assessing others' attitudes and interpersonal compatibility. For instance, people discuss film preferences in social networking and online dating sites to decide whether their views are shared by others' (2014: 111–12). The etiquette of exhibiting story preferences acts as a display to both potential friends *and* romantic partners; sex, mateship display and selection are all so intimately entwined with storytelling practices that they cannot be ignored. Like all of the functions of narrative art explored in social narratology, 'The sexual display and socialization accounts can peaceably sit side by side as long as one does not try to frame either explanation as all-encompassing' (Taberham 2014: 221). Likewise a synergy of these approaches could offer a more holistic picture of our complex motives for story engagement; these motives should not be seen as separate from one another, as we can derive a variety of gratifying experiences from a single narrative, sometimes which appear contradictory. For example, a film can both titillate and moralise about titillation at the same time. I agree with the sex positivists that we need to accept all of these functions of story as productive in their own ways – theories of sex positivity could help us achieve better tools to discuss sexual fear, timidity and shame in story with less fear, timidity and shame around the subject itself.

All of these imaginative and ludic narrative functions, from the autotelic to the seriousness of play, from fantasy to narrativised sexual play, regularly sit alongside our more serious concerns rather than being separated out into singularly affective narratives. I now move to look closer at the correlate mental work of fiction, and how it might produce pleasure or rewards in cognitions that are germane to our flourishing in the world.

Mental Work, Memory and Need for Cognition

As we have established, different people have different appetites for the various cognitive processes fiction guides us through. An appetite for open-endedly effortful cognitive tasks is measured by the 'need for cognition' personality variable (c.. Cacioppo et al. 1996). As these needs change from person to person, writers like myself who value stories that offer difficult cognitive tasks – narrative puzzles, challenges to reason and opportunities for elaboration – should not universalise this disposition, or presume that an appetite for the interpretive work of avant or other experimental fictions is somehow superior. Nonetheless, we can still point to some of the positive functions of narrativised mental work, and its results. In particular, we can use stories **to exercise advanced pattern recognition, explore the limits of our cognition, hypothesise, perform mental experiments and guide our comprehension of abstruse concepts**. Pattern seeking has long had survival benefits, from the physical to the social (Boyd 2009: 88), and story remains a place to exercise advantageous pattern recognition, or what Boyd calls 'cognitive play with pattern' (14). But stories can exercise cognitive processes that are not directly social or moral, and that move beyond appeals to naïve physics: we can make complex scientific and mathematical problems easier to grasp, for example, by procedurally laying out their terms in an analogous narrative. Further to Boyd's work on cognitive play and its relation to pattern recognition, Peter Swirski has written extensively about all manner of thought experiments in *Of Literature and Knowledge* (2007). Swirski notes multiple intrinsic links between science and story; each framework for understanding the world, and its associated cognitions, opens up new tools to explore the other. The exploration of science through story can have a pedagogical element – consider Raymond Smullyan's use of logic puzzles to teach mathematical concepts in a popular book such as *The Lady or the Tiger?* – as well as being a process of discovery for both storyteller and audience. For example, one can find a solution to a problem by crafting a narrative around it, or alter existing narratives to meet the demands of their own particular problem.

Rationalising the appeal of avant-garde film, Taberham writes that avant narratives stretch our discernment of meaningful patterns to a radical degree: 'On occasion, the more indiscernible the patterns are, the more rewarding their identification may be' (2014: 225). Considering the relatively recent emergence of modernist art in human history and its concurrence with globalising technologies such as electronic-telegraphic transmission, auto and air travel, it may be that our skills at recognising more complex patterns in social products like stories and artworks *were* in fact advantageous as our social context expanded and became more complex. We needed new complex stories to understand new social patterns that made up the globally connected world we describe, and social comprehension can confer a survival advantage. However, some levels of creative inference working from abstractions (especially graphical or non-semantic abstraction) are so removed from description of a specific context that they can be hard to explain. Taberham echoes many cognitivist-evolutionary theorists in postulating the function of avant art as a mental work that is pleasing as a pattern-recognition superstimulus, although, he is at pains to point out, it is not adaptive, offering no survival benefit of itself (226–7), and its marginal appeal makes it 'inefficient' as a sexual display (221). This assumes that traits are only adaptive if they have pan-cultural appeal, or make us attractive to all potential human mates, but traits can also be selected for and passed on within niche communities, and this heritability is still part of human evolution. Once removed from broad appeal, according to the universalisms of such evolutionary psychology, a trait can no longer be considered part of the selection process. Yet the technical skills in arts production that we identify as mateship or fitness display are very often culture-specific, and they will speak to niche communities and become adaptive within those environments. That virtuosic behaviour may demonstrate one's intellectual skills as much as one's technical skills. Punk music may not demonstrate virtuosic technical ability, but it demonstrates a raft of intellectual and creative values that speak to the social needs of a specific community and will thus be attractive traits within that community. This is similar to avant art, a creative expression of intellectual prowess and invention that will be selected for in communities that place value on the social skills it signals, and thereby be a heritable trait (perhaps intellectual passion in the case of punk, and intellectual restraint in the case of an avant cinema phenomenon like the slow film). Deterministic flattening of the myriad contexts in which humans have thrived produces unitary explanations, and it is an example of how evolutionary psychology can limit itself to a narrow or ad hoc notion of environmental fitness that neglects the complexities of culture – we adapt to the cultures we create, and can become 'fit' for an environment that includes intellectual values apt for the circumstances they emerge within. This includes all sorts of cognitive feats demonstrated in narrative that have unclear practical applications, yet demonstrate a mental ability or disposition that is valued by peers.

Of course, there are also complex concepts and cognitive feats in narrative that have clear utility. For example, reminiscence is a complex task of tying together multiple cognitions into a coherent narrative; so **story can also be used as a memory exercise**. Shared reminiscence – when memories are externalised and negotiated – is a directly communal storied activity with all manner of social utilities and benefits (Alea and Bluck 2003). Sharing family stories, for instance, can aid children's socioemotional knowledge development (Van Bergen et al. 2009), cognitive developmental processes and wellbeing outcomes (Fivush et al. 2006), and collaborative recall can have benefits lasting our whole lifetime, including in aged cognitive decline (Barnier et al. 2014); the foundation of memory and identity is the crafting of a story of social causality.[3] Maurice Halbwachs noted in 1950 that the individual's recollection was inseparable from group memory (*The Collective Memory*), and psychologists now recognise that memories are equally inseparable from their expression or externalisation (Hirst et al. 2014). Autobiographical memories are one place where social storytelling practices and the construction of internal stories are aligned – and they all contain traces of fiction (our memories are all somehow reconstituted and fabricated). As William Hirst et al. put it, 'Remembering is, if you like, communicating' (2014: 275). Additionally, the transactive nature of story can act as a socially distributed cognition or extended mind (Sutton et al. 2010): we accumulate collective information in stories, and so they do some of the work of remembering that an individual themselves might be unable to perform.

Family reminiscence, including the prompting of open-ended questions of narrative construction and context, is also important in the development of literacy, and thereby comprehension of fictions (Peterson et al. 1999). It may be apparent how autobiographical memories are storied, and therefore how distributing and negotiating memories as nonfictional narratives can have benefits in social cognition, although we might equally inquire how fiction in turn helps us craft causal narratives that connect meaningfully to our lives. Various scholars have queried the experience of rewatching or re-engaging in narratives we have already completed (Bentley and Murray 2016; Weispfenning 2003). Why are we able to experience the affect of a familiar narrative more than once, and how does it change on multiple readings or viewings? Some sports viewers, for example, are able to enjoy revisiting favourite matches despite knowing the outcome. This experience points to a particular kind of investment in the players, be they sportspeople or characters that we reclaim a proximity to. We want to empathically walk in their shoes again, but how does their fate provoke us if we already know the events and emotions that will follow? Rewatching is a particular kind of dramatic irony – one that encompasses the whole piece. Bentley and Murray's (2016) research qualifies participants' self-reported goals of rewatching: social rewatching (such as showing a friend); mood management or regulation (although this is not particular to the rewatching experience, knowing a narrative makes its emotive content more dependable); and nostalgia. They also note that fans of specific content will rewatch to gain mastery of complex storyworlds and thus build a 'social connoisseurship'. This self-reportage points to a simple answer to the question of a familiar narrative's ability to provoke emotional responses we have already been through: we might remember the thrust of a narrative and those few points impressed upon us, but we are liable to forget or overlook its cadences and nuances. We rediscover the affective path it leads us through upon rewatching – the emotional variation from one instance to the next, its affective causality. John Weispfenning theorised that television reruns provide the comfort of generational narratives, making sense of our shared history especially in times of social change (2003: 172). In rereading, there is cause for reflection on a story's emotional causality afforded by distance from any suspenseful immersion, and a subsequent feeling of mastery provides comfort. Again, we should keep in mind personality variation: different viewers with different memories and different tastes for drama will exhibit a range of desires, and some do not like to rewatch a narrative at all.

In Patricia Meyer Spacks's *On Rereading* (2011), returning to favoured novels aids a reflective self-narrative construction: we monitor our reactions to a familiar story, and so the story provides a benchmark for the way we have changed over time. We can even use such stories to critique the views of our former self, and in this way clarify lessons learned, and also compare our own social development with the development of historical events in the world. There are, thus, two types of memory being exercised here: the memory of narrative events, words, images and our response to them, as well as the memory of who we were at that time that may have led to these interpretations.[4] This chimes with literature on the bidirectional link between memory and identity (Wilson and Ross 2003) and similarly points to story's nostalgic potentialities as being part of the process of attaching to a causal narrative of the self and our development.

At the same time, **we use stories to forget**: not just to forget our daily trials, or forgetting as aversive mood regulation, but also in order to replace memories with new versions of events, or reduce the importance of painful and inconvenient memories. This has benefits in the creation of new identities (Connerton 2008: 62), or even just as a way to prioritise information (64). Paul Connerton's work also points out many of the more socially imposed narratives that attempt to inspire forgetting in a populace: to erase criminal conduct or painful cultural memories (60–2) or to sell new products by diminishing remembered attachments to the old (66). We might also protect our self-concept and social status by forgetting people (64) and events (67) that humiliate or do not reflect favourably on ourselves. Without these mechanisms, we can end up deeply unhappy (Price and Davis 2008). Kurt Vonnegut's *Slaughterhouse-Five* grapples with these questions: the use of fantastical fiction as a site of transaction with our traumatic memories, what we need to forget and what we choose to remember. Perhaps, more speculatively, even phenomena like collaborative inhibition – when groups working together recall fewer unique events or less information – may have some social utility, too, in paving the way for an empathic connection between mutual narratives of reminiscence.

Notes

1. Theorists including Boyd and Joseph D. Anderson (1996) insist on story as a kind of play that extends beyond sensorimotor development and into further cognitive feats, adult activity and lifelong engagement with narrative; their arguments find support in the earlier work of Jean Piaget ([1945] 1962), as well as Sue Taylor Parker and Michael L. McKinney (1999). Since Johan Huizinga's formative text *Homo Ludens* (1944), theorists from Boyd to Roger Caillois ([1961] 2001) have advanced notions of play as the foundations of human culture.
2. Gilliam points to a complication of technical achievement even while he goes about trying to emulate the beauty and power of his favourite oil paintings within the film frame: 'I wanted it to be painterly,' Gilliam said of *Doctor Parnassus*. 'I didn't want it to feel like anything naturalistic or even crude and cut-out. There were models, too, and photographs of real things stuck

in. It's still a mess, the way I work' (Covert 2010). Thus Gilliam's integration of digital effects functions in a similar way to his cut-out animations from Monty Python and his convoluted art direction: although vibrant and neuroaesthetically appealing, his effects disturb by putting ease of perception just out of reach, clouded as they are by proximate and often anachronistic technologies.
3. On another level, the unity of storytelling and memory is much simpler: observe the saying-is-believing effect. In vocalising or externalising a thought, we ourselves come to believe it (Higgins and Rholes 1978). So even more fundamentally, we use story to reinforce and attach to our own memories.
4. As well as these two types of memory, one might conclude here that there are four levels of autobiography worked through in narrative: when we first respond to a story we explain our sense of self through its evaluation (deeming it good or bad, for example, tells us more about ourselves); if we return to the narrative, it might become entrenched in a grander history of the self, or a personal corpus; where that corpus is shared or a particular work becomes canonised, it can tell of a shared history with specific others (for example generational identity); and finally, if that story is distant enough (for example a narrative belonging to another time, centuries or millennia ago), it might speak to a shared history with general others, even all of humanity.

CHAPTER 6

Ethics and Conclusions

Symbolic Memory, Social Roles and Ethics

The final chapter in this social narratology connects all of the narrative experiences explicated so far to our ethical considerations: how do we use narratives to derive prescriptive meaning from our observation of the world, and from our understanding of nature, when neither our phenomenology nor our scientific reasoning can ever offer us reliable instruction for acting in the world? This discussion first requires an understanding of how memory cognition supports our ability to read narrative symbols that contain ethical information.

Many of the symbolic functions of narrative we have already covered connect symbolism to social roles and our co-construction of communal ethics. All of these functions of narrative in some way acknowledge the value of symbols in storytelling – narratives tend to codify their meanings, and most narrative events in fiction point abstractly or symbolically to their utility in our real lives. But we also use story to **sort out what we need to know and what symbols we need to privilege in memory and consciousness**. In fact, Eva Jablonka and Marion J. Lamb (2005) list symbolic inheritance as one of the four components of human heredity in their book *Evolution in Four Dimensions* (the others are genetic, epigenetic and behavioural). Symbolic inheritance is different from behavioural learning or transmission as symbols (including language and fiction) can provide latent (202), translatable (203) and infinitely variable information in a rule-governed, self-referential system (199), which is part of the heritability that will shape who we are.[1] Pre-existing symbols allow for human cultural evolution. Thus we are constantly metonymically linking together cultural handles and iconography, and fusing memory connections to swiftly access the cultural shorthand language we need to communicate, and indeed to comfort one another with mutual understandings. When engaged with media, we are always negotiating what is culturally expedient for use in our own communiqué. This might be a primary social usage of television and celebrity: 'the discussion of, for example, stars of film and sport, produces a basis on which people transitorily associated can find something personal to talk about' (Gluckman 1963: 315). In a globalised context, mobile populations need ways to swiftly access mutuality with the vast number of strangers they meet; the comfort we receive from knowing the same stories and characters on television is one example of this function of narrative, as are rock-pop classics that anyone can sing along to at a karaoke bar.

For Zengotita in *Mediated*, a pervasively ironic reflexivity has crept into popular (in particular televised) media, which fulfils this function of enforcing a comforting sameness, simultaneously serving to pacify (2007: 63) and ignite feelings of business, work or achievement (191). We feed the story addiction and feel like we are working, purposeful, when we learn, discuss and endlessly reappropriate cultural symbols. Likewise, when we debate musical acts and bands we like and do not like, another level of tacit conversation may be occurring as we discuss how similar we are merely via common knowledge of the music, the stories around the music, and acknowledgement of the music and its related stories as important – a narcissism of small differences.[2] This is another way of experiencing oneness, but it is ordered by our recognition of cultural symbology, which we learn through narrative, and which also privileges assumptions of importance or status: an image of Popeye, for example, might be identified as more important to commit to memory than an image of an obscure cartoon figure from a non-American country, simply because we may need to refer to Popeye later amongst peers. The implications of this process in asserting dominance point to the sale of symbols as a transnational imperialist device, and reinforces why culturally hegemonic practices remain a constant field of study. It would do some good to recall, however, the socially derived utility such processes rely upon: it is impossible to operate as a social being now without being complicit in privileging such symbols in memory and consciousness, or we risk a lack of connection with others. Chamorro-Premuzic et al.'s (2014) etiquette of film preference exhibition is dependent upon mutually known narratives – their mutuality is potentially an even more important predictor of friendship potential, partner selection and ingroup statuses than the way we feel about those narratives. Dominant cultural symbols become part of our deepest social spheres, with direct utility in our sense of connectivity with others. Even if we wanted to reject them, we cannot do without them. This genuine need is what is being exploited in all forms of cultural imperialism.

Clearly the process of negotiating which cultural handles are pertinent to commit to memory also extends to a familiar cultural-ethical discussion, concerning who we would like to be together: we use stories to discuss what our togetherness should be, and what values it should be based upon. Deciding which symbols we will use and interpret in this task plays an important role in the process. It also points to the way **stories reinforce and demonstrate adherence to social roles, or reflexively prompt social role renegotiation**. Examples include gendered reactions to scary films, in which women are more often required to demonstrate empathic fear and men fear mastery, providing comfort for female viewers (Zillman 1998: 197–8), or diegetically, those same films can demonstrate comparable social roles in their narrative events, such as the reprehensible trope of the hapless woman twisting her ankle and the enterprising male saviour coming to her rescue. Both offer demonstration, adherence to and reinforcement of social roles. This aspect of narrative has often been portrayed as a one-way mass media social control mechanism rather than a dialogous relationship between audience and storyteller, although this view is complicated by the fact that we exhibit genre and story preferences that tailor to pre-existing self-schemas (Chamorro-Premuzic et al. 2014). It is very difficult to change attitudes with story, rather than fortify existing dispositions. However, the net effect of a mass media appealing to the same social roles is clearly part of a process that normalises identities as universal, natural types – as with gender essentialism or heteronormativity – whether or not we see media norms as a genesis or a symptom. We could refer to this as the 'echo chamber' effect: if the film market appeals to prevailing social roles in order to sell products, it leaves little room for the potential function of narrative to reassess social roles that go out of date as our cultural environment changes. Yet there always remain storytellers whose conscience outweighs the need for wider distribution, more than willing to circumnavigate market demands and tell a story they are passionate about. These stories can often involve a direct engagement with, and renegotiation of, prevailing social roles.

Exclusive focus on mass media, too, can lead us to neglect quotidian experiences that contribute, in some respects much more substantially, to our self-schema or concept of our social selves. Many of these are storied. One of our primary storied means for the reinforcement and performative demonstration of social roles is gossip; so **story can be a form of gossip**. Volumes of literature on the subject of gossip have been published since early anthropological accounts by figures including Paul Radin (1927), Melville J. Herskovits (1937; 1947) and Elizabeth Colson (1953), propagating later reflection on those works (Gluckman 1963: 307). Gossip can be understood both in non-fictive terms (peer group gossip, as we traditionally know it), and in the use of certain narratives as objects of gossip, such as discussion around the events of a television show to demonstrate an epistemic mutuality. Celebrity gossip also blurs apparent boundaries between the fictive and non-fictive: readers of gossip magazines can be aware of the highly dubious nature of the claims made, and yet still enjoy entertaining the notion of the stories as actualities (McDonnell 2014: 86). Gossip itself is always a storied act, but fictions can also mimic gossip, appealing to the same discursive formula that peer group gossip exists within: discussions around soap operas are able to somewhat seamlessly fit into the same kind of conversational mores as peer group gossip, for instance. High production television serials like *Game of Thrones* offer a similar utility – the questions that circulate after the release of new episodes still gravitate around who did what to whom, and the morality of their actions. There can be differences, though, in the levels of moral relativity or fortifying certitude about transgressions that such shows exhibit or incite.

Gossip clearly has similarities with a foundational function of story: spreading second-hand information between peer networks, so that information-gathering did not have to be direct. However, gossip is clearly more complex than that, as it spreads information specifically focused upon the social behaviours of others, and human conflicts of interest render this kind of information particularly unreliable. In fact, theorists like Robin Dunbar (1996) have posited gossip needs, emerging initially as a form of allogrooming, to be the adaptive genesis of storytelling behaviours and thereby language development itself. Gossip is a kind of hyper-attentiveness to social interactions, the storied nature of which elevates its impact and sense of purpose. As the mutuality of attentional focus in narrative audiences can build feelings of rapport with other observers, so too can the alignment of information, interests, salient personalities, reactions and emotions in gossip generate ingroup cohesion, perhaps with even more efficacy than other storied activities. Although not exclusively so, the primary knowledge communicated through stories is social in nature (Mar and Oatley 2008: 182); the information provided in gossip is both assiduously, directly social (gossip leaves out narrative events that do not speak directly to moral interactivity) and personally relevant. This makes it a very powerful social tool, especially when identifying indiscretions that may lead to ostracism. Gossip does not just ask us to be hyper-attentive to social events, but in particular singles out negative appraisals of players within those events (Anderson et al. 2011), aggressors and antagonists we might avoid. We should naturally be wary, then, when fiction enters the realm of gossip: identifying aggressors and negative traits of real-life figures (in biopics for instance), or those that allegorically summarise a maligned group (from German or Russian 'bad guys' in Hollywood cinema to the current portrayal of Islamic antagonists). These narratives have gossip value while remaining unspecific about a particular individual; they can similarly generate aversive responses to those perceived as transgressors, which is also a primary function of gossip (Anderson et al. 2011).

Conflicts within stories open a space where we can imagine possibilities for change, and in particular change as a response to social and ethical dilemmas (even if the efficacy of human agency is later defeated or revealed to be inconsequential to larger forces at work). Mar and Oatley describe the reader's process of comprehending character thus:

> the psychological effects of character include the pleasing surprise of recognition, the satisfaction of being able to understand visible behavior in terms of deeper principles, the insight of seeing both others and ourselves in terms of human attributes that are both valuable and also problematic, as well as the possibility of some movement in our mental makeup. (2008: 182)

This means that our conception of and reaction to character, the information it communicates and its abstraction to social principles is an entrée to ethical discussion, especially given a narrative that stresses our capacity for psychological change. As well as provoking character evaluations, we can **play out responses to ethical problems** in narrative. Stories offer us ways to imagine the consequences of actions, even actions that are impossible to take (like superhuman feats). The consequences we explore reflect moral reasoning. Charles Taylor's ([1989] 2006) storytelling as moral identity extends to a projection by which we can imagine future moral identities. Locating oneself within a framework of moral goodness, 'requires a narrative understanding of my life, a sense of what I have become which can only be given in a story. And as I project my life forward and endorse the existing direction or give it a new one, I project a future story, not just a state of the momentary future but a bent for my whole life to come' (48). This conceptual view of story as a projection with which to explore possible ethical direction is made politically palpable by Augusto Boal, who used 'legislative theatre' in Brazilian parliament to invite voters to act out solutions to a social dilemma to see where it took them. This is similar to the way Mette Hjort invites us to extend cinema hermeneutics to address real social needs in 'Community Engagement and Film' (2014). Videogames can also focus their narrative interactivity on moral causality: the entire interface of *The Walking Dead* videogame (Telltale Games,

2012), for example, is the making of moral and social decisions, primarily in conversation. After their consequences are revealed, the game focuses upon retrospectively explaining one's decisions and ethical positions (which usually stress the pressures and limitations in which those decisions are made, and question how we can 'own' our ethics when they are so mutable given differing circumstances). Here again we can see the potential value of play in moral development: storied play can be focused not only on imagining ethical consequences, but also on the work of explaining subsequent responses to ourselves and others. Mar and Oatley also go on to clarify how the act of projecting feelings is connected to the imagining of consequences: 'narratives allow us to try out solutions to emotional and social difficulties through the simulation of these experiences' (2008: 183). So we imagine an aversive scenario that calls for change, project possibilities for intervention, and imagine consequential emotions and meanings by trialling out potential actions in narrative. The consequences portrayed are a moral reasoning – this is how the end of a story can come to matter to us so much. Endings point to consequences that will not be further questioned, and are therefore one of the best suggestions of an ethic stories can provide, even where the story might explore many other quandaries, responses, causes and effects along the way.

So finally we use story to **ask ethical questions: how we ought to live**. These questions, and story's remit to answer them, also introduce the possibility of 'imposing social control and, hence . . . achieving power' through moralistic narrative (Sugiyama 2001: 241). It might seem obvious that one function of narrative can be to demonstratively articulate and offer perspectives on particular ethical problems, but we might also consider the possibility that ethics are embedded in *all* narrative and drama involving one or more living things. As Martin Price puts it in *Forms of Life* (1983), all novels and the characters that populate them are forms of life that we imagine, and because they live, they have a moral dimension; this interior moral dimension is in itself another entirely necessary 'form of life' (50–1). As soon as a living thing is present in a narrative, an ethical tension exists, as we read its purpose and consistently ask what we would hope to happen next and how it is achievable through agency, the many pathways of which translate to an *ought* question. It is very difficult to come up with a plot point that does not spur an ethical question about how we should behave; it is the implicit internal examination undergone whenever something happens involving a living entity. According to Booth, narrative ethics are a universal subject because story is at the genesis of the human and the means by which humans reinvent themselves, and now the 'daily barrage of narrative to which we are subjected' heightens the need for ethical criticism (1988: 39). If it is clear how ethics are inextricable from narrative (even those that purposefully frustrate ethical intelligibility or minimise ethical evaluations within the diegesis), and if we accept that our quotidian engagements with story media are proliferating, then it also makes sense to ask how we should value the relative ethical strategies employed by various contemporary narratives, and what we want from narrative ethics. In relation to the contemporary philosophy of cinema, Robert Sinnerbrink says, 'despite the evident concern with the "unethical" aspects of cinema throughout the history of film theory, it is striking how few theorists have attempted to explore the positive ethical potential of the medium' (2016: 28). Narrative humanism, with its emphasis on articulating positive ethical potentials, can perform this exploration.

We have established that storytelling is a kind of ethical thought, and one that may rehearse responses to problems arising in the world. However, this points to some problems in the relation of ethical thought to ethical action as we also might have rehearsed ideologies that we fail to act upon – when we act, we can fail to meet our own moral standards, or choose to ignore or overlook ethical discernments previously abstracted from and rehearsed in fiction. We might read a book detailing the plight of sweatshop workers, for example, but still knowingly buy textiles that support the industry. It remains difficult to politicise our thoughts rather than our actions: one can spend a lifetime studying complex ethics and still behave reprehensibly toward others (not me though, I swear). This means we have a need for stories that can make clear the precise relation between complex moral thought, and potential moral action.

To briefly recap, humanist storytelling emphasises difficult, multifaceted ethics and complicates intuitive responses to familiar problems, especially punitive responses – it challenges the comfort of seeing justice prevail, threats brought under control, and order occurring independently of our personal efforts, brought by a hero, heroes, or nature. It asks us to think twice about our closely held principles; in short, it promotes a sharper view of one's convictions, in order to improve our understanding of one another. In humanist story ethics, we have to be challenged to refine what we think about a human problem – if a conclusion is easily drawn from the narrative without articulation of its contingent complications, it is potentially reductive, failing to encourage deeper thought about the human. Stories can entertain pre-existing moral predilection, or seek to complicate the ease of our moral responses, considering a quandary from multiple perspectives, with due compassion for the lives of all involved, and 'humanism holds that the tool of compassion is not by nature apologist or lacking in attention to culpability and pragmatic response to culpability' (Moss-Wellington 2015: 107).[3] Yet any questions that lead us to evaluate an individual's moral worth are decentred in humanist narrative, as we are focused upon social interaction and the collective forces that drive behaviour, not the punishment of bad behaviour. As humanism does not totalise human identities into moral categories in order to dole out reward and punishment to the deserved, its ethics are emphatically consequentialist.

It is tempting to conclude, after all this, that what we need is simply more moral doubt – complications of our ethical solutions. But what happens when we need to conclude on a course of action? As Kwame Anthony Appiah points out, shared moral language and mutual values are essential components in reciprocally beneficial outcomes:

> Folktales, drama, opera, novels, short stories; biographies, histories, ethnographies; fiction or nonfiction; painting, music, sculpture, and dance: every human civilization has ways to reveal to us values we had not previously recognized or undermine our commitment to values that we had settled into. Armed with these terms, fortified with a shared language of value, we can often guide one another, in the cosmopolitan spirit, to shared responses. (2006: 30)

The best stories can do, I submit, is to provide a space to test our convictions and our hypothetical, narrativised moral responses against both simplicity and validity, an arena by which courses of action can subsequently be confirmed or denied against these principles. The arts unite phenomenological and moral knowledge through striving, giving rise to moral *possibilities* rather than actualities (Soper 1986); their completion is up to the individual after the narrative closes and we are once again called upon to act in the world. We may consequently, at the very least, be primed for more complex eventualities, and ready to face the difficulty of sticking to our convictions when self-interest intervenes.

Conclusion

So again, we arrive at an ethic of striving rather than perfection. The development of moral language requires striving and mental work; as a case in point, Darcia Narvaez's (2002) research finds that children apply pre-existing, context-contingent moral schemas to literary narratives (as do adults), yet they rarely comprehend morals the author intended to convey. To my mind, this points to the complex sociality of storytelling, in that we use narrative to develop a moral language in concert with others; again, stories are a springboard into discussion not only about the actual, but also about possible morals arising from the story, and a child is probably much more likely to receive moral instruction from a parent or guardian than an interpreted narrative. Caregivers and children instead might use the narrative together in conversation as a point of reference for emergent moral knowledge; the story itself may not be the primary conveyor of information, so much as the effort put into discussion around the story, and that effort breeds a familiarity with moral conversations that will help the child navigate more complex social interactions as they gain independence. While it may be unsurprising that a brief intervention teaching reading skills fails to surmount children's moral misreadings (Narvaez 2002: 166), these skills should be thought of as developing over many years, with effort. When we read a picture book to children, for example, we may discuss the story with them to clarify alternative interpretations, yet this does not mean they will have an immaculate comprehension of moral storytelling within six weeks. Narvaez speculates: 'There may be moral developmental hurdles that prevent a young child from comprehending an author's theme until sufficient developmental structures are in place' (166–7), however these developments will need a context in which to flourish, a reason for their development. Stories provide a safe context for such developments. Comprehension of intent may become easier over time, although we still interpret and discuss our interpretations with others, a learned advanced sociality.

We are thus returned to a primary humanist value: the striving and effort of complex understanding is more important than moral perfectionism, and emphasising ongoing development keeps us open and adaptable to human difference and change. This connects the mental work of fiction to its potential for a complex empathy: it takes effortful care to remain alive to how other people's stories are alive (cf. Price *Forms of Life* 1983; Frank *Letting Stories Breathe* 2010), adapting and changing as they confront new environments in which new stories will be relevant. The primary ethical appeal of the narrative humanist, then, is that we should never allow our conception of one another to become complete, to reach an end in which we think of another lifeworld or culture as static; we achieve this through stories, those mutating transactions that speak of incessant mutation, that diverge and require a comparison back to those moments we diverged from.

There will doubtless be objections to this taxonomy: story functions I have or have not included, that I have made too much of, or not enough of, or those that seem too indistinct to be separated into more than one function. These are all the problems of taxonomy, and I should reiterate before closing that I do not expect this first attempt at a social narratology to be in any way comprehensive. I expect it to be extensive enough to inspire imagination, however, and to lay the groundwork of untotalisable unknowing at the same time as offering space for new descriptive insights, the openness to discovery that humanism relies upon. In the spirit of humanism, it invites complication and extension.[4] I hope to retain this sense of open wonderment, but also prompt attention to many of these uses of narrative in practice, as I address a case study of the human drama on film. The remainder of this book concerns the millennial suburban ensemble dramedy as an example of humanist narrative practice. Where I have so far only described the theory of humanism, I turn now to demonstrate its application at two levels: an expansive cinematic genre reading, followed by a close reading of a single film.

Notes

1. We should keep in mind that biology, like all sciences at their vanguard, is an open debate rather than a holistic or closed explanation, and so these Lamarckian notions of 'soft inheritance' are still in question (Dickins and Rahman 2012: 2916).
2. This term has been reclaimed by figures like Glen Owens Gabbard (1993) to demonstrate its prevalence in loving relationships. Gabbard's narcissism of small differences might provide a model for understanding this narrative function among friends and acquaintances, too.
3. There exists an attendant fear of the loss of culpability, especially in legal settings, when we admit biological explanations. But if we see our genes and environments as co-dependent and their effects as indivisible, this makes little sense. Understanding criminal or unethical behaviour as a product of both our sociobiology and the world it is expressed within should lead us to a consequentialist rather than a retributivist ethic. We can identify culpability and still explain its emergence without resorting to punitive rather than pragmatic measures.
4. Literary scholars have been famously hostile toward empirical or otherwise systematic approaches to narratological inquiry (like functionalism), and I hope that I have demonstrated too that these approaches just offer some new vantage – they do not ordinarily totalise their findings as the summation of narrative's meaning in our lives – and that they will not obliterate, and indeed can be harmonious with, traditional hermeneutics.

PART III

GENRE CASE STUDY: THE SUBURBAN ENSEMBLE DRAMEDY

CHAPTER 7

An Introduction to the Millennial Suburban Ensemble Film

The suburban ensemble film had been hinted at prior to the turn of the millennium, yet only really began to coalesce into a recognisable cinematic mode or genre with identifiable conventions as the 1990s drew to a close. Some of the more successful titles include *The Kids Are All Right* (Lisa Cholodenko, 2010), *Little Miss Sunshine* (Jonathan Dayton and Valerie Faris, 2006) and what is arguably the inciting feature in a wave of such films entering production, *American Beauty* (Sam Mendes, 1999). Although seldom recognised as a genre in its own right, beyond being identified by critics as 'humanistic drama' as we will see, the conventions are familiar: a cross-section of an American neighbourhood with concerns equalised across a transgenerational multi-character cast, contrasting personality types, gender, sexual, ethnic, ideological and other differences. The shift in independent filmmaking – to ensemble cast family and domestic studies with a focus on performance rather than perceptible or ostentatious technique – was not impulsive or abrupt, or without precedent, but a gradual development is observable throughout the 2000s, possibly as film investors began to recognise the potential for return on films experimenting with the inexpensive yet high-profile *American Beauty* formula. The film grossed $356 million worldwide against a $15 million production budget (Box Office Mojo) and won the Academy Award for Best Picture. A pioneering example of the influence, prestige and financial success possible in studio-independent hybrid modes of production, DreamWorks borrowed practices 'from the indie/ specialty realm, from budget to handling to textual qualities' (King 2009: 195). *American Beauty* emerged from a major studio, yet spearheaded a trend that would traverse modes of independent and Indiewood production, gathering momentum throughout the 2000s.

Along with a realist or representational mode of expression and suburban context, characteristics of the genre include ensemble casts often featuring no distinguishable protagonist; concentration on the ways in which families mediate dysfunction and ultimately get by after traumatic events force reconciliation; a feature-length transition from sardonic displays of familial conflict to sentiment; a converse upsetting of sentimentality with humour; admission of painful or repellent desires and taboos, usually followed by a deflation of the shame they incite; recurrent themes of adultery and ephebophilia; comparative fusion of coming-of-age and midlife crisis drama; observational, performance-based comedy of manners, coupled with politically aware satire; coverage which concentrates the viewer's attention on character and performance; interventions of the real in comical situations, whereupon we are called to imagine the characters' broader lives outside of the comedic diegesis; a critique of consumer culture obedience, aspiration, status and class anxiety in the suburbs; a concurrent attempt to understand the roots of narcissism and promote humility; anatomisation of ennui, depression and 'affluenza' (cf. Harmon 2006) in the suburban malaise; and communally prompted redemption, resulting in a new political awareness and liberalised care. Being a low-cost domestic mode, the suburban ensemble film also features a predominance of early career and first time filmmakers working on limited budgets.

In 1999, three suburban ensemble dramedy films were released: *Election* (Alexander Payne) in April, followed by *American Beauty* and *Mumford* (Lawrence Kasdan), both in September. Although *American Beauty* was by far the most successful of the three films and can claim the clearest lasting impact on future productions, both *Election* and *Mumford* are important in the development of suburban cinema in their own ways. The first half of the decade saw the release of a diverse range of films from Rose Troche's *The Safety of Objects* in 2001 to Mike Binder's *The Upside of Anger* in 2005. The second watershed year was 2006, with the much darker *Little Children* (Todd Field) and ensemble dramedy-road movie splice *Little Miss Sunshine* both receiving awards attention. Films like *Lymelife* (Derick Martini, 2008) cast a critical eye over early influential texts, referencing *American Beauty* in particular and revisiting some of its questionable gender politics (Beuka 2004: 242; Karlyn 2004 passim) and haughty spirituality (Hentzi 2000: 49). By the middle of the decade, the genre was recognisable enough for its own conventions to be satirised in works like *The Chumscrubber* (Arie Posin, 2005) and *A Serious Man* (Joel Coen and Ethan Coen, 2009). Latter works include *The Kids Are All Right* and *The Oranges* (Julian Farino, 2012).

There were predecessors. Although *American Beauty* could be considered the watershed moment, an earlier breakthrough is evident in the release of *Parenthood* (Ron Howard, 1989) a decade prior, then an unconventional script both in its narrative structure and resolve to scrutinise the inherent drama in our everyday familial relations that other films overlooked or sidelined (I take a closer look at *Parenthood* in the final part of this book). These multi-character family dramedies were for a long time isolated examples, however. For now, I will trace some of the more generic predecessors, as the suburban ensemble film has amalgamated conventions from a number of filmic traditions, including coming-of-age and teen films, infidelity dramas, televisual family sitcoms, the family crisis drama, generational reunion pictures, and some of the pioneering post-Production Code ensemble works of the New Hollywood era. Following from an introductory history and taxonomy of the suburban ensemble dramedy's influences, this section looks at the politics of suburban representation on film, discussions around its affective formula, in particular the implications of sentimentality and satire's interdependence, and finally the political context from which this particular ensemble form emerged at the dawn of the new millennium. First, however, as the suburban ensemble dramedy's polyphonic storytelling presents something of a narrative fusion of genre forms spanning the preceding century, I turn to an archaeology of some thematic elements it juxtaposes and revises, including various iterations of domestic melodrama and comedic genres. The following proliferation of genres and styles suggests from the outset the filmic histories millennial suburban ensembles are steeped within, and in many cases talk back to; this taxonomy should then place the suburban ensemble in a historical context, providing the grounds for further discussion of its politics.

The Thematic and Generic Heritage of the Millennial Suburban Ensemble Film

A number of dramatic ensemble film forms were popular in the years leading up to the millennium: the episodic family genealogy film, often emphasising romance or theistic identity, such as István Szabó's *Sunshine* (1999), released the same year as *American Beauty*; the social issue ensemble drama, such as *Traffic* (Steven Soderbergh) in 2000, or what Hsuan L. Hsu describes collectively as the 'Los Angeles ensemble film' (2006: 134–43);[1] and Alejandro González Iñárritu's butterfly-effect cinema sustained throughout the 2000s, a popular version of the 'network narrative' (Silvey 2009), 'fractal' (Everett 2005) or 'hyperlink' (Quart 2005) cinema, in which seemingly disparate people are revealed to share causal connections. In an overwhelming majority of these films, the tragic or melodramatic modes far outweighed the comedic, and suburbia was rarely a primary consideration (urban spaces are much more prominent in the above examples). These phenomena were continuous with a trend of proliferating multi-protagonist films throughout the rapidly globalising 1980s (Azcona 2010), and of course with countless multi-focalised literary and theatrical traditions before that. Nonetheless, surveying all of these ensemble forms, it does appear that the turn of the millennium initiated special interest in our connectivity and shared meaning. This is perhaps unsurprising considering plentiful evidence that temporal landmarks, no matter how apparently arbitrary, spur searches for meaning (Dai et al. 2015; Alter and Hershfield 2014), and this phenomenon could also help explain the high volume of influential film productions released in 1999, a year Geoff King positions as the coming-of-age of Indiewood filmmaking (2009: 191–2). Other ensemble pictures became popular in the millennium's first decade: the seasonal, such as *Love Actually* (Richard Curtis, 2003) or *The Family Stone* (Thomas Bezucha, 2005); the thriller, including Quentin Tarantino's works and *Rashomon*-influenced (Akira Kurosawa, 1950) polyphonic perspective films like *Vantage Point* (Pete Travis, 2008) or *Elephant* (Gus Van Sant, 2003); musical adaptations; Rodrigo García's women-centric hyperlink vignettes; political history revision narratives, often humanising peripheral characters, such as *Bobby* (Emilio Estevez, 2006), *Battle in Seattle* (Stuart Townsend, 2007) or *Lions for Lambs* (Robert Redford, 2007); and one-off experiments like *Timecode* (Mike Figgis, 2000). Nor can the popularity of ensemble filmmaking be considered an exclusively American phenomenon. Notions of global connectivity in popular films such as *The Edge of Heaven* (Fatih Akin, 2007), Michael Haneke's *Code Unknown* (2000) and Susan Biel's cinema vivify transnational causality and thus present a broader political reach. Finally, the success of Paul Thomas Anderson's Los Angeles ensemble *Magnolia* (1999) also paved the way for a number of connectivity films throughout the following decade, often employing a similar romantic irony and narrativised reflexivity with abstruse purpose, such as *Happy Endings* (Don Roos, 2005), *The Rules of Attraction* (Roger Avary, 2002), or *Thirteen Conversations About One Thing* (Jill Sprecher, 2001), all of which present as some manner of temporal-causal puzzle.

There were two suburban period pieces prefacing the ensemble dramedy genre in the years prior to *American Beauty*: *The Ice Storm* (Ang Lee, 1997), a parable of child neglect during the sexual revolution, and

Pleasantville (Gary Ross, 1998), somewhat more facetiously taking aim at mediatised ideals of 1950s suburbia. These were both accounts of midcentury suburbia, the lasting images of which are, as Steven Mintz (2003: 353), Stephanie Coontz (*The Way We Never Were* 1992) and Arlene S. Skolnick (*Embattled Paradise* 1991) all assert, inaccurate representations of the breadth of family living arrangements across America at the time. The white picket nuclear family was never the standard, and is thus a case of ersatz nostalgia, or 'nostalgia without lived experience or collective historical memory' (Appadurai 1996: 78). Drawing on ideas from historiographer David Lownethal, suburban media narrative theorist David R. Coon agrees: despite the imprecision of so many of our presumptions of postwar suburban demography, nostalgic visions of the suburban archetype are still motivated to create demand for neotraditional development and related policy goals, as well as to criticise these goals (2014: 30–68).[2] The archetype – or suburban façade – remains a fabrication we continue to discuss as if it were a real rather than psychical space, or 'symbolic ecology' (Hunter 1987: 199), yet Coon suggests that in 1998, *Pleasantville* and *The Truman Show* (Peter Weir) anticipated a trend in self-reflexivity around suburban image construction. Understanding suburbia in these early examples of the genre meant understanding homogeneity – whiteness, family standards and upper-middleness, for example, were tied to the geographic imaginary of extant postwar sociospatial iterations, even if the reality was increasingly divergent.

It is arguable, though, how much the late 1990s suburban films reveal an unacknowledged psychical construction of suburbia, or merely extend popular fantasies founded on a suburban stereotype. Robert Beuka claims 'these films also represent a perpetuation of the two-dimensional view of suburban life that has characterized the dominant perception of suburbia' (2004: 14), displaying both affection for and chastising attitudes toward the fantasy of a postwar uniform suburbia. *Pleasantville* and *The Ice Storm*, for example, in different ways cautioned against idealising a sexually confused past, both emphasising their suburban settings as nodes in the history of sexual repression. David E. Wilt points out that *The Ice Storm* riffs on themes of suburban sexual dissatisfaction explored in 1960s exploitation cinema such as *Sin in the Suburbs* (Joe Sarno, 1964) and *Suburban Roulette* (Herschell Gordon Lewis, 1968) (2003: 484). However, again, our image of sexual unknowing in these eras is exaggerated (perhaps compounded by the Production Code's distortion of thematic candour): early multi-character coming-of-age melodramas such as *Peyton Place* (Mark Robson) in 1957 and *Splendor in the Grass* (Elia Kazan) in 1961 tackle sexual repression lucidly, as well as providing another humanistic suburban ensemble template.

Between renewed interest in the family unit under strain in the 1960s to 70s, surprisingly giving rise to 'some of Hollywood's most searching explorations of family life' (Mintz 2003: 359), and its resurgence after 1999, American cinema often reimagined the US suburban context within the canon of popular genre film. Examples include the much-discussed family- and home-under-threat in post-1960s horror and suburban Gothic,[3] through to the more pointed suburban gender politics in hostage/siege dramas such as Roger Donaldson's *Cadillac Man* and Michael Cimino's *Desperate Hours* remake (both in 1990), or the less-observed gender role redefinition of comedy features such as *Mr. Mom* (Stan Dragoti, 1983), in which the climax sees both parents (played by Teri Garr and Michael Keaton) hastily patching together a deal to co-work and co-childrear, out of necessity to mitigate the slapstick chaos unfolding around them (the settlement comically coincides with a sudden end to their suburban entropy). The generational studies of reunion films *The Big Chill* (Lawrence Kasdan, 1983) and *The Return of the Secaucus Seven* (John Sayles, 1979), as well as Barry Levinson's 'Baltimore Films' and later, Whit Stillman's 'Yuppie Trilogy', all provided another blueprint for ensemble works that emphasised social inquiry. Sayles's influence in particular should be noted: a pioneer of creative funding methods for American independent filmmakers of the 1980s and 1990s, Sayles was already known for his various experimentations in ensemble cinema. After exploring the urban ensemble drama with *City of Hope* in 1991, Sayles wrote and directed a number of fascinating and highly political hybrid films: he crossed the small town ensemble with a Frontera Western mystery in 1996's *Lone Star*, and with the survival film in 1999's *Limbo*, before reaching perhaps the closest he would come to a purist suburban ensemble with 2002's *Sunshine State*, a look at development politics in Florida, and then returning to the small-town ensemble detective story with 2004's *Silver City*. Although his works never quite mimicked a recognisable genre form, as his recognition of human hybridity in all its forms permeated not just his casting and dialogue but his approach to genre also, it is clear that Sayles's filmmaking throughout the 1990s provided another model for the millennial suburban ensemble dramedy. There is discernible hope for a developing global fairness in Sayles's reiteration of inevitable hybridity across such a variety of narrative spaces (Moss-Wellington 2015: 199), which may be carried from Sayles's influential ensemble templates to later suburban pictures, too.

Reaching back further, the voluntary ratings system that succeeded the Hays Code in 1968 clearly opened the door for New Hollywood maturity, capable of more candid representations of domestic politics. There are clear precedents in the early work of John Cassavetes, Mike Nichols and others. Robert Altman in particular experimented with (monogenerational, non-suburban) fusions of comedy and drama across an ensemble cast with *MASH* (1970) and *Nashville* (1975). Before this, we can trace the humanising of suburban lives to figures including Frank Capra, particularly in the enormously influential *It's a Wonderful Life* (1946). We can also trace family and drawing-room drama on the stage from Henrik Ibsen and Eugene O'Neill to Tracy Letts today, whose *August: Osage County* was adapted into a suburban ensemble film by John Wells in 2013. Although all of these works contain elements that would turn up in later American indie cinema, the suburban ensemble dramedy as genre, with sustained conventions of its own, did not cohere until the turn of the millennium.

Perhaps one of the clearest generic threads prefacing the suburban dramedy cinematic form can be witnessed across family crisis dramas, from the affecting narrative efficiency of *Kramer vs. Kramer* (Robert Benton, 1979) to *Ordinary People* (Robert Redford, 1980) and palliative dramas like *Dad* (Gary David Goldberg, 1989), right up to *One True Thing* (Carl Franklin) and *Stepmom* (Chris Columbus) in 1998. Of course, these films tend away from comedic relief, lean to melodrama, and mostly fixate on parental concerns rather than equalising our sympathies across generations or neighbourhoods. They also may have got it wrong: in the crisis drama, we often we see family trauma (particularly the loss of a child) tearing families apart, where research demonstrates that shared dysphoric experience is actually more likely to bind communities through identity fusion (Whitehouse 2013: 284) and promote cooperation (Bastian et al. 2014).[4] Many films of this ilk, however, do take gender role definition as a springboard for drama – in particular *Kramer vs. Kramer* and *One True Thing* – and this remains a key component in most millennial suburban ensemble works. Later, Alexander Payne fused the family crisis drama with ensemble dramedy conventions in both *The Descendants* (2011) and *Nebraska* (2013). The latter, perhaps less humanistic than many of Payne's works, exemplifies an in-vogue fantasy of small-town and semi-rural suburban existentialism, permeating films as diverse as *Fargo* (Joel Coen and Ethan Coen, 1996) and *The Good Girl* (Miguel Arteta, 2002). Each offers discriminatory visions of a mundane world the very provincialism of which diminishes human worth and potential – a barren aesthetic and moral landscape, and its parallel physical and human geography, generates parochial ennui.

Sexual politics play a substantial part in many of the millennial suburban dramedies, in particular infidelity, and deconstruction of a contemporary confusion around young sexuality and pubescence. Therefore another precedent can be witnessed across infidelity dramas, from *Brief*

Encounter (David Lean, 1945) to *Strangers When We Meet* (Richard Quine, 1960), both considering the context in which the infidelity takes place, and of course *Lolita* (Stanley Kubrick, 1962). Recent melodramas may seem to be a useful reference here, from the knowingly ham-fisted excesses of Todd Haynes's didactic suburban critiques, including Douglas Sirk homage *Far from Heaven* in 2002 and 1995's *Safe*, to the outrageously popular high-production soaps of HBO. The emotional arc of a majority of suburban dramedy films seems derived in no small way from television, perhaps as television provided an early model for the family ensemble, across which further structural influences were carried. Indeed, feminist media theorist Lynn Spigel has underscored just how much of our historic presumptions of suburbia were carried through television in *Welcome to the Dreamhouse* (2001). However, as the millennial suburban dramedies resist melodrama in favour of diverse attempts at realism, and a pathos tempered by humour, I see more in common with family sitcoms such as *Roseanne* and socially conscious predecessors such as *The Mary Tyler Moore Show*, *All in the Family*, *Diff'rent Strokes* or *Good Times* than TV serials such as ABC's *Desperate Housewives* or *Big Love*, both of which attempt to 'transcend' geographic specificity in suburban depiction (Coon 2014: 223), and thus wind up as hyperbolic misrepresentation.[5] *Roseanne* pioneered a kind of dramedy in the family sitcom format that has clear threads to this day: the gags are often cruel, the characters overtly aggressive toward one another, but when they are faced with the complex ethical dimensions of a particular social dilemma and struggle to devise their own resolution, each short story concludes with opportunities for sentiment, as each character's attempts to do the best they can demonstrates a genuine care for one another. The format was carried through cartoons such as *The Simpsons* to today's *Modern Family*, albeit gathering excess ironic address along the way, which by the time of *Modern Family* would overwhelm and undermine any social critique or sincerity. Of course, the difference remains that *Roseanne* admitted class and regularly foregrounded financial concerns. These influences are, sadly, now dwindling in related sitcoms; where they are apparent, class too often becomes farce, as with series like *Raising Hope* or *The Middle* (Grabowski 2014). Equivalent contemporary programmes are drained of sentimentality until only the humour remains, as in the pathos-hostile *Family Guy*; these productions demonstrate a tendency to bigotry, complicating the notion of sentimentality as conservative praxis, assessed later in the following chapter.

As coming-of-age and teen films involve a liberal dose of family relations, many of the conventions also have crossover with the suburban ensemble dramedy. Some films, such as *Juno* (Jason Reitman, 2007), *Dirty*

Girl (Abe Sylvia, 2010) or *The Way Way Back* (Nat Faxon and Jim Rash, 2013) straddle the border between the suburban dramedy and coming-of-age film. These pictures have absorbed a progression in teen-revolt dramas from *Rebel Without a Cause* (Nicholas Ray, 1955), and of course *Peyton Place* and *Splendor in the Grass*, along with milder coming-of-age ensemble features like *American Graffiti* (George Lucas, 1973), through to rebellion-hysteria pictures *Suburbia* (Penelope Spheeris, 1984) and *Over the Edge* (Jonathan Kaplan, 1979), in which the youths' disgruntlement explicitly stems from the town-planning self-interest of their parents. This was followed by Francis Ford Coppola's S. E. Hinton adaptations, then via John Hughes and the 'brat pack' to Richard Linklater's more sober reflections on youth rites of passage. Concurrently to Linklater's early youth studies, films such as *House Party* (Reginald Hudlin, 1990) began to chart changes in racial and spatial mobility, as ethnically mixed characters 'traverse a landscape that runs the gamut from inner-city "projects" through lower- and middle-class suburban fringe neighbourhoods to the upper-middle-class suburbs' (Beuka 2004: 216–17), and Lasse Hallström extended his own rite-of-passage filmmaking to variations on a multi-character suburban perspective for the humanistic features *Once Around* in 1991, *What's Eating Gilbert Grape* in 1993 and the more episodic Bildungsroman *The Cider House Rules* in 1999. Hallstrom's later films, however, waned in humanist subject matter.

Post-Hughes studio teen pictures too, such as *Easy A* (Will Gluck, 2010), now include more screen time and consideration of parents, teachers and other adults in the lead teen's life, which indicates a trade in genre conventions has begun to take place (perhaps also taking cues from the broader suburban critique of independent predecessors, such as Hal Hartley's teen romance films). On the other hand, pictures like *The Kids Are All Right* and *Enough Said* (Nicole Holofcener, 2013) take a dramatic moment in teenagers' lives (moving out of home to college) and focus on the way in which the parents displace their anxiety around the lifestyle shift to relationships with their partners and peers. The latter splices the kids-going-to-college movie with romantic comedy conventions. The suburban ensemble dramedy does not necessarily require inclusion of family: some films, such as *What Goes Up* (Jonathan Glatzer, 2009) and *Best Man Down* (Ted Koland, 2013), include very little to no family relations, focusing on the relationship between children and adults who are related by extra-familial acquaintance. *What Goes Up*, like *Election*, could be seen as representative of another movement in this cinema: the focus on adults in high-school contexts. Some include a breadth of young people and their teachers, and some, such as *Juno* or *Butter* (Jim Field Smith, 2011), examine how a central character relates to a breadth of adults and peers around them. Others again, such as *Mumford* or *The Station Agent* (Thomas McCarthy, 2003), include little or no lead child or teen roles. Many of these films test the boundaries of the suburban ensemble dramedy, which is, like all genres, permeable. In summary, coming-of-age cinema could be seen as symbiotic with the suburban ensemble dramedy (often sharing a suburban context and considering the meaning of family): early teen cinema could be seen as inspiring a suburban ensemble formula of humour and pathos, and in turn teen films have featured larger ensembles with a greater breadth of character types receiving attention alongside young protagonists. For now, though, I will stick to analysis of those films that work squarely within the confines of the suburban ensemble rather than Bildungsroman or teen cinemas that have incorporated suburban ensemble influences.

So the suburban ensemble dramedy presents an amalgamation of several genres, both antecedent and concomitant. It borrows their conventions and fuses them into something comparative and new. Wilt compellingly identifies the longstanding influence of another convention in exaggeration of the relatively mundane activity of home maintenance and renovation, extrapolated to a (usually comedic) nightmare (2003: 482). Examples include 1948's *Mr. Blandings Builds His Dream House* (H. C. Potter) to 1986's *The Money Pit* (Richard Benjamin). Aspirational-conformist suburban aesthetic gags were once the bread and butter of satirical fantasy filmmakers in the suburban Gothic tradition, too: Tim Burton opening *Beetlejuice* (1988) with a spider crawling over a model dream home, for instance, and *Edward Scissorhands* (1990) with cookie-cutter suburban rooftops of alluring toybox colours. The 'imaginative construction of suburbia as uniformly dull or relentlessly gaudy' (Millard 1994: 186) endures as a fantasy of cultural specificity and diversity of taste lacking in the suburban populace. *Neighbors* (John G. Avildsen, 1981), *Parents* (Bob Balaban, 1989) and *Serial Mom* (John Waters, 1994) also reach for a cynical fantasy show of suburban horrors via camp hyperbole. Joe Dante draws attention to the inherent solipsism of these images in *The 'Burbs* (1989) when, in one of the most underrated film openings in cinema, we zoom in from the Universal logo (aspiring to considerations of the global) right into a darkened, pristinely art-directed film set of a suburban cul-de-sac (parochial considerations are now inescapable), where a hilariously extrinsic trophy home-cum-Gothic-mansion looms over the street. Composer Jerry Goldsmith's disconcerting, alien percussion blends into ominous string arrangement clichés recognisable from recent thriller films, culminating in the classic, over-the-top Gothic organ to craft a truly unique experience projecting the viewer into the suburban uncanny.[6]

These hyperbolic images of material conformity, once a dark gag exposing absurdity in the media fantasy of the suburban façade, were imported right into the realist dramedy in 1999 with *American Beauty*.

Finally, the concept of the façade in suburban representation is a long-standing cliché of particular interest to these filmmakers, many of whom challenge its summary of suburbia as a front for depravity or vice, while others, such as writer/director Derrick Borte in *The Joneses* (2009), uncritically replicate it. The imagery associated with the suburban façade has also been increasingly loaded with irony, revealing a growing discomfort with its uncomplicated deployment. Despite enduring appeals to 'look closer', as in *American Beauty*'s publicity campaign, or strip back appearances to 'shatter the illusion' and expose 'what is hidden underneath' (Coon 2014: 18–19), we are already familiar with what is hidden underneath. The discourse and tropes of an intellectual 'special access' cajole us into thinking we are being granted an exceptional vision of deeper truth, when all we are witnessing is dog-eared manipulation of fantastical socio-spatial iconography masquerading as truth, repeating the viewer's preconceptions: 'look closer' assumes the on-screen suburbs are a reality hiding a truer reality. A central tenet of both *Pleasantville* and *The Truman Show* is that there is a real world outside of the suburban ideal or utopia, and the notion has extended in American antisuburban cinema since their release in 1998.[7] Coon admits these spaces are as bogus as the West of the Western, or the crime-addled urbanity of a noir thriller (2014: 19–20), or what Beuka refers to as a suburban 'imagined environment, a landscape of the mind' (229). 'Despite the range of options available,' Coon says, 'storytellers tend to return to one particular vision of suburbia more than any other. As a result, the image of the suburb as a middle-class bedroom community continues to dominate our cultural imagination, even as the reality of suburban life becomes increasingly difficult to define' (222). Reliance on some veracity of the suburban façade as a real-world phenomenon in a film like *The Joneses* lays bare the didactic elitism of its reductive fantasy, totalising all suburban lives as unfulfilling, vapid and concealing corruption, duplicity, or human ill. *New York Times* journalist Stephen G. Freedman uses the films of Todd Solondz to point out how this antisuburban cinema implicitly frames its concerns as polarised, ideological war between those who struggle in the confines of suburbia, and those who epitomise it:

> Solondz, a native of New Jersey who calls his production company Suburban Pictures, means to speak for the misfits in a monochromatic world . . . Such compassion, though, relies on cheap shots against whatever or whomever represents the suburban status quo. The white-collar father in 'Happiness,' a Cheeveresque figure with his car phone and rep tie, cannot simply be unmasked as a hypocrite

or a souse; no, he turns out to be a pederast who rapes his son's playmates. When Mr. Solondz's camera in 'Dollhouse' surveys a suburban home, it lingers over a veritable catalogue of bad taste – gaudy afghans, mismatched paneling, green shag carpet, cabinets stuffed with Yodels and Ring Dings. This kind of satire, far from seeking to jar an audience out of its complacency, sneers along with it from a superior distance. (1999: 1)

After the millennium however, a new breed of films, largely independently produced, have taken the time to reclaim and explore humanising character possibilities within the suburban cinematic context.

None of this is to suggest a complete expulsion of antihumanism from suburban depiction in cinema after 1999. Filmmakers like Derek Cianfrance with *Blue Valentine* (2010) and Mendes with *Revolutionary Road* (2008) extended 'yet another presentation of the suburban world as a hopeless trap for clueless people who had wanted more out of life than marriage' (Basinger 2012: 353). The image of suburbia as prison sustains. Across the history of suburban cinema, a number of films, unpleasantly asserting their misogyny as comedy, also reveal an impulse to blame, punish or deride women (at worst offering their simulated abuse as nihilistic catharsis) for a perceived awfulness seething under the suburban façade: from *Blue Velvet* (David Lynch, 1986) to *American Beauty*, and to an extent *The Stepford Wives* (Bryan Forbes, 1975), these films identified the suburban malaise as a female problem, the regressive mores and routines particular to women's domesticity (*The Stepford Wives*) and women internalising or sustaining the worst of American competitive exceptionalism (*American Beauty*); this cinema often went on to scorn and degrade their female characters for such crimes (*Blue Velvet*). They are part of an ongoing suppressive characterisation of women's domesticity as operating outside of real labour, productivity and political relevance (McHugh 1999: 193). Susan Saegert critiques this sustaining misconception of the suburban, private and parochial as feminine and the urban, public and productive as masculine in 'Masculine Cities and Feminine Suburbs' (1980).

American Beauty's inclusion of elements of aesthetic fantasy also reveals a key development unfolding throughout the ensemble dramedies of the 2000s: the gradual relinquishing of extra-realist style (a realism occasionally interrupted by presentational flourishes, dreamlike sequences or editing bombast, particularly evident in the early works of Alexander Payne). Concurrently, we see a movement away from the distancing irony associated with filmmakers like Wes Anderson and Solondz, through a more romantic irony and eventually to a clear reaction against postmodern ironic distance.[8] As the suburban ensemble developed as a recognisable cinematic mode, it would eschew the ironic and metafictive address still lingering in *American Beauty* and *Election*, supplanting remaining distancing techniques with a much more prominent sincere realism, proximity to and care for character. King notes that in *Little Miss Sunshine* and *Juno*, 'Ironic distance and foregrounding of quirks tends to give way to a more direct appeal on this ground that seems to be intended seriously and unironically' (2014: 42). Some films, perhaps most markedly *Juno*, chart this course within their own structure: beginning with overt quirky irony, having the irony challenged with interventions of the real, moving through sincerity in order to deal responsibly with the awakened drama, and ending with a kind of mediated irony, a kinder self-awareness that does not permit dismissal of human frailty or the manner of irreverence postmodern irony appears to invite.[9] The difference, then, is that the suburban ensemble dramedy is a predominantly realist mode: the object of our attention is the narrative's ethics rather than its construction, or the pleasure of identifying the hand of a cinematic auteur like Solondz or Anderson in the aesthetics of a film world.

This realist tradition is also what differentiates the suburban ensemble dramedy from millennial hyperlink cinema such as *Happy Endings* or *Thirteen Conversations About One Thing*, perhaps its closest ensemble relative unfolding on a similar timeframe. In these pictures, the hermeneutic confusion propelled by ironic devices – such as 'register alteration, exaggeration or understatement, contradiction or incongruity, literalization or simplification, and repetition or echoic mention' (Hutcheon [1994] 2003: 152) – becomes a metaphor for contemporary identity confusion, whereby we must likewise make meaning from complex, splintered communities with ambiguous interpersonal cause–effect structures. In this way, they wield the techniques of narrative irony (fudging intentionality to explore open-endedly interpretive spaces) to represent an existentialism particular to the encroaching digital era's splintered causal relationships. The suburban ensemble dramedy consequently sought to answer the questions of shared meaning-making raised in ironic connectivity narratives, and by earlier examples of the suburban ensemble form. This left two very different forms: the suburban dramedy's focus on human drama and earnest approach to quotidian moral predicaments, offsetting its sentiment with satire and its irony with pathos, while smart and connectivity cinema remained tethered to presentational or otherwise aestheticized modes of address, analogising oblique personal causality with indirect formal techniques, along with the films of cult drawcard directors like Anderson and Solondz.

There is a sense in which the films I am concerned with could be designated *domestic* ensemble dramedies rather than *suburban*. However it is important to note that even those that particularise their locations are working with and against visions of suburbia inherited from previous works (rather than the everysuburbia of films like *Little Children* and *The Oranges*). Their geographic particularity upsets notions of uniformity across the medium-density living arrangements broadly designated as 'suburban' – for example the small town or semi-rural suburbia of *Mumford* or *Junebug*, or the different versions of suburbia within greater Los Angeles that are presented in *The Kids Are All Right* (Horn and Cholodenko 2010).[10] Later films increasingly talk back to a notion of suburban homogeneity resurrected and propagated at the turn of the century, so in their geographic specificity they are still engaged with a critique of suburban media. *Lymelife* is emphatically set in Syosset, Nassau County, yet references the everysuburbia of earlier films including *The Safety of Objects* in its model houses, materialist symbolism and dark aesthetic, and *American Beauty* in its synonymous narrative structure; *Little Miss Sunshine* takes place mostly on the road, but still works within the template inherited from these earlier suburban films. As the suburban critique retains such a primacy across all of these works, I prefer *suburban ensemble* to *domestic ensemble*.[11] In this case, however, I leave out urban ensembles such as the work of Holofcener and Kenneth Lonergan's *Margaret* (2011). The suburban ensemble dramedy is effectively one kind of domestic ensemble that emerged in the millennium.

Historicising a mode of filmmaking or cinematic genre is, of course, not without definitional problems. As many philosophers have pointed out, the nature of genre is, like all categorisations of human activity, and like the human itself, porous. Considering the seemingly infinite ways we can group texts – by form, ideology, use or purpose, for example – any categorisation will always be vulnerable to alternate classifications. But nominal problems never completely invalidate the use of problematic terminology in scrutinising cultural adaptation or change; despite the challenges, it still behoves us to take note of commonalities and chart patterns in ever-changing cultural formulae, as the narrative that genre language directs us to is one of human adaptation and transformation. As John Frow puts it, succinctly: 'Instead of being "in" a genre, texts are transformative instantiations of genres', and so genres introduce a range of discursive tools around cultural transformation (2007: 1633). Genre identification is an act of historicism and can potentially reflect the complexities of cultural shift, involving multi-causal interactions which can be economic, symbolic, socially direct or reciprocally influential: 'a genre develops according to social conditions; transformations in genre and texts can influence and reinforce social conditions' (Thwaites et al. 1994: 100). As Daniel Chandler writes: 'An interpretative emphasis on genre as opposed to individual texts can help to remind us of the *social* nature of the production and interpretation of texts' (1997: 5). That is, genre identifications are yet another kind of storytelling focused on the complexities of social interaction (and are thus subject to the same responsibilities as any other narrative act).

While the genre anatomy detailed so far points to some of the interactions between the suburban ensemble film and other, related filmmaking tropes, there remains a distinct subgenre of humanist filmmaking, or a mode of creation bringing together humanistic ideological traits (respecting our struggles to get along) within a particular format (suburban; multi-focalised; shifting affect), which is recognisable even with its permeable boundaries. After Janet Staiger (1997; 2008), genre identification is in itself a political act, and we can probably learn more about the development of narrative conventions and related psychology if we avoid extrapolating from perceived patterns into alleged purity in genre labelling, and perhaps by privileging an examination of the ways filmic works *resist* presupposed generic boundaries. We do not want to rob filmmaking of its explorative nature by anachronistically applying categorical intent to each motion picture, thus it is important to identify problem works and canonical in-betweens. Some of the films I look at significantly overlap with other genres, such as *Election* (the high school or teen film) and *Little Miss Sunshine* (the road movie), and others innovate subtly within more recognisable genre confines, for example *The Oranges* and *Lymelife*. All, however, ask where we might take film next, to remain relevant and intriguing. In a Darwinian sense, hybridity is life – mutation, trial and error, mixing components. Genre hybridity is a story of human hybridity, of cultural evolution and changing interests. These texts began as an experimental mix not only of genres, but also of the disparate characters, plots and themes associated with genres, and so they continue to scout future imagined landscapes; domestic, reformative, emotional, cerebral and visceral.

Taking a cue from the exploratory spirit of these filmmakers, my approach to genre articulation takes joy in the very instability of the suburban framework it proposes. This heuristic method of genre archaeology nonetheless calls attention to the way narratives of human movement are encapsulated within modes of filmmaking that align momentarily, broadcasting a unity of interest among storytellers perhaps just for a decade, before stemming to explore emergent concerns arising in emergent contexts.

Notes

1. Hsu describes these films as categorically melodramatic, sociopolitically mysticising and principally urban. Hsu's principal example is *Crash* (Paul Haggis, 2004).
2. To borrow Svetlana Boym's (2001) terms, it is possible to have reflective rather than restorative nostalgia; that is, a nostalgia that has no need to retrieve a version of the past, but rather remains responsive to transience.
3. See in particular Robin Wood 'The American Family Comedy: From *Meet Me in St. Louis* to *The Texas Chainsaw Massacre*' (1979).
4. Sara Albuquerque et al. found that 'a child's death can cause cohesive as well as detrimental effects on a couple's relationship' (2016: 30) and Astri Syse et al. (2010) found no general association between childhood cancer and risk of parental divorce.
5. Similarly, the American soap opera presents another domestic ensemble template, yet its sustained melodrama unleavened by intervening affect and preclusion of broader socio-political reflexivity distance soap conventions from the suburban dramedy. Perhaps again, the sitcom *Soap* could be seen as a more influential text than any purely dramatic television narratives.
6. This musical pastiche was, in some ways, an experimental self-parody of more serious-minded genre scoring conventions that Goldsmith himself had employed across previous features (Clemmensen 2009).
7. Another formal difference is that films like *The Truman Show* and *Pleasantville* begin with a falsely idyllic absence of conflict and then incrementally reveal schisms undergirding their suburban context – in this way they 'reveal' suburbia as fraught. Later suburban cinema, from *American Beauty* onward, begins from the assumption of suburban friction and increasingly works inversely from conflicts toward their resolution, shifting the narrative focus substantially.
8. Figures including Anderson, Solondz, Noah Baumbach, David O. Russell, their contemporaries and their independent predecessors, like Hartley – variously labelled the directors of 'smart cinema' (Sconce 2002; Perkins 2012: 132–56) and members of an ironically named New Sincerity (Olsen 1999: 17) – have worked with ensemble family casts, yet they tend to operate outside of realist modes and emphasise the inventiveness of their artifice, and as Kim Wilkins suggests, many present an amplification of meticulously orchestrated eccentricities, disclosed through 'hyper-dialogue' or evasive, perhaps pop-ironic verbosity, behind which lies an ongoing existential meditation (2013: 413).
9. In fact, at times the clichés of the American 'smart film' are antithetical to the humanistic ambitions of the suburban ensemble dramedy: 'In each film, the suburb is rendered as a veritable totalitarian state that denies individuality and represses freedom through its institutions of work, school and family. Limited detail is given on the particulars of any character's job: all are sketched in broad, cartoonish terms of boredom and surveillance' (Perkins 2012: 141).

10. 'Suburban' does not simply mean the outskirts of the urban, rather it is an arrangement of housing density that produces changes to the geographies it is iterated within; this is why I include small-town suburban ensemble works like *Mumford* or *Junebug*. Human geographers, of course, continue to point to the instability of all of these terms (Brenner and Schmid 2014: 749–52).
11. Plus it sounds a lot snappier than the technically correct *residentially dispersed ensemble dramedy* . . .

CHAPTER 8

Discussions: Affect, Sociopolitics and the Ensemble Narrative

I have already begun to chart how the heterogeneities of the suburban ensemble dramedy contradict notions of an insidious suburban unanimity familiar in popular media. Suburbia, in reality, is many things to many people. The suburban ensemble intervenes in the treatment of suburbia as merely a symbol of dystopia, lifelessness and corrupt ideals, rather than a place where people live. I now turn to a comparison between the literature and public debates around suburbia, the interpolations the suburban ensemble film makes within antisuburban discourse, and the ways in which these films reflect polymorphic shifts in suburban geography after the postwar era. This in turn reveals the class politics that cluster around suburban discourses; suburban settings are a good place to look for some of the enduring issues of class that recur in American cinema.

Scholars from Elaine Tyler May (2008) to Robert A. Beauregard (2006) and Kenneth T. Jackson (1985) write of suburbia as the locus of American exceptionalism, and either symptomatic of or propelling America's worst divisive economic behaviours. Robert Fishman, for example, inflammatorily labels the suburbs *Bourgeois Utopias* (1987). This reading is not new: Coon and Beuka summarise a wave of literature from the 1950s onward indicting suburbia as homogeneous and oppressive (Coon 2014: 9; Beuka 2004: 6), which they both suggest influenced the cinema of suburban critique in ensuing decades, starting from pictures such as *No Down Payment* (Martin Ritt, 1957) and carrying through to New Hollywood dramas such as *The Swimmer* (Frank Perry, 1968), as well as the mid-century films of Douglas Sirk. Critics have traditionally drawn from histories of postwar suburbia to inculpate suburbia today. Many of the contemporary antisuburban arguments, where they similarly treat suburbia as a metaphor to stand against rather than a dynamic social phenomenon to understand, conceptualise the move to majority suburban living as concurrent with conservative values perceived to be burgeoning across America, in lieu of any compelling causal account – with the exception, perhaps, of Jackson's views on suburban inefficiency (1985).[1] Fishman, for example, historicises suburbia as a zone of exclusion (1987: 4), and many other suburban critics focus on examples of blatant postwar exclusion in planned communities, such as the discriminatory socioeconomic experiment of Levittown, New York, which comes to stand for all iterations of suburbia thereafter.[2] The application of an all-encompassing motive for suburbanisation, however, should be challenged. The initial postwar boom provided:

> a practical alternative to [economic] hardships in the city. A severe housing shortage in urban centers was soothed by Federal Housing Administration (FHA) construction loans and low interest mortgages provided through the GI Bill. (Spigel 2001: 110)

Such policies were driven by a need to accommodate growing populations outside of cramped and increasingly unaffordable cities, but were explicitly segregationist. Accounts like these complicate visions of the postwar suburb as economically elite utopia (perhaps that title should belong to those who could continue to afford city dwellings in wealthier localities), yet at the same time provide cases of consciously administered exclusion and homogeneity.

Although the phenomenon of suburbanisation has been an indicator of developing affluence in many countries (Jackson 1985: 303), this does not mean that excessive wealth has been concentrated within the suburbs, or that segregation has remained static rather than changing shape. The isolated postwar examples we continue to draw on tell only a small part of the story of American suburbanisation in the second half of the century, so we cannot speak of current iterations of suburbia as if they are the same thing. A myopic focus on postwar suburbia leaves us powerless to explain how the ethnic makeup of the suburbs has since begun to balance (Coon 2014: 8) despite a history of explicitly discriminatory housing policies (Lamb 2005), especially throughout the 1980s and 1990s (Palen 1995: 132) as the invasion-succession model of black American suburbanisation reversed (Lee and Wood 1991). Nor how narratives of inclusion and superordinate goals in suburbia may have worked to challenge historic geographic segregation initially for European and Hispanic immigrants in the 1970s (Massey and Denton 1987), followed by black Americans in southern states throughout the 1980s (Stearns and Logan 1986), and in northern states thereafter so that in 1995 'the all-black suburbs . . . tend to be not poor but middle-class or even affluent communities' (Palen 1995: 133), and at the same time extreme wealth (and its opposite), from which ethnic groups are largely excluded, was consolidated in *urban* centres (Conzen 2014). Nor can it explain how narratives reinscribing essential differences worked to resegregate ethnic communities across both suburban *and* urban spaces in the years leading up to the subprime loan crisis (Wells et al. 2012: 128). Migration patterns inverted: 'white flight is reversing course, moving toward central cities, where black population is declining' (Freilich et al. 2010: 9), and America's momentum of spatial hybridisation reversed along with it. We should recall, too, that the mortgage crisis disproportionately affected inner-suburban (Ekers et al. 2015: 36–7) and exurban homes (Freilich et al. 2010: 10), driving further disparity between high-income, predominantly white urban-dwellers and the rest of the nation – a trend beginning long before the crisis (Leinberger 2008: 71).

Some of America's most impoverished constituents now live in various suburban arrangements on the outskirts of larger cities, and as Beuka notes, African-American identification in media narrative has struggled to move out from urban centres (and the often violent dramas associated with them), and so now appear inconsistent with these demographic changes (2004: 215–16). In 1999, Freedman cited rap music as an example, and in particular the urban crime narratives of the suburban-raised Ice Cube. Freedman says:

> suburbia has evolved in startling ways, becoming ever more varied by race, class and ethnicity and eluding the grasp of all but a handful of perceptive artists and entertainers [. . .] The counterbalance to the successful movement of immigrants and minorities into suburbia, though, is the deterioration of inner-ring suburbs. These communities, clinging to the borders of cities, have been growing poorer, more segregated and more troubled for decades, losing population nearly as rapidly in some cases as urban ghettoes. (1)

He goes on to stress the diversity of these new suburbias in the face of continued homogenising media images. Black identity mobility is revealed as compromised both by nostalgia for a time when people knew their place, and the particular comfort of knowing how to identify the 'other'. If ethnicity onscreen can only signify a preselected range of spatial identities, agency of selfhood is curtailed for the comfort of those who may feel threatened by nonstatic and dynamic humanness afforded to ethnic others who might surprise us by not acting in the ways designated by screen cultures, or those who feel safe in the sense of historic antagonism these recurring images of racial polarity provide.

In suburban ensemble cinema we begin to see a move away from the exclusionary dystopian archetype that characterises *American*

Beauty and suburban works from the turn of the millennium, with black American examples of the genre such as *The Cookout* (Lance Rivera, 2004), often presenting more as comedy than dramedy, Sayles's ethnically hybrid features such as *Sunshine State*, and films explicitly scrutinising the process of a developing inclusivity in the suburbs, the political forces that work to keep ethnic marginalisation alive, or the ways we might rally against such forces by stressing a better nature, such as *Butter*. These films can also be connected to early ensemble examinations of integration politics and racism in American suburbia, such as *The Intruder* (Roger Corman, 1962). To an extent they chart the progress of, and resistance against, spatial mobility and equality in the United States, and the difficulties of sustaining a narrative of positive hybridisation while essentialist separatism moves in and out of vogue. Earlier domestic ensemble experiments depicting black social class and identity heterogeneity, such as the Chicago-set family ensemble melodrama *Soul Food* (George Tillman Jr, 1997), remain pegged to predominantly urban locales.

Unfortunately, however, all of these works tend to be the less famous examples of the genre, revealing both an industry-wide problem of racism by subtle omission, as well as American audiences' presumed reluctance to move past visions of the suburbs as wholly white. Reiterating the postwar fantasy of an all-white suburbia could probably be conceived as a method for Hollywood filmmakers to excuse themselves from maintaining a standard of all-white casting, indulging homogeneity under the pretence of critiquing homogeneity. However, increasingly in noted examples of the genre, race-consciousness is not only evident but also key to comprehending these films: for example, in *The Kids Are All Right* we are invited to complicate our identification with the lead characters when they vilify a Mexican gardener, and their petty racism is contrasted with their children's open-mindedness – the generational disjunct here may be a suggestion of some kind of progress. Although the lead characters remain white in popular films such as *The Kids Are All Right*, racial complications are not ignored: the suburban façade archetype as white exclusive utopia is slowly being abandoned. Despite the suburban dramedy genre's decline in recent years, isolated examples such as *Black or White* (Mike Binder, 2015) now tend to focus on ethnicity and spatial politics. As reviewer Nathanael Hood wrote:

> I cannot remember the last time I saw such a wide variety of American blackness represented onscreen: blacks living below the poverty line, affluent blacks, upwardly mobile blacks . . . black criminals, black judges, black lawyers, black musicians, black mothers, black fathers, black children. Rowena herself is a

self-made businesswoman who operates six businesses from her garage in South Central and supports upwards of a dozen relatives living in her home. But in a grim touch of economic realism, they live just across the street from a crack-house. (2015)

It may have taken some time for American filmmakers to cultivate sensitivity to these demographic changes, but perhaps media representations of black suburbia have now begun to reflect the diversification of identity we originally struggled to admit for white residents. Of course, there are other ethnic groups in America with even less onscreen visibility: indigenous Americans and Arab Americans would count among these omitted groups.

At times, this increasingly outdated narrative of suburban exclusion is also taken to encapsulate a problem of 'The West' in general, as a contemporaneous suburbanisation occurred in various iterations across Western nations over the globe. As with so many American cultural exports, the clichés of America-specific suburban development have become a benchmark for the self-analysis of other English-speaking nations. Suburban narratives and images in Australia, for example, 'point to the influence of an American suburban imaginary when thinking through our own geographic context' (Moss-Wellington 2016). Suburban desegregation occurred in different trends, and at different speeds with a varied level of permanency in different countries, yet the American cultural discourse of suburban homogeneity was often imported uncritically as a parallel narrative across Western nations. Iconography such as the suburban façade proliferated in global histories and narratives of municipal development, despite local contingencies and challenges presenting as enormously diverse. Historian Mark Peel explained the cultural myth of suburban homogeneity in Australia with a vivid personal anecdote:

We were puzzled when people talked about 'monocultural' outer suburbs. Most of our neighbours were migrants or the children and grandchildren of migrants. In our part of the estate, Koreans, Filipinos, Greeks, Indians, English, Dutch, Samoans and New Zealanders were mixing as neighbours, partners and friends. It was post-multicultural, in a way. And rather than abstract tolerance, it meant managing the concrete problems and opportunities that came from living with different people. It was farmers' children moving in from Gippsland who lived next door to the grown-up children of Vietnamese refugees moving out from Springvale and Clayton. (2007)

This is the very source of the contradiction much suburban cinema now attempts to unravel, with perhaps a little less distanced censoriousness than aforementioned literature. While the green living and efficiency arguments may have merit, they are expounded into hyperbolic, incendiary and unjustified value judgments by figures including the dogmatically outspoken star interviewee of feature documentary *The End of Suburbia* (Gregory Greene, 2004), James Howard Kunstler, and at worst are generalised again to the alleged retrogression of suburban inhabitants, their parochialism and their lack of intellectual capability (a familiar and recurring stereotype, as identified by Coon 2014 and Felperin 1997). Kunstler's speech on 'The Ghastly Tragedy of the Suburbs' is an example of how this dialogue has permeated the mainstream. After cherry-picking some of the worst examples of brutalist *urban* buildings (occurring in civic spaces), he blurs a distinction between his critique of suburban sprawl and imposed, demeaning public architecture. Worse, he then blurs the distinction between the homogeneous lifelessness of environment and inhabitant, without pause to reflect on the economic realities of population increase and suburban growth. He instead leaps straight into classism. Reflecting on an image of a semi-rural suburban home, he says:

> This is really, in fact, a television broadcasting a show 24/7 called 'We're Normal.' We're normal, we're normal, we're normal, we're normal, we're normal. Please respect us, we're normal, we're normal, we're normal. But we know what's going on in these houses, you know. We know that little Skippy is loading his Uzi down here, getting ready for homeroom. [Laughter] We know that Heather, his sister Heather, 14 years old, is turning tricks up here to support her drug habit. (2004)

This gobsmacking conflation of identities with allegedly unenlightened living arrangements is indicative of the way we have come to popularly imagine suburbia. Richard Porton describes how a more personalised anti-suburban rhetoric infiltrated the political discourse of the American intellectual left: '[New Left] students rightly perceived that suburbia partially reflected a boring, bureaucratized conformism, but stupidly attacked workers who merely yearned for some of the creature comforts that the much maligned "consumer society" promised' (1993: 12). Antisuburban attacks on the cultural integrity of an American working class became an accepted part of radical thinking.

The lack of specificity in describing vastly divergent conditions of suburbia internationally appears to lead us directly to a process of dehumanisation by robbing a majority of identity specificity. The suburban ensemble dramedy makes the case that suburbia is a majority experience (Hayden 2003: 3; Hobbs and Stoops 2002: 33, for demographic evidence), and therefore entails human diversities not accessible by this level of debate. Peel continues to expose the bigotry in Kunstler's presumptions:

> There's a difference between arguing that an outer-suburban estate manifests something that is wrong in our culture and arguing that the people who live in it are causing what is wrong in our culture. There's a difference between criticising

people for their choices and criticising the context that limits and defines their choices. There's also a difference between lecturing people about what they must do – lower their expectations, accept less, sacrifice more, be more like us – and talking about what we all have to do . . . There's no doubt that what is called 'McMansion-land' has social and environmental consequences. There are real costs, for the people who live there as well as everyone else. If nothing else, there are long drives to work on crowded freeways. But these problems are symptoms and examples of larger forces. (2007)

Peel goes on to anecdotally suggest that people are now driven to suburbia because they cannot afford access to the more moral and green urban alternative – the cost of an environmental conscience precludes many. So if suburbia is a zone of exclusion, then we may ask who is being excluded. In a way, these films constitute a claim that suburbia is merely a backdrop to the drama of our lives: it may be a problematic backdrop, but the norms of suburban living and the way environments *project* a homogeneous lifestyle are not what matters. Scratch beneath that surface and you will find that people are not homogeneous, and that they matter to other people more than their houses matter to them.

The point is not that all suburban residents are compromised at the hands of urban elites; it is that it does not quite make sense to talk of the suburban life as a discrete and unchanging phenomenon, and so metaphorising the lives of those living in suburban arrangements, as do many of the early suburban dystopian works, is inherently problematic, and at worst a class violence. Terry Eagleton once disparaged humanism as 'a suburban moral ideology' (1983: 207). Eagleton meant that focusing on what he calls 'largely interpersonal matters' (ibid.) prohibits us from focssing on the larger political forces that shape lives, and shape privilege. In a sense, he was merely offering yet another suburban slight: humanism is politically impotent, and the suburbs are somehow humanistic, therefore suburbanites are also impotent. Yet in synonymising humanism and individualism, Eagleton suggests that our understanding of one another's daily circumstances necessitates lenience toward their self-interest. This antihumanism is the strategy by which theorists might excuse themselves from curiosity, investigation and articulation of one another's lives, and instead treat them as abstract phenomena calling for distanced evaluation, such as the suburb-as-metaphor; it is a claim that invalidates local and situated knowledge (and at the same time, an interest in human narratives also provides us with a stake in the welfare of others who are affected by the political systems we study, so that our political ideals and theories do not become too divorced from their lived impact). It also invalidates entire disciplines seeking to document such knowledge like anthropology, and suburban ethnographies like the work of M. P. Baumgartner (1988), all of which use immersion in the personal to *specify* how larger social and political forces might play out in our lives, with a degree of care and nuance, an understanding that suburbia is more than just a metaphor and contains many iterations of group interaction. At this level of theory, humanism and suburbia are reduced to symbolic sketches and lose their specificity as any lived practice, contrived into a mundane whole to rally against. For example, Greg Dickinson (2015) reduces the suburbs to a 'rhetorical spatiality' rather than a lived experience, and refers to its 'topos' to deliver abstract backhanders at emotionally inferior residents, chiding them for wanting a 'good life' (cf. Berlant 2011). There is a kind of affective classism in Dickinson's claim that 'the enforced normality of the suburbs distances, abstracts, even makes impossible access to true feelings, deep emotions, or passionate experiences' (2015: 49). Similarly, a volume like *Visions of Suburbia* features multiple chapters in which humanism and suburbia are fused into a repugnantly facile museum feature, far distant from the real work of tut-tutting global political abstractions (Silverstone 1997: 175, 190). Suburban residents are still depicted as homogeneous in order to maintain elite theories of governed identity, robbing a majority of any sovereignty of meaning in their own world, their own place. This looks a lot like an intellectual colonisation – the very crime literary humanism has long been admonished for. It is bad spatial analysis when a standardised geography can be presumed to delete the human complexity of its inhabitants. Thus, metaphorising people's lives can be a kind of class violence.

So how, then, do suburban ensemble films circumvent this trend? Coon argues that 'viewing suburbia as a cultural construct helps to reveal the individual ideals and values that define it, and which are less apparent when suburbs are viewed as merely physical spaces' (2014: 10), but the millennial suburban ensemble insists that there are no individual ideals and values that define it – at least not any more. It is now evident that from this position we can displace blame for America's political ills to the *symbology* of suburbia, which is bracingly generalised, remains historically fixed despite rapid, profound human spatial-psychological mobility, permits ignorance of immeasurable human detail, and is thus inaccurate. Focus on suburbia strictly as cultural construct allows us to turn away from the reality of its diverse iterations and peoples, and perpetuate the same inadequate cultural analysis extended from the postwar era. Coon insists upon polar, perpetually at-war representations of the suburbs as utopian or dystopian, even after admitting their complication (2014: 15). This is typical of scholarship on suburban depiction in recent cinema; for example, Claire Perkins fixates on utopias in her chapter on the suburban smart film (2012: 132–56). Yet in the suburban ensemble dramedy, the suburbs are neither utopian-imposed custodial community nor dystopian exclusionary zones, as the multi-character casts emphasise a momentum of inclusivity, challenging one another to include and accept a greater field of others. This new cinema explores the middle ground, where so many of us live; the suburban ensemble dramedy paves a way to move beyond the binarism of utopian/dystopian analysis, which has dominated and framed the debate on suburban media for so long.[3] Freedman pointed to this inadequacy as early as 1999 in his piece 'Suburbia Outgrows Its Image in the Arts', and following Freedman, Beuka does at least suggest some ways we might move past 'didactic essays on the dystopian aspects of suburbia' (2004: 15): humanistic geography, with its emphasis on the lived landscape rather than the physical land, or Foucault's concept of heterotopia in 'Of Other Spaces'.[4] This is not to suggest that these films avoid the necessary symbolic language of any narrative – it is simply that they afford spaces for the viewer to challenge and think past the more corrosive archetypes of antecedent suburban media.

So suburbia changes, but its popular image remains largely static: it becomes a kind of summary of our anxieties of negative social change. Beuka synopsises these anxieties as 'cold war-era fears over mounting social conformity' (2004: 234) and Wayne Brekhus similarly describes the projection of majority 'averageness' (2003: 6) serviced by the suburban stereotype, the everyfamily or everycommunity.[5] But to ignore the shifting topography of the suburbs means we are missing the most salient point: the fascinating mutability of human life and culture, the ways in which we adapt environments to suit our needs and in turn adapt to them. The ensemble dramedy represents an awakening to polymorphism in suburban media depiction.

Suburbia may be the setting, but the commentary in these films is on personal and political relations at large; our quotidian suburban experiences are an appropriate zone of conflict as this is precisely where so many of us will feel the impact of, and perhaps impact upon, sociopolitical phenomena of the day. Where these films raise similar geographical issues to suburban critics – to what extent suburban living directs regressive behaviours or values – they are not as quick to reach a verdict, or indeed conclude that the suburban turn is so dire. The question of whether or not suburbanisation is a good thing is decentred from these narratives; rather, what is in question is how we make meaning in our lives *given* a sociopolitical climate in the suburbs. The location that comes to matter is the community and the family – the heart is where the home is – not the figuratively conjured suburbs. In this way, suburbia can never be reduced to a mere metaphor that in turn summarises the lives of suburbanites. The community, family and domestic spheres are never an uncomplicated site of privilege, as they are forced to be in any utopian/dystopian reduction to an idyllic suburbia or its opposite. In his conclusion, Coon is willing to admit that texts such as *The Kids Are All Right* represent a new breed of suburban depiction, circumnavigating the familiar typification:

> Instead of focusing on the particular behaviors, mores, and values generally associated with suburbia, these texts emphasise the tense conflicts and humorous predicaments that their characters face, with suburbia serving as a largely unremarkable background . . . Although these texts do not draw attention to suburban norms by making them the focus of their stories, each of them quietly challenges assumptions about the social identities and family structures of suburban residents. (2014: 222)

Considering how often the drama documents lives in transition through conservative values to a more cosmopolitan position – consider self-help author Richard Hoover's (Greg Kinnear) character arc in *Little Miss Sunshine* – we could also derive the idea from these films that the current political and psychical manifestation of American suburban living is transitory (cf. the awakening of responsibility to various others in *American Beauty*, *The Safety of Objects*, *Little Children*, *Smart People*, *What Goes Up* and all of Thomas McCarthy's films, as well as the destroy-and-rebuild values arc of Alexander Payne's cinema). They suggest another dominant political ethic is possible *within* a majority suburban context; speculatively, this could then be a force for spatial-architectural change if enough people no longer saw the suburbs as suitable to their needs, or a 'right to the city' extending beyond the city (cf. Lefebvre 1968; Harvey 2013). During the final reels of many narratives – *Junebug* (Phil Morrison, 2005), *City Island* (Raymond De Felitta, 2009) and *The Oranges* for example – suburban living is revealed as appropriate for some and not for others, as some characters flee the suburbs (to the city in *Junebug*, to university in *City Island* and to participate in overseas development programs in *The Oranges*) and some stay; these films accept that people's appetites can change as much as the places they inhabit. In fact, they emphasise a capacity for lifestyle change associated with ideological shift, so the suburbs, whilst not demonised, are neither valorised nor assumed as immovable norm. It is a hope akin to Dolores Hayden's imaginative suggestions for working with existing suburban potentialities and spaces, closing her historical work *Building Suburbia* (2003), or the public policy suggestions in Wim Wiewel and Joseph J. Persky's volume on *Suburban Sprawl* (2002). Rather than indicting the old, they look to the new. They also demonstrate that versions of suburban life are not suitable for everyone; this is not a new utopianism, just a call to work with what we have. Changing needs built the suburbs, and changing needs will lead to further geographic change.

Almost all suburban ensemble dramedies are, at least to some extent, about trying to find a mutually beneficial way through social dilemmas arising from context-driven behaviours (although the instructive context is presented as more social than spatial, without making absurd distinctions between the two). On the one hand, it is refreshing to see films dealing with moral situations isomorphic to everyday experience, that a majority audience can presumably recognise and apply to their own lives; this can validate our lived experience rather than providing an impression that real life is happening somewhere else, that we are somehow secondary. On the other hand, this validity can still be questioned if the lives we are leading are by their nature globally exploitative, and remain exploitative – so one can ask whether the constituents of middle-class America really need any more of our sympathy than they already command. Filmmakers such as Kenneth Lonergan, especially with *Margaret* (2011), and Glatzer with *What Goes Up* are actively raising these issues, as we will see.

There are more troublesome characteristics thrown up by realist ambitions coupled with a fantastical view of middle-class living arrangements. Much more has been written on the aesthetics of aspiration, and how American cinematic conventions might compel a competitive individualism or normalise the unattainable. Noël Burch (1982), for example, presents classical Hollywood editing norms as hegemony, but I believe the more obvious example is pertinent: production design standards in which the alleged Everyfamily is placed in upper-class environs. Wilt points out that as early as the 1960s:

> the suburban state of mind was by now so ingrained that many films were set in suburbia without comment. As with television, the norm was now a detached house in suburbia, often larger and somewhat more luxurious than those in which the audience lived. (2003: 484)

Demographic shifts offer a partial explanation: 'from 1940 onward suburbs accounted for more population growth than central cities' and 'in 1960, the proportions were nearly even' (Coon 2014: 8). Reviewer Leslie Felperin describes how this phenomenon of 'suburbia without comment' means that suburban cinematic depiction 'is seldom allowed to convey the character, specificity and local identity that cinema allows cities and countryside alike' (1997: 15).[6] A number of volumes have attempted to wrestle back the diverse iterations of suburbia from media stereotyping and draw a more complete picture of geographic variation from the first suburbs of early nineteenth century Boston (Binford 1985) to now; these include *Expanding Suburbia* in 2000, edited by Roger Webster, and publications associated with new bodies dedicated to mapping urban morphology, such as the International Seminar on Urban Form (ISUF). We still must remain careful not to homogenise American suburbia: films from *City Island* to *Lymelife*, *Junebug* and *Mumford* emphasise the particularity of suburbia in their differing locales (often these films stress isolation as an incubator for drama). While the suburban ensemble dramedy attempts to remedy such discriminatory universalising with focus on exactly this specificity and human diversity, the form rarely provides an exception to the rule of production design identified by Wilt, and many are equally guilty of propagating unreasonable aspirational norms as any other Hollywood genre cinema.

This is not true across the board, however. In 1998, at the beginning of the suburban cinema renaissance, Tamara Jenkins suggested an alternative vision of suburban habitation with *The Slums of Beverly Hills*, a picture some of the ensuing ensemble dramedies more closely resemble:

> After shooting the interiors of the apartments, people got concerned it looked too depressing. It was like, 'Oh, all the walls are so bare. Can't we put some color in there?' I'd told the production designer that these apartments are bare except for what the previous tenant left behind. They said, 'But it's a comedy.' I said, 'You read the script; poverty is not funny.' (quoted in Freedman 1999: 1).

Jenkins's experience points to two primary factors influencing production design standards in American cinema: foremost, we often forget the career interests of the majority of film workers beyond the director. The entire art department may be looking to develop their reel with attractive designs, advance recognition of their work, and use any notoriety to access further employment opportunities (in part the product of a casualised workforce moving between contracts). It might, thus, not only be within the publicity interests of art department workers and production designers to build what they feel to be appealing – often an inflated view of the living standards one might expect to find the characters in – but these interests can also chime with the concerns of studios, production houses and film investors. The high-publicity-value *Housesitter* (Frank Oz, 1992) variety of design decadence may also attract awards consideration. Secondly, Jenkins's experience could reveal more about how, and from which social echelon, the industry drafts its employees rather than how it fashions them. The living standards depicted may accurately represent the high salaries of film departmental heads, and therefore appear to its makers as realistic – the segregation of Hollywood film workers from a majority American experience is clearly going to have an impact on the kinds of story told. These are all undesirable, although far from unique, effects of American income inequality. Unfortunately these conditions may keep many filmmakers from realising a truly class-critical vision; however, there are plenty of exceptions within the suburban dramedy cannon (I look at *City Island* and *Junebug* as examples of such class-consciousness, below). As most suburban ensemble dramedies also permit specificity of place in lieu of an imagined or purely symbolic geography, it is also harder to accuse them of generalisation. These filmmakers may not indulge the pretence of speaking for all of America, but they still choose predominantly upper-middle contexts to analyse. Although fixation on elite classes in the dramatic arts is certainly not new, it remains problematic.

Some films share these qualities, however are set in recognisably urban locales, usually looking at upper-middle family relations and class anxieties, such as *Every Day* (Richard Levine, 2010), or the films of Nicole Holofcener. Holofcener's cinema is excellent at unearthing our discomfort with the invisibility of status markers, and they draw compelling lines between status and gender inequality. The dénouements in her scripts, however, often worryingly dismiss these concerns in favour of a return to the improvident, inward-looking norm of consumerist guilt annihilation, building and protecting one's pack and possessions – see *Friends with Money* (2006) and especially *Please Give* (2010) for examples. Nevertheless, these films do assert urban dwellings as the grounds of the upper-middle class, which is consistent with global socio-spatial class divisions (Coon 2014: 5), rather than the conventional depiction of a suburban fringe as the locus of 'bourgeois utopia'.

Many of the suburban narratives I am looking at foreground class relations, questioning our responsibilities to one another while avoiding moralistic blame or vitriol, such as Phil Morrison's release *Junebug* in 2005. *Junebug*'s outsider art dealer, Madeleine (Embeth Davidtz), is confronted with the disjunct between her idealism of southern suburban eccentricity and the reality of the ordinary nuance of lives within the communities her gallery selectively represents (in turn, these communities read her own Chicagoan intellectual elite mores and behaviours as equally eccentric). Madeleine's contract negotiation with the outsider artist (Frank Hoyt Taylor) recalls Julia S. Ardery's commentary on the industry's economic anomalies and duplicities: 'folk art's popular success and institutionalization throughout the 1970s and 1980s have continually depended upon barring folk artists themselves from substantial gain, and on locating and nominating to folk artist status creators ever more socially disadvantaged and personally frail [sic]' (1997: 331). The loser must remain the loser for the reductive narrative of marginal authenticity to perpetuate. Madeleine's version of acceptance of the semi-rural suburban, Christian working-class communities she engages with is dependent upon the safe spectre of maverick psychosis, a reduction via which she can overlook the complex humanity of the majority. While visiting both a potential client and her newlywed husband George's (Alessandro Nivola) family in North Carolina, she comes to realise the meaning of her class in tense relations with the community, especially George's brother (Ben McKenzie) and mother (Celia Weston). Madeleine privileges her relationship with the artist she is attempting to woo and sign to her gallery over the unfolding of a genuine family event – her sister-in-law (Amy Adams) gives birth to a stillborn child. This, however, comes after the family rejects Madeleine by not driving her to the hospital, so the undertone of classism is reciprocal.

Likewise, the film contrasts communication of intent through words and actions; Madeleine finds words easy to manipulate, for example, while the southern community demonstrates care through deed. Madeleine says 'I love you' to her employees on the phone in loveless situations while George's father (Scott Wilson) speaks little, and yet still manages to transmit love for his family (for example, using wood carvings as gifts). In *Junebug*, demonstrative and highly codified verbal communiqué are synchronised with working and upper classes respectively. George's brother Johnny finds all of these communications difficult, thus not allowing us to elevate either as uncomplicated social intercourse. Johnny misreads Madeleine's clumsy attempts at ingratiation via sexualised kinetic overcompensation as a genuine advance, and also in one of the film's most affective scenes (with strings fading in softly in the background), attempts a demonstration of care by taping a documentary on meerkats for his wife, but fails and ends up taking out his frustration by yelling at her. The true outsider of the film may be George, however, who straddles an uncomfortable border between classes, living with tension from his envious brother and a community that feels he should come home, and his own sense of belonging in a culture and class within Chicago that he has no roots in. He is curiously and unexpectedly absent for much of the narrative, which focuses instead on relations between Madeleine and George's family. An example of what reviewer Mark Bourne calls 'the faith [*Junebug*] shows in handing us small puzzles' (2007), George appears to vacillate between his stringent family values, and expressing relief when he escapes from them – a recognisable ambivalence, no doubt, for many viewers. His position never crystalises, but instead changes each time we see him, an expression of the divisive convolutions of American class culture.

In Raymond De Felitta's *City Island*, another film foregrounding class concerns, a family's-worth of characters perform a secretive dance around one another, and all of their duplicities are variously related to status anxiety or class-bound pride. Vince Rizzo (Andy Garcia) takes acting classes at night, but would rather his family believe that he is engaged in another, more class-appropriate vice, such as gambling. He also conceals details of his illegitimate son Tony (Steven Strait), primarily because his association with Tony's unreliable mother reveals background in a class he has struggled to distance himself from. Thus Vince is stuck between a tall poppy syndrome (embarrassment in the presumption of educational and cultural mobility), and the humiliation he sees as inherent in his working-class background, a 'hidden injury of class' (cf. Sennett and Cobb 1972) that undermines self-confidence. The identity contradiction manifests in familial conflict. Daughter Vivian (Dominik Garcia-Lorido) will not tell her parents she works at a strip club to pay her university fees, as she lost her scholarship due to marijuana use; the implication is that she struggles with the family's hopes for her to move beyond their working-class roots. Family tensions regularly focus on access to education and whether or not one is 'smart'. In fact, the only character whose problems turn out to be relatively unproblematic is Vinnie (Ezra Miller), a teenager whose fat fetishism is presented as somewhat more detached from class anxieties, making the shame easier to deflate. The characters' uncertainty around their place in the social strata of America at large is contrasted with a relatively fixed identity in their locality: the Bronx's City Island.[7] As in many of these films, the real home (or valuable mutuality) is revealed to be family at the explicative conclusion. The tensions and guilt they have experienced exist in a shared context, spatial and familial, and are therefore familiar and understandable to all involved. They have a mutual language to resolve these issues. When contrasted with the power of familial and community care, class shame ceases to have such power over their lives. The picture closes with bonding through shared sentimentality.

So class issues in millennial suburban cinema rarely remain uncomplicated: the suburban façade can normalise upper-middle living arrangements in some cases, but in the ensemble feature is more often used to reveal prejudice and class tensions in a variety of specific zones we problematically generalise as American suburbia. Along with films like *Junebug* and *City Island*, hybrid pictures including *The Slums of Beverly Hills* and *Duane Hopwood* (Matt Mulhern, 2005) also interrogate our assumptions of class indicators in suburban spaces. However, as sentiment is taken to be synonymous with class unconsciousness for many theorists – especially in the apparent sentimental celebration of familial norms (Loukides 1991: 97) – the following section deconstructs the use of sentimentality in the suburban ensemble film.

Drama in the Comedy: The Problem of Sentiment and the Possibility of Affective Equilibrium

Sentimentality has a long history in literary theory, and more recently writers including Lauren Berlant (2008) have extended its reach to media and film critique. Famously summarised by James Baldwin as 'the mask of cruelty' ([1955] 1984: 14), the experience of sentimentality has earned a particularly poor reputation as being synonymous with bigotry. The philosophical underpinnings of sentiment – seeking higher truth in the internal, the bodily and meta-physiological, sensation and feeling – translated to a literary tradition that, to critics such as Baldwin and Berlant, has appeared to value self-congratulatory and self-justifying emotional excess, a means by which a privileged few were attributed the humanity of higher feeling (a more profound interiority, and connectedness through superior affect) at the expense of others. Berlant reinforces a contemporary conflation of humanism and sentimentality, using both as bywords for prejudice: 'the critical literature on sentimentality has now long refused the appearance of apoliticism brandished by sentimental humanism, connecting it to racist, imperial, and exploitative alibis for control' (2008: 282).

On the other hand, in a 1999 article June Howard points up the shedding of sentiment's philosophical heritage of mutual empathy and emotional imagination:

> In postbellum America, the literary was often defined against sentimentality and the domestic culture of letters. Prestigious writing gradually and unevenly became less openly emotional and more ambitiously intellectual, less directly didactic and more conspicuously masculine. Antisentimentalism is an important part of that story, especially for literary studies. (73–4)

In its translation from philosophical doctrine to literary form, Howard argues that sentimentality was conflated with domesticity and the feminine.[8] Any principled opposition to such a form then had to propose alternative authentic emotional states that sentiment could not reach; thus antisentimental analysts are still imposing hierarchies of acceptable affect.

A concomitant reappraisal of antisentimentalism can be witnessed in another unlikely source: by constantly shifting focalisation and thus representing a range of mental states, ensemble dramedies move us between satiric, realist and sentimental filmmaking modes, asking us to consider a greater range of affective possibilities in tension and in flux. Of these kaleidoscopic affects, sentimentality stands out as a significant place of transition – we move through sentimentality, and it has purpose in both fortifying and broadening our field of community identification, responsibility and sympathy. Stoking sentiment, as we will see, is a means, a tool, not an end in itself. Surely it matters what the object of sentimentality is, what we are sentimental *about*. Berlant, however, suggests that even the most radical of these humanist narratives, upon reaching for sentimentality, allow us to relax into apoliticism and dismiss critiques of structural disadvantage, as the sense of relation and belonging they provide is rarefied and protected, concealing conservative values, gender and class privilege.

The development of a suburban ensemble dramedy mode in American filmmaking after *American Beauty* provides an interesting case study in the use of cinematic sentimentality for progressive thought: in such films the audience is rarely allowed to feel sentiment until a progressive conclusion is reached, a relational mutuality founded on respecting difference and striving for equality. Sentiment may allow us to feel comforted by a conviction, but if this conviction is that sometimes life is hard and surprises us, yet we can turn to our families and communities and look after one another for consolation, or that we need to think generously about one another's misdemeanours and a breadth of different humanness, then is such an apparent pause in reflexivity doing anyone any damage? Could we not instead call this kind of sharing 'consolidation' or 'solidarity'? Coherent self-narratives are unavoidable and it is impossible to live suspended in a state of constant reflexive self-regard, so if we are to share conviction through sentiment, which in effect asks us to relax into a mutual value (or what we imagine to be a mutual value in order to reinforce it), then the value itself should be assessed, not the notion that we may respond with sentiment in the first place. Being specific regarding the *particular* values we should question is a humility that remains vulnerable and open to discovery, where binaristic admonishments of others' sentimental optimism or masochistic fantasy of the good life (Berlant 2011) merely permit us to be unclear about the conditions of identity flux and politicisation, about thoughts, actions, causes, and the way we transmit ideas about our selves through storied behaviours.

Berlant assumes a binary between the idealism she locates in sentimentality and a depressive realism, which, she says, 'in contrast, [is] more accurate' (McCabe and Berlant 2011). This is a dubious fortification of a negative bias, extrapolating favourable self-diagnosis of a controversial psychological effect to generalised cultural theory, from which any pessimistic sociopolitical prognosis could be asserted as being 'more accurate' (one may exhibit depressive realism, but one cannot be a depressive realist any more than a cultural theory can be buttressed as such). The binary between sentimental idealism and depressive realism is imaginary. Brian Wilkie points out some of the classist undertones in these readings of the literary sentimental (1967: 570–1) and spins a neat analogy for thinking about elitist antisentimentalism, or the claim to an attitudinally superior cognitive bias in cultural analysis that is allegedly provided by depressive realism: 'Sugar is as much a fact of life as vomit; one is a soft fact and one a hard one, if you will, but both are facts' (572). This concept of humanness is clearly limiting, but we should note too the humour sitting alongside a drive to earnestness, honesty and realism in Wilkie's account, as this affective balancing act is an important component in the suburban ensemble dramedy. Most of the millennial suburban ensemble dramedies recognise that neither bias, focusing on one affective state and not the other, would be superior or more realistic – instead they illustrate the possibility of affective balance or equilibrium. Films such as *Little Miss Sunshine* or *The Kids Are All Right* use such recognition to their advantage, yoking human insight from the affective spectrum they are able to cover. *Little Miss Sunshine* features a family moving through rage, contempt, grief, sarcasm, scepticism, flippancy, cheer, hope, disappointment, love and sentimentality, yet they are permitted all such responses, as is the spectator. *The Kids Are All Right* features reflection on the heredity of bias to particular emotional states, as two children with lesbian mothers meet their biological father, prompting consideration of the unknowable inheritance conditions, genetic and cultural, of varied personality traits and coping mechanisms.

Sentimentality, then, is not 'unearned', to borrow a descriptor popularly attributed to James Joyce. These films use sentiment to find a place where we do not know exactly how to feel or what to think, as we could equally be laughing or crying, feeling shock or understanding, and embracing or rejecting characters and their actions. Screenwriters Lowell Ganz and Babaloo Mandel have demonstrated this on a number of occasions, especially in *Parenthood* and their follow-up film *City Slickers* (Ron Underwood, 1991), which similarly portray sentimentality and humour as alternating coping mechanisms, their characters juggling negative and positive biases in dealing with crises both existential and physical. We feel the pull of emotional excess – sentiment – but it is charged with conflicting knowledge and feeling. This delicious tension, the space where we are not certain exactly what a film is eliciting from us because, in a kind of affective verisimilitude, its dynamism precipitates no correct response, is a curiously empowering place to be – it exists elsewhere in cinema too, from the horror comedy to the political romantic comedy. Here we can reach a zone of sanctioned affect where that affect is not prescriptive, and by stoking a lifelike confusion, we can think more generously, receptively and open-heartedly on the subject at hand.

More specifically, we need to scrutinise the grouping of repartee, oft-unkind riposte and performance gags with genuine attempts at unpacking socio-ethical problems to comprehend the purposeful interlacing of drama and comedy in the suburban ensemble film. This could be seen as extended from the fluidity between social commentary, sarcastic jibe and demonstrations of familial care in the lineage of television sitcoms from *Roseanne* through the *The Simpsons* and *Modern Family*, as described above. The tension between pathos and associated moments of bathos shows up both our attempts to dismiss that which troubles us with jest, and our impulse to become absorbed by our own woes. We are permitted both states, but encouraged not to remain too long with either condition, as we are prompted to use one to upset the other – to challenge affective inertia – in our search for answers to difficult ethical situations. The technique promotes a kind of sifting through affective responses to find what is appropriate, yet none are considered inadequate or incorrect, and all emotive responses are potentially useful in finding a way forward.

So sentimentality is not in and of itself an affective coherence. We can have an affective incoherence – an 'incompatibility between conceptual and embodied affect' (Semin and Smith 2008: 215) – in features that engage sentimentality. In fact, sentimentality before, after and alongside other emotive responses may increase the scope of the upset and reflexivity available, potentially even leading to a reduced reliance on stereotypes (cf. Huntsinger 2013). At the same time, as George McFadden argues, affective incoherence nourishes laughter as the critical viewer wonders 'how sense and nonsense are combined to make comedy, and what kind of adult behaviour correlates with the zany and outrageous activity on the stage' (1982: 156). Our affective experiences in narrative, however, should be recognised as separate from unmediated lived experience – we recognise a level of intentionality in emotional cues, so we might refer to *attempts to achieve* the state of affective incoherence in art by another term: a challenge to affective inertia, or a call to affective mobility. Again we should look at sentimentality as a tool or device that can be put to use in this capacity, and not merely as a generic code (which might in any case more accurately be called melodrama).

As just one example, many of these films demonstrate how anger can be a force for positive change, as long as we do not indulge its permanency. *The Oranges* stands out here, repositioning as redemptive possibility the antagonism of people we might otherwise scorn as immoral – in this case an adulterous, intergenerational couple (Leighton Meester as Nina Ostroff and Hugh Laurie as David Paige) whose affair spurs family and friends to reimagine their own lives. Sentiment is just one of the responses we move through to patch together our best moral resolution. *The Oranges* makes counterintuitive use of a gentle, pensive, acoustic score at moments of expected melodrama and audience disparagement, and its focalisation shifts between characters of differing perspectives; later we learn how the indiscretions of some characters have productive effects on others. The couple's exploration of moral ambiguities justifiably enrages those implicated, yet ultimately moves everyone along a continuum of affect – including laughter, attempts at deflating their torment, and sentimentality, allowing them to access redefined communal attachments and potentialities. Without moving through anger, they may not desire change; without levity, they may remain in depression or the inertia of resentment; without sentiment, they may refuse to work together to revise relational responsibilities. This process allows them to attach to a new life less complacent and more fulfilling than before. The perspectives on anger offered by the suburban ensemble dramedy, though, are far from homogeneous. As we have seen, *Junebug* and *City Island* look at anger arising from class friction, and conflicting demonstrations of belonging required by different communities, families and locales (semi-rural suburbia in North Carolina or the Bronx's City Island, for example).

Problematic as the community may be in identity politics and Berlantian theory, as all community entails some kind of exclusion, Darwinian humanists such as Ellen Dissanayake suggest that such problems cannot be used to dismiss inextricably human impulses:

> we evolved to need mutuality with other individuals, acceptance by and participation in a group, socially shared meanings, assurance that we understand and can capably deal with the world, and the opportunity to demonstrate emotional investment in important objects and outcomes by acts and experiences of elaborating. (2000: 168)

Belonging is part of everything we do: it is an intrinsic condition of human sociality. Exploitation, however, is different – there are periods, places, thoughts and actions that have varying degrees of exploitation, so it must be subject to change. The need for belonging is everywhere in equal measure, in intimate publics as in cosmopolitan fealties. As Frans de Waal notes:

> Individual interests may be served by partnerships (e.g., marriages, friendships) that create a long-lasting communal 'fitness interdependence' mediated by mutual empathy. Within these relationships, partners do not necessarily keep careful track of who did what for whom (Clark & Mills 1979), and derive psychological and health benefits not only from receiving but also from giving support (Brown & Brown 2006). (2008: 292)

Belonging is not simply part of life; it is also positively correlated with health outcomes. In denying these human needs, we risk devising an unworkable and self-defeating ethic to live by, thereby proffering dissatisfaction and disappointment. We imagine ourselves as ethically bound to a community in order to reach mutually inclusive goals. This can apply to a cosmopolitan communal adherence too. These films position sentiment not just as mutuality, but also as an important part of our communal governance, diplomacy or decision-making processes, which can lead to outcomes of care for *a broader spectrum* of otherness, and certainly do not preclude ethical or political action – this is realised in philosophy and deed by all of the protagonists at the conclusion of *Little Children*, for example. Vigilante ex-cop Larry Hedges (Noah Emmerich) realises he has a duty of care to Ronnie McGorvey (Jackie Earle Haley) when he discovers that Ronnie has attempted self-castration following struggles with paedophilic desire, stigma and the death of his mother; and a couple involved in an adulterous affair, Brad Adamson (Patrick Wilson) and Sarah Pierce (Kate Winslet), must confront the inherent self-absorption of their elopement plans, stemming from a belief that they have missed out on earlier formative experiences, to ultimately reclaim a wider sense of belonging and accountability (Moss-Wellington 2018: 99). Often the sentimental component of these films is focused on mutual redemption, a political awakening into a new communal care: the characters' comprehension of their interdependence helps them reconstruct their identities to be more broadly considerate of others. Dan P. McAdams's (2006) research looks at how narratives of redemption promote generativity, or concern for the welfare of future generations (c.. Erikson [1950] 1977: 240); in fact, McAdams suggests such narratives are integral to maintaining generative values beyond the present self (2006: 82). He writes that 'high scores on generativity measures are positively associated with indexes of prosocial behaviour and productive societal engagements', which include 'interest in political issues and involvement in the political process' (84). The sentimentality of personal redemption within a community – in which we come to care more about community – may help shape our behaviour in positive ways, whether or not it is founded on a mythical, optimistic or entirely imaginary public.

Ed S. H. Tan and Nico H. Frijda (1999) argue that sentiment and crying are inherently submissive, in that they express a giving up of personal autonomy to be overwhelmed by emotion. This could contribute to a kind of idle acceptance that Berlant sees as unconducive to political action (although it remains unclear how emotional acceptance necessarily generalises to political idleness). Yet many narrative events can propel such a feeling, including those related to attachment and separation (56), morals and justice (58), or awe-inspiring stimulus (62), and again these emotions are transitory. If sentiment and weeping are submissive in one instance, the excitation transfer from such a state may later be leveraged to more rousing ends, and those ends do not necessarily need to be reinforced attachment to an imaginary public or exclusive group.

For Berlant, the sentimental inspires an imagined group cohesion which is bigoted, oppressive or incorrectly aspirational, but to sustain this view we must resist recognition of the many different ways we can imagine ourselves as akin to others: group identification is different from identity fusion, which is in turn different from tolerance, and surely there are many more social glues.[9] All of these recognised varieties of communal identity construction, and the spaces in between them, may be the object of sentiment, and may drive compassionate behaviours.

Harvey Whitehouse's work makes an important distinction between group identification and identity fusion, encompassing different levels of personal accountability felt to others, and different activations of self-identity. Blending all kinds of group cohesion and identification into a single problematic process without scientific recourse is a dangerous route to simplifying, and thereby dehumanising the ways people operate together. A spectrum of degrees of adhesion to social identities and fused groups should also be recognised across local experience and extended imaginings, and shared ideology does not necessarily have to follow from either cohesion, especially with extended fusions (in Berlant, imagined publics). Whitehouse writes:

> Recall that one of the hypothesized features of local fusion is that personal experience, on which my sense of self is at least partly constructed, provides the main reference point for sharing a common bond. So extended fusion would seem to be a more tentative kind of fusion of self and other. Since it depends on external sources as well as direct personal engagement (e.g. testimony rather than experience) it carries less conviction. (2013: 286)

This could also translate to ideological conviction. Although we see strong methods for generating a fusion by which we might favour peers in a large anonymous grouping – such as routinised doctrinal rituals – it does not necessarily follow that we will all adopt the same *values* in any grouping (consider the breadth of dispositions even among one's immediate family), so we may be looking in the wrong place if we are to politicise communities and imagined publics to this extent. Communities can be established by interaction rather than shared ideology, which should be seen as a set of behaviours constituting a kind of community self-governance that crucially complements state and market, as Bowles and Gintis argue (2002); and communities can exist even without the perception of relationality or commonality, as Robert J. Sampson explains (2006: 153). Although we still see social groups influencing values and neighbourhood effects in ideological contagion, it seems that contact with peers is still key. As in Nicholas A. Christakis's 'Three Degrees of Influence' theory of social influence outlined in *Connected* (2010), the attitudinal and behavioural contagion we exhibit is reduced with each degree of separation from direct contact. No modelling of community per se *mandates* shared values or privilege, so we cannot assume imagined communities control the genesis of political attitudes.

Suggesting an excess beyond the detail of cohesion we have so far been able to gather data on, Whitehouse also mentions that:

> While individuals are only capable of fusing with a small number of groups (typically two or three at most), it is possible to identify with a great many different groups. This means we can build a complex division of labour in which we shift flexibly between roles as changing social situations dictate. There is no limit on the size of groups with whom identification is possible. (2013: 288)

For some, group cohesion appears to be *the* problem, but for others with perhaps more faith in the concurrence of local community fealty and political cosmopolitanism, a fair scientific deconstruction of the diversity of human group identification may suggest opportunities for reducing civil and global conflicts, poverty and exclusion.[10]

Thus, even though some community fealties may be problematic, this should not mean that all of our communal behaviours are – even some exclusionary social groupings are impossible to avoid, and some condoned ostracism is necessary to live. Ignoring strangers on public transport, for example, is not without purpose. But this does not mean we will refuse ethical responsibilities to others outside of our social circles. Tolerance is another kind of group cohesion in which we neither identify with nor aggress against an outgroup, and thus encompasses a kind of communal responsibility without affinity. The strictures on social grouping and how we think about our social groupings are therefore inadequate. Even if Berlant accepts a version of communal belonging, this level of debate cannot tell us what conditions of belonging make our relationality acceptable; thus we are all prescribed a suspicion of our inherent and varied attachments to others. Sentimentality, then, when it allows us to feel comforted by feelings of connection to others in our community, is not the problem. However we can still ask if conceiving of oneself as 'special' because of these feelings is reasonable: a number of urban ensemble dramedies, such as *Margaret* and the films of Nicole Holofcener, actively ask this question.

I conclude that the antisentimental ethic proposed by Berlant is an unfair condition to saddle viewers and readers with, and constitutes, paradoxically, another attempt to restrict parts of our identity – in this case our affective identity – for ideological reasons that spuriously relate to how we actually treat one another. To summarise, we can see sentimentality as a device rather than having intrinsic ethical value. The communities we may attach ourselves to via sentiment are not merely imaginary; communities also constitute behaviours we exhibit to one another. The need for belonging is a pancultural phenomenon and cannot be realistically appraised as a surmountable problem. Further, identifying with members of one's community does not necessarily mean we will fail to exhibit kindness or ethical inclusivity to outgroup members. The use of sentiment in stories, in acknowledging a breadth of otherness, may also work to *extend* our cosmopolitan actions by humanising others, and encourage us to find points of ethical identification with and commitment to a broader range of living entities. Berlantian affect theory needlessly restricts identities and attitudes that do not translate to political or compromising actions, and can thus be seen as arguably prejudicial.

Comprehending how the suburban ensemble film engages with sentimental experience allows us to access an alternative to Berlant's political-affective binaries. The affective spectrum covered in the suburban ensemble dramedy permits concurrent diverse emotions in tension with associated ideas and attitudes, and opens up a place to truly consider how we might behave *given* our troubled relationships with peers.

American Millennial Sociopolitics and the Ensemble Narrative

Although propagation of the suburban motif, and visions of suburbia as quintessentially American political iconography, reach back at least to the 1950s and 60s if not earlier (Wilt 2003: 484), Coon points out of the past two decades, 'it is notable that such a large number of high-profile suburban films . . . have appeared in such a short period of time' (2014: 3). The retreat to domestic concerns may seem like an apolitical gesture to a surface reader of these films, yet politicoethical upheaval runs deep throughout. Resistance to a direct political prescription could also be off-putting to some theorists, however instead we witness onscreen representation of a specific, contemporary political confusion and disillusionment, and tandem inquiry as to how we might navigate the despair of political uncertainty and associated feelings of inconsequence. Having now explored the class politics of suburban media and outlined an ethics of mixed emotion in dramedy cinema, the remainder of this chapter explores how the suburban ensemble film – and especially its multi-focalised structure – spoke to mounting political disillusionment at the end of the last century.

Although it would be reductionist to equate the breadth of concerns covered here to a handful of American historical events, selectively conjuring political occurrences to rationalise the emergence of a broader cultural phenomenon, one still might speculate that a collision of the political and personal had already reached its zenith in American media at the height of the Lewinsky scandal. As Thomas de Zengotita put it: 'no one ever called attention to his privates, literally or figuratively, with the splendid abandon of Bill Clinton. His whole persona was performance intimacy. In the long run, that is what will make him the archetype of leadership for the media age' (2007: 153). In 1999, the same year as *American Beauty*, Payne's adaptation of Tom Perrotta's novel *Election* provided the perfect filmic example. Perrotta said, 'so much of it has to do with what I was seeing out of the Clintons during the '92 elections: that politics is personal, the "character issue'" (Veis 2009).[11] We had effectively been taught that the extraction of political and personal relations was to play out on a battlefield of sexual politics. It may seem little wonder that political discussions on film would increasingly take sexual misdemeanour as a springboard. However, we could equally say that the synthesis of (once more easily distinguishable) right and left politics into a blur of populist opportunism and seemingly condoned narcissism (culminating more recently in the shock of the Trump presidency) also directed us to a re-evaluation of personal beliefs. We had been purposefully confused: successive administrations moved to conceal an agenda of incremental neoliberalism by directing public debate to questions of political presentation rather than conviction. From Ronald Reagan to Arnold Schwarzenegger and now Donald Trump, the unconcealed conflation of Hollywood and politics permitted what Bernard Manin has termed 'audience democracy' (1997: 223), in which voters react to issues generated by celebrity politicians rather than exercise any agency to set a people's agenda. This reduction of the voting populous to reactive 'audience' has embroidered and cemented the strategic discourse of economic liberalism, eventually leading to Trump's obliteration of any need for a coherent ideology beyond self-interest. When the political became so much more about character and celebrity, our attention was so diverted that any dubious political compromise became plausible.

As Ben Dickenson explores in *Hollywood's New Radicalism* (2006), filmmakers responded to this disillusionment in a variety of ways. Cinema began to trace how such confusion and abuses of civic trust affected our lives. If we could no longer identify a continuum of political conviction or evaluate what a public figure stands for, if after Francis Fukuyama's *The End of History?* (1989) we had no leaders discussing a meaningful alternative, if we have been unwittingly inaugurated into a kind of political anomie, and critically, if we in fact *require* mistrust of all media channels that communicate political values (leading eventually to ideologically targeted fake news on social media), then how do we even begin to *discuss* such values anymore? These films all explode any remaining certitude in our political identities, and then go about building our values back up from rock bottom. We cannot forget that in the 1990s, America had seen a huge disturbance of suburban voting norms, as Seth C. McKee and Daron R. Shaw reflected in 2003: 'the factors that led to GOP dominance of the suburbs have dissipated . . . This context varies so dramatically by region that we would be surprised if suburban voting patterns do not vary more significantly in the future than they did in the 1990s' (144). The changing demography of the suburbs is a deeply political subject, and these filmmakers have recognised it; not just in the transformation of identity, ethnicity, sexuality, equality, ideology, and associated imagery, but also direct electoral influence. Across these films, there is the sense that we need to rediscover a political identity in order to truly combat the pervasively impracticable conservatism stewing in our adherence to politicised media cues. Characters in these films attempt to match their unquestioned ideals to a lived reality, fail, have to explain themselves to others, and in so doing discover a more generous way of looking at one another that suggests (usually without prescribing any particular behaviour or action) the possibility for a new political identity that will respect the diversity of our lives and moral challenges. The social critique of such suburban cinema can be summarised thusly: our political assumptions and debates no longer seem to match the reality of contextual and personal diversity they must address.

In his 2004 'Declaration of Independents' for *Variety*, Payne wrote:

> Whether Bush and his corrupt gang are reelected or not – and especially if they are – these times ensure increased demand for films with human and political content. Art is all we have to combat the fearsome, awful animal side of man that today controls events. To portray real people with real problems, real joys, real tears will serve as a positive political force, a force for comfort and possibly for change. With the inhumanity forced upon us by governments and terrorists and corporations, to make a purely human film is today a political act. To make a film about disenfranchised people is a political act. To make a film about love is a political act. To make a film about a single human emotion is today a political act. And bad things happen when good people fail to speak up. Intelligence and humanity should not be 'specialty' items. (2004: S7)

From Reagan into the bloody results of the Bush Junior years, these domestic filmmakers saw themselves not only as responding directly to the accumulative dehumanisation of their era, but also to the environment of cynicism and disengagement that made such regimes (and their worst results, terrorist retaliation and corporate dominance) possible. The most sensible way to talk about all of these issues on a level that seemed pragmatically relevant to mainstream American audiences disaffected by political distancing rhetoric may, to some filmmakers, seem to be a look at the misalliance of our political values and our everyday lives, in the family and at home. This approach recalls the 'politics of kindness', whereby generous listening to others' lived emotional experiences renders political points clearly impactful, and asks how our better nature could help us overcome the ills foisted upon us by an increasingly remote and exploitative elite – through thinking generously of others, it searches for our agency.

Coon notes that many suburban storytellers have clearly stated in interviews that they were reflecting upon the disparity between suburban images they grew up with and the more complex realities they lived through (2014: 225–6).[12] Somewhat like Stanley Cavell identified across remarriage comedies in *Pursuits of Happiness* (1981), this genre is a philosophic inquiry into the sociopolitical and moral upheaval encroaching on our everyday lives; its narrative conventions service questions regarding how we can live well despite the ideological and domestic uncertainty of our epoch (in his case, the Depression; in this case, a politically splintered, incrementally unequal, disempowering, media-drenched, trust-poor and above all confounding new millennium). The filmic responses, in both cases, continue to cite a kind of maturation of human relations based upon a relinquishing of beliefs and practices that keep us from a deeply satisfying connection with others. Concomitantly, an urgent cosmopolitan question arises: to whom do we owe responsibility? The concentric circles of accountability found in these films – to partner, to family, to neighbourhood, to distant family and friends, to nation state and to globe – display characters actively juggling these interests in their daily lives, and position difficult cosmopolitan ethics as unavoidably quotidian. Thus we must also keep the political nature of ensemble narrative empathy equalisation in mind when we discuss these films, as it is a cornerstone of their intervention against Hollywood individualism (the emphasis on individual triumph over collective or collaborative agency).[13]

Globalisation puts pressure on cosmopolitan ethics, which may help explain the millennial trend toward ensemble film narratives, which have the ability to 'stress a sense of collectivity and community at odds with the structure of protagonism that otherwise characterizes Hollywood cinema' (Mathijs 2011: 89). Lorraine Sim makes a similar point in her analysis 'Ensemble Film, Postmodernity and Moral Mapping':

> Through its use of the ensemble form, *Babel* reminds us that a recognition of our responsibility for, and connection to, others is particularly important in the era of postmodernity as our lives become increasingly intertwined with the lives of more and more strangers who – while often geographically or socially distant – are, through the forces of globalization, ever more proximate in ethical terms. (2012)

Both Sim and Vivien Silvey (2009) point to recent ensemble narratives' attempts at complex cognitive mapping in new and unfamiliar social spaces. Sim's analysis becomes more specific when she addresses

Zygmunt Bauman's work on the ethical splintering that characterises postmodernity, the narrativised investigation of which she describes as 'moral mapping'. In *Postmodern Ethics* (1993), Bauman emphasises the increasing invisibility of the outcomes of our personal actions, the elusive connection of social consequences to their respective agents, and cognitive limitations in summarising moral causalities: 'The scale of consequences our actions may have dwarfs such moral imagination as we may possess' (18). In a global world, our moral certainties are rendered increasingly ambiguous, are pluralised, and when called upon for revision, the resultant insecurity is existentially felt. Thus, Sim (2012) suggests in order to avoid 'floating' responsibility into a colossal global bystander effect, we resort to the kind of moral mapping ensemble narratives are apt to provide. The ensemble mode, then, regularly appears as another narrativised humanist ethic: again we find ourselves constructing hypothetical others to understand and talk through our moral effect on the world, with respect to local contextual contingencies. The films I am looking at do not merely represent onscreen the existential feeling of this millennial condition (as do the fractal or hyperlink narratives discussed in the preceding chapter), but also develop from the political roots of confounding and depreciative feelings of disempowerment into questions about how to live within a causally entangled and variegated world – open contextualised ethics.

The suburban ensemble dramedy in particular features polyphonic, intergenerational perspective-taking through alternating focalisation, which could be seen as comparable to the real family narratives discussed by Fivush et al. in 'Personal and Intergenerational Narratives in Relation to Adolescents' Well-Being' (2011). The films not only recognise and represent this activity, integral to familial wellbeing, of collectively determining a family narrative; they may also be a good way to reflect on one's own family narrative-building practices. As Fivush et al. point out, for example, family narrative is instrumental in the teaching and learning of gender identities, particularly for adolescents: 'That adolescent males and females tell stories about their parents' childhoods that differ by parental gender suggests that adolescents are understanding and propagating the gendered roles their parents are narratively portraying' (52). The kind of reflexivity asked of us in the ensemble narrative can politicise this process. It encourages us to wonder at others' internal states and perspectives, and thus how this information will help us co-construct identities more equally, as well as providing a simulation of the kinds of story we tell in our own lives, a model for connecting our own construction of self-histories with their behavioural consequences. 'The multi-character drama is inherently positioned against individualist monocausality' (Moss-Wellington 2015: 119), and the alternating focalisation of an ensemble format, at its best, is itself a striving for egalitarianism, and systemically resists elevating the concerns of one above another.

So I prefer to acknowledge that maybe this cinema arose precisely because we *did* have a lot to work out, a kind of a cry against a climate of apathy burgeoning in the wake of ideas such as Fukuyama's absurdly bowdlerised modernisation theory and the publicity narratives of successive presidential offices, sold so proficiently to us by an elite. We needed to be self-reflexive about consumerism, gender politics, humility and narcissism at large, because we had been ignoring these problems in popular narrative by pinning them to bygone eras, as in the examples in the years leading up to *American Beauty* (*The Ice Storm*, *Pleasantville*). Even within more fantastical near-future settings, as in *The Truman Show*, the politics were still displaced and not quite *our* problem. It has been curious to see the extent to which *EDtv* (Ron Howard, 1999, again in collaboration with Ganz and Mandel), which tackled the real psychological torment and contractual immorality that astonishingly endures in reality television production, has been largely forgotten in cinema analysis in favour of *The Truman Show*'s pessimistic fantasy of such abuses being clear, visible and unheeded.

Above all, this cinematic movement offers trust in people to work things out on their own *despite* an unpleasant political reality. In this way, it attempts to restore agency to the majority. Another way to put this is that the suburban ensemble dramedy works from a reasonable scepticism levelled at outmoded institutions, public and private (for example academe in *Smart People*, systems of justice in *City Island*, business enterprise and the workplace in *In Good Company*), foremost among these the family. We sympathise with the cynic, then move through a trajectory of comprehending the human grounds – through practical situations where we need support from one another – for rebuilding trust and integrity into our communities and the structures that bind them, demonstratively expressing how humility, understanding, acceptance of complexity and the will to cooperation make this possible. This cinema both validates a sceptical point of view of our political status quo and asks where we can proceed from here.

The final part of this book uses a close reading of progenitor text *Parenthood* to demonstrate how these concerns play out across an ensemble film narrative.

Notes

1. Jackson's history of American suburbanisation is slightly less moralistic than others, and his critiques focus on the energy waste of sprawl.
2. Levittown was a planned postwar suburb, built 1947 to 1951, the developers of which explicitly advertised its exclusion of black residents. The resultant controversy bolstered its advertising appeal and status, spawning imitators. Levittown became a symbol of suburban homogeneity, which is at times more liberally applied to contemporary suburbia, or suburbia in general.
3. See Coon (2014), Beuka (2004), Perkins (2012), Fishman (1987), Smicek (2014), Joanna Wilson (2015) for examples.
4. However the latter may be misguided, as Foucault's oblique description of space as cultural mirror stresses the influence of excessive regulation ([1984] 1986: 27), which anthropologist M. P. Baumgartner avows is an untrue characterisation of legal process and law enforcement in the suburbs, where moral self-regulation is a prevailing standard (1988: 134).
5. We might even catch a whiff here of that particularly American paradox: a fear of perceived economic threats to individual liberty that in turn obliterate liberties (the phobic language of which peppered neoliberal campaigns against Obamacare, for instance).
6. Catherine Jurca has made a similar point of suburban literature in her work White Diaspora: The Suburb and the Twentieth-Century American Novel (2001), and urban cinematic counterparts have been much discussed by figures including Pamela Robertson Wojcik (2010), Steve Macek (2006), Merrill Schleier (2009), Mark Shiel and Tony Fitzmaurice (2001).
7. *City Island* can also be seen as part of De Felitta's continuing documentation of the Italian American experience in New York and New Jersey in films such as *Two Family House* (2000) and documentaries like *'Tis Autumn: The Search for Jackie Paris* (2006).
8. Carl Plantinga goes a step further: 'The wholesale denigration of sentimental emotions is an expression of masculine bravado at best and of rampant sexism at worst. To denigrate the emotions caused by sentiment's concerns is to denigrate the concerns themselves' (2009: 193). The claim finds support in the work of Flo Liebowitz (1996) and Molly Haskell (1987).
9. For example, Lakin et al. 'The Chameleon Effect as Social Glue' (2003); Bastian et al. 'Pain as Social Glue' (2014); Van Vugt and Hart 'Social Identity as Social Glue' (2004).
10. This is what Whitehouse suggests in 'Three Wishes for the World' (2013).
11. Author and screenwriter Tom Perrotta is an important figure in the history of the suburban ensemble dramedy. He wrote the novels both *Election* and *Little Children* were adapted from; he also co-wrote the screenplay for *Little Children* with Field. More recently, options for his 2007 novel *The Abstinence Teacher* have been associated with filmmakers Jonathan Dayton and Valerie Faris (*Little Miss Sunshine*) and Lisa Cholodenko (*The Kids Are All Right*).

12. Again, this political problem is mirrored in the research on news media and public trust. Stephen Coleman et al. found that 'public trust collapses when journalists are perceived to be reporting on social groups, areas and practices that they do not understand. Distrust happens when the news fails to address the world as the public recognise it, leaving them feeling like outsiders looking on at a drama that even the leading performers do not care if they really comprehend' (2009: 2).
13. For more on cinematic individualism, see Richard Rushton on Hollywood and the 'unified subject' (2013: 94).

PART IV

CLOSE READING CASE STUDY: *PARENTHOOD*

CHAPTER 9

Parenthood: A Humanistic Close Reading

Halfway through *Parenthood*, director Ron Howard's 1989 collaboration with screenwriters Lowell Ganz and Babaloo Mandel, is a scene in which the disturbed and secretive pubescent teenager Garry Buckman-Lampkin (Joaquin Phoenix) asks his working, single mother Helen Buckman (Diane Wiest) if he could live with his estranged father for a while. Emerging as we do from a sequence in which Helen reacts with comic surprise to her new son-in-law Tod Higgins (Keanu Reeves) shaving her daughter Julie's (Martha Plimpton) head, the audience is caught off guard by the question, and the swift change in mood. The ensuing scene encapsulates the way the film rewards close listening to lives in domestic environments. Using a detailed analysis of this scene's coverage, set and sound design as a starting point, as well as recourse to two major extant studies, both published in 1999 (Kristin Thompson and Joseph Kupfer have both devoted chapters to its narrative structure and virtue ethics, respectively), the following chapter studies *Parenthood*'s treatment of the domestic politics, ethics and psychology of family relations from a humanistic perspective, and considers filmic representations of emotional contagion, social transaction and co-authored family narratives.

A detailed description of the coverage in Garry and Helen's central scene provides a foundational example of the film's language of domestic realism, focusing upon close attention to transactive social contagions, and the way family narratives are articulated collectively through the spaces we live in. Before moving into an analysis of the social psychology of the narrative structure, I first look at the film's visual and auditory representations of emotional contagion, as well as potential creative contagions in collaborative filmmaking labour and the work of ensemble casts.

The Domestic Realism of *Parenthood*

As Helen and Garry's scene begins, Garry is introduced in a medium long shot, appearing tentatively behind Helen as she prepares to leave for work; she manages a local bank. He sticks close to the walls as if being in the open space of the house might be hazardous. The camera tracks Garry, moving along the wall and away from his mother as, in a preemptively defensive tone, he tells her the house is 'getting crowded' since Tod moved in. When he finally asks if he could stay with his dad for a while, Garry is positioned as far from his mother as possible within the dining room, a large table between them, standing awkwardly with his back against a monolithic white cabinet, hunched, arms crossed, and looking up sheepishly, head slightly bowed, aware of his vulnerability but seemingly unaware that he is being dwarfed by a looming domestic object (a technique employed more than once in this film to convey parent–child power relationships in a space governed by parental agency). He occupies a portion of the left of the frame, walls, tables, chairs and cabinets all larger than his own figure – the wide set-up of Garry alone, before we move into progressively tighter eyeline coverage.

A stillness follows: a long beat with a hushed buzz track, a kind of showdown of information-processing while both of them survey an inevitable oncoming sadness. This disappearance of background noise sustains throughout the scene, crafting something of an auditory bubble around a private two-player drama that speaks to the fragile acoustic intimacy made possible in close domestic settings. In the ensuing shot of Helen, Wiest manages to convey not just trepidation, but also the agony of not knowing what to do in these charged moments of parenting, so loaded with contradiction (Kupfer 1999: 102). She is both surprised and unsurprised, as she has speculated on her son's desire for connection with his father but wanted to suppress it; she wants to prevent him from the painful rejection she envisages, but also knows she must respect his agency and cannot prevent him from being hurt; she is both longing to hold onto 'that little boy who never left my side' and aware that she must take a step back to allow him to explore the world on his own terms; she knows the aching trials of growing up, but not his specific trials, and not how to ease them.

Reviewers recognised that such attempts to convey the realism of mixed emotion were key to understanding the film. *New York Times* critic Stephen Holden observed Wiest's, 'anxious longing, exasperation and pained tenderness . . . Even being the most sensitive parent, the film reminds us, has its limits. No matter how hard you try, you can't live your children's lives for them' (1990: 234). As Kupfer puts it in his chapter on virtue in *Parenthood*:

> Child-rearing involves a tension between protecting children and fostering their growth and independence from us. Cushioning the blows our children are bound to receive must be complemented by helping to prepare them to meet the world on its own terms. Complicating the work of raising children is the fact that not only do the children change but the world changes as well. Consequently, parents cannot always rely on what has worked in the past as they respond to their children's growth. (1999: 92)

What is being asked of Helen here is a manner of humility particular to childrearing:

> Humility is essential to raising children because parents must deal with the fact that they cannot protect their children from all harm. In addition, parents must accept their ever-diminishing control over children who are becoming increasingly self-governing and involved in a world outside the home. (97)

Garry's arms remain folded as he briskly makes his case: he clenches and unclenches his fists nervously, and positions his body away from Helen and toward the kitchen, where he will soon use the phone to call his father. When Helen advises Garry against calling his father, telling him 'you don't know your father like I do', she does so in an uncharacteristic whisper, a resigned but tense monotone, and it is evident she knows her resistance to the idea is a matter of procedure more than guidance. 'I don't know him at all,' Garry snaps, using reassertion of his familiar role – reactive and righteous defiance against his mother's authority – as a kind of courage, and the impetus to move toward the kitchen.

Howard and cinematographer Donald McAlpine shoot this as Garry's over-the-shoulder POV. As he walks to the phone, the camera swings around Helen and pulls away from her while she watches on, her eyeline just above and behind the camera, and then finally the movement ends behind a framed glass divider separating the kitchen from the dining area. The foregrounding effect emphasises the distance between them: neither can stop the motion that has started, now, and they only see each other refracted through the glass, not quite in separate rooms, not quite in the same room, in the same house for now, but one of them is looking for a way out. Helen quietly, haltingly provides the number, and Garry looks up to receive the information, both defiant and afraid, reading her face once more, a last moment of emotional contagion as Garry fails to resist mirroring his mother's doubt before he turns away and dials. With each shot of Garry the coverage is slightly tighter, but it is only now, when he turns his back to Helen, that we have the first uninterrupted close-up. Behind him, Helen sits down to silently watch, her hand covering her mouth to protect against an impulse for intervention.

Garry's voice already has a desperate, raspy quality when he has to introduce himself to his own father, but then he stumbles over his words when he asks, 'well. . . would it be ok if I stay with you for a while. . . a few months?' We have a final shot from Helen's perspective, her son behind the glass huddled over the phone, protecting himself from her gaze. In the final close-up, we do not hear Garry's father's response; we just witness it on Garry's face. The camera is trained on his reaction, and all peripheral details have fallen away. Garry's lip quivers, he squints back tears, and his voice cracks as he acquiesces without retort, and meekly says, 'ok'. At this cue, Randy Newman's bittersweet string section fades in softly underneath, not cloying, not sad, not certain, but still comforting in its resignation, encouraging us to accept the melancholy of the circumstance without being overwhelmed by it, an example of Newman's 'tender, melodic writing [that] ultimately defines the score' (Clemmensen 2009). Helen mirrors this resignation when she sadly and quietly curses her ex-husband under her breath. When Garry hangs up and emerges from behind the glass divider, he can barely face his mother to say, on the verge of crying, 'he didn't think it was such a good idea.' Helen reaches out to her son, says 'oh sweetie', and tries to approach, but Garry walks in the opposite direction around the dining table to avoid her embrace, heading for the exit. 'I've got to go,' he says, and disappears through the front door. Helen hangs her head. As Thompson puts it, 'Garry's abrupt departure, rejecting Helen's consolation, leaves dangling her inability to cope with his problems' (1999: 266), but also her struggle to be released from shouldering the blame for her ex-husband's neglectful behaviour. Both are left alone to process their pain: Helen in her home, and Garry somewhere outside of it.

The first thing this scene demonstrates is the film's foundational quotidian humanism, locating drama and meaning in the everyday life of an extended family in personally charged situations we might otherwise read as unextraordinary, or are omitted from more conventional dramas. Comprehensive description of the filmic resources used to trace a quietly unfolding everyday tragedy reveals rich human detail: domestic politics, the push and pull of emotional contagion in proximal spaces, navigation of and bartering for control over shared familial space, the internal lives we struggle to share even when living so closely with relatives, the quiet pain of tacit kinship rejection, need and desire (in physical contact, in positive attention, in mere presence, in accommodation of one another's needs and verbal demonstrations of love), and an intersubjective chemistry of hope. Garry, for instance, can read his mother's sense of futility, and on one level knows the answer he will likely receive from his father, but has chosen to ignore this intuition and call him anyway. Her only choice is to mirror this hope back to him, and let him own it for this short time, even in her apprehension of its consequences. The domestic realism of the suburban ensemble mode challenges us to read nuance and infer intersubjective politics from everyday events seldom represented onscreen. *New Yorker* reviewer David Denby's close reading of Weist's performance provides a good example of how sustained attention might increasingly reveal conflicted affect:

> Weist has those crinkled eyes, her clipped, harried look, and her nervous smile, greeting each outrage from the kids with a beseeching grin. The way she plays Helen, she's a mother whose every instinct tells her, despite much hurt feelings, to stay available, stay open – they'll come back. Weist's soft hopefulness, combined with anger underneath (which comes bursting out in weird, almost unconscious little jokes), gives the performance its pathos and its comic tension. (Denby 1989: 80)

Denby recognises that the film's true conflicts and drama are discovered only within such close attention, as they are largely internal and closely, quietly, often subliminally held by each protagonist, iterated in domestic spaces where we feel the curious blend of estrangement and sanctuary.

In evaluating the cinematic devices employed to construct environments that resonate with social detail, it pays to scrutinise the creative exchanges occurring between various film workers (inherently social in nature too) rather than isolate contributions; for example, the production designer and the ensemble cast. Scholarship on production design has traditionally emphasised its haptic materiality and contributions to film texture over its practical use (Donaldson 2014: 82); however Howard and his actors use designer Todd Hallowell's interiors to examine behaviour in familiar domestic settings, exposing not just individual character identities with symbolic art direction (the work of Christopher Nowak with decorator Nina Ramsey), but also the particular methods we use to negotiate physical contact and verbal exchange within these proximal environments. Helen has to read Garry's cues when he puts objects between them, yield to his threats of complete withdrawal, and resist approaching to comfort him. After the call to his father, when he is in need, Helen attempts to enter the space Garry has carved for himself, but he uses the dining table as a shield against contact, choosing to leave the house to feel the pain on his own terms rather than hers.

Hallowell's design speaks of controlled domestic space: Helen's attempt at ordering the chaos of work, life and family commitments, the way she projects her upper-middle identity, and implicit material requests for her rebellious teenaged progeny to fall into a commitment to the life she envisioned – a commitment they can no longer provide for her. Garry sits uncomfortably among the objects of this world, but has learned to navigate them. In this scene, we witness a testing of the boundaries of learned behaviours in a controlled environment, or what some sociologists might call (somewhat hyperbolically) the tyranny of the home: 'Even its most altruistic and successful versions exert a tyrannous control over mind and body. We need hardly say more to explain why children want to leave it and do not mean to reproduce it' (Douglas 1991: 303). Yet crucially, negotiation is still possible here. Although they are playing their own familiar roles in this location, Garry is attempting to redefine his role and his relationship to his mother through the domestic space; the phone call to his father is just one among many attempts at escape.

Both of Helen's children use their rooms as a protective shell of private interests against their mother's interventions of order. When we first meet Helen's family, we are provided access only to Julie's room: 'Indeed, we immediately learn that, like Garry, Julie has turned her room into a secret domain within her mother's house. Tod emerges from under the bed . . . She plays loud music (the equivalent of Garry's lock on his door) as the two begin to make love' (Thompson 1999: 255). When we finally catch a glimpse of Garry's room later in the movie we see, perhaps unsurprisingly, an entropic mound of toys. But they seem largely neglected: there is an archaeology of puberty here, with forgotten beloved items still in transition, still held near despite Garry's growing interest in pornography and his developing sexual shame, putting his boyhood toys at a distance. As Joëlle Bahloul muses, for adolescents a closed door (or locked door in Garry's case) can conceptually contain their liminal space of self-perceived dirt or impurity (2012: 263). The room's chaos may represent something of his inner tumult, and the layers of deteriorating and forgotten playthings speak to the discomforts of pubertal transition and a past he is reluctant to leave behind; however, the props are also used practically by the actors. When an insouciant Tod picks up a pair of bug-eyed toy glasses in Garry's room, he demonstrates a casual affinity with Garry's world, and Garry subsequently trusts Tod enough to talk to him about sex. The chaos in Garry's room somewhat connects with that of his aunt Karen (Mary Steenburgen) and uncle Gil's (Steve Martin) house, which is equally messy, and contrasts with Helen's more orderly settings of feature pieces and imperial furniture. When Garry mentions his uncle Gil, he does so somewhat ruefully, as if Gil's family had something he wishes he had in his own – Garry clearly imagines them as more carefree, and Gil as a man who is not struggling under the weight of his own domestic chaos.

The set's lighting, too, will affect our reception of the relationships that are bartered within its confines. Although it appears sunny outside, the light inside Helen's house is strangely muted, with half-drawn timber window shades blocking some of the exterior sources. McAlpine's darker yellow-brown palette, suggesting the languor of a late afternoon rather than the brightness of a new day, implies another kind of control within this space – a subdued affective control out of step with the radically exploratory dawning of teenaged identity, but which Helen's progeny might take cues from in managing their own privacy and self-containment.[1] Moreover, it speaks of the situation this family has reached, struggling to let light in.

The domestic study is not purely visual, however: the space between Garry and his father is suggested in close attention to Phoenix's vocal performance, and rejection and absence are represented in the complete omission of his father's voice from the soundtrack. Garry's huskiness indicates not only the discomfort of acclimatising to a transformed voice during pubescence, but also the self-handicapping behaviour of swallowing one's words, defensively adapting to laryngeal change by overemphasising constricted qualities, becoming quieter and raspier, potentially a kind of adolescent transitional dysphonia (Morrison and Rammage 1993: 428–34). Garry is clearly uncomfortable with being heard; his vocal norms usually service attempts to slip by his family members unnoticed, but now he has to adopt firmness and feigned confidence within the vocal confines he has set for himself, and those of male puberty. His lack of familiarity with assertiveness shows in abrupt vocal shifts: he becomes suddenly louder for a single sentence without changing pitch when he challenges his mother, or when he must interrupt his father's initial rejection to plead for a moment of his time, in lines such as 'I don't know him at all', or, 'It'll only take a minute.' However, he lowers his voice mid-sentence, as if changing the volume took enormous effort, or was not what he intended. Interestingly, studies have found that the absence of a father predicts early onset of pubertal indicators such as vocal change, potentially as a father's absence induces hormone-altering stress (Bogaert 2005: 544). There is a sense that Garry is struggling with a maturation that he feels underprepared for, in vocal change but also in onset of masturbation, which we later learn he feels is a shameful activity and is a primary source of much of the avoidant behaviour he exhibits toward his mother and sister. Simultaneously, editors Daniel Hanley and Michael Hill explore social space using pauses and their attendant opportunities for reflection: the temporality and rhythms of nonverbal conversation and communication that occur in between utterances, as well as the time the audience is allowed to spend considering a character's interiority and emotional processing before moving ahead with the narrative.

For the most part, the scene maintains a standard of conventional, naturalist two-character conversational shooting, yet at times Howard chooses grander or delicately presentational cinematic gestures – potentially conspicuous indoor dolly shots and camera movement, domestic objects obscuring parts of the frame or played symbolically against the characters, and incidental strings intervening on the soundtrack – which would not be out of place in, for example, one of Alfred Hitchcock's apartment-bound domestic thrillers such as *Rear Window* (1954). Recalling analogous techniques in *Rear Window*, we might be so focused on the anxiety induced by a sequence that we could conceivably fail to notice the way the camera moved to ratchet tension. In *Populism and the Capra Legacy*, Wes D. Gehring (1995) calls Howard a 'contemporary Capra Auteur' and singles out *Parenthood* as a primary example: '*Parenthood* seems to soar because it pushes the Capra envelope into new areas' (85, 107; see also Thompson 1999: 250; Holden 1990: 234; Kempley 1989: D1).

Howard had absorbed these classical Hollywood techniques through years of work on film and television since his early appearances on *The Andy Griffith Show* and *Happy Days*. He was by now renowned for employing them in fantasy settings, having previously directed films including *Willow* (1988), *Cocoon* (1985) and *Splash* (1984), and receiving early filmmaking opportunities with budget genre producer Roger Corman.[2] In the production notes to the DVD release of *Parenthood*, Howard wrote, 'After directing films which were very theatrical in theme, I wanted to do something more organic, something I could feel' (2003). I have already noted some of the film's very tactile environments – feeling here comes to mean the corporeal, as well as emotional 'feeling' bound to the corporeal. In *Parenthood*, the more presentational cues of early Hollywood are sparingly used and balanced with predominantly realist stylistic choices. Grander gestures are underplayed, focused as we are on the nuance of the performances, the characters, and the interpersonal politics of each scene. In later interviews, Howard indicated that electing to do a realist piece 'stretched' him as a director (Wayland and Howard 2010). Working outside of genre filmmaking was a challenge; because disparities in a realist diegesis are more intuitive for the audience, they might then be more discerning (and less forgiving) of perceived contrivances.

Parenthood also employs some overlap of the real with daydreams, imagined and projected realities – expressionistic gestures that are uniquely bound within the film's realism. As Gehring observes, 'Like *Wonderful Life*, *Parenthood* begins with an inspired scene of fantasy born of sadness' (1995: 101). The film opens with protagonist Gil Buckman daydreaming about being a boy (Max Elliott Slade as Young Gil) attending a baseball game with his father Frank (Jason Robards), who pays an usher (Ganz) to mind his child. Young Gil motivates pop psychological concepts to explain to the usher that he is in the middle of a daydream, and that the usher does not exist, being an amalgam of ushers he was left with as a child, at which the usher becomes comically irate: 'that's great, you have a family and I'm a goddamn amalgam!' The sequence elegantly (and uncannily) introduces a number of elements the film will be working with: serious concerns raised in comedic settings or punctuated by jokes which deflate solemnity; a tandem question regarding how we might balance hard work with playfulness in childrearing (Young Gil mentions that his father taught him to see parenthood as 'a prison rather than a playground'); family politics and attempts to make progress through superior childrearing (Easton 1989: 5); the collapsing and overlapping of generational identities to explore shared meaning in intergenerational collectives; frictions between confounding social realities and our simplified interior fantasy lives; the power and importance of imagination as a social tool (Kupfer 1999: 100); critical engagement with some of the contemporary pop psychological concepts of the era (such as the 'positive male influence'); the way we group memories together or 'amalgamate' them to narratavise family experience and develop moral goals (Gil promises to be different from his own father); the difficulty of finding the place for humanistic sympathy in this process;[3] and affinity with the uncanny and bizarre, engendering yet another affective tension throughout the film as we are asked to reflect upon some of the absurdities of family life, even while we acknowledge the seriousness of family ethics.

As Thompson points out, the film begins with an absurdity of temporal displacement not only as the child spouts pop psychology, but it also becomes 'doubly odd' in its anachronistic twist: 'the scene seems to be set in the 1950s, while the "positive male influence" is palpably a modern term' (1999: 250), confounding the usher further. Gil's wife Karen soon punctures the daydream and brings him back to the present, explaining that the ball game is over, at which Newman's Oscar-nominated song

'I Love to See You Smile' commences and the opening credits roll over a sequence, gently slapstick and comically observational, both lovingly and astringently depicting the trials of loading a family into a car to go home, drawing the film's beginning laughs from the recognition of a parent's end-of-day weariness.

Daydream sequences permit interior lives to be projected and realised. In *Parenthood*, they are largely used to poke satirical fun at our internalisation of the cultural-psychological pressures of caregiving, such as all-or-nothing thinking (binaristically conceptualising a child as either succeeding or failing in life) or dysfunctional perfectionism (obsessing over best childrearing practices to the detriment of one's progeny). Gil's later daydream sequences register cognitive associations between perfectionism, existential and catastrophic thinking.[4] Howard makes use of these more fantastical elements without saturating the overarching realism, quotidian insights of his cast and crew, or guidance of the spectator's focus toward the work of the performers and dialogue – the actors' efforts to communicate meaning, both internal and social.

The film's ethic of close listening to causation among the variety of lives found in proximal domestic spaces meant that performance would always be one of the film's pivotal narrative devices. Consequently, Howard's method for working with his ensemble cast is key to how the narrative polyphonics would be received. Reviewers commented on Howard's thespian-centric coverage (holding the camera on his actors and letting them do much of the communicative work) which allows performers to be 'uniformly expressive – using every second onscreen to give their characters dimension' (Novak 1989: 17). Other reviewers saw that the film was 'first and foremost, a showcase for wonderful acting' (Boyar 1989). Ernest Mathijs (2011), on the other hand, thinks that ensemble casts are more likely to exhibit a kind of groupthink in their performance style, which he calls referential acting. The connectivity stressed in such filmmaking may make actors more likely to reach for popularly recognisable types, and distribute them to colleagues through the sheer pressure of achieving an artistic unity, or some kind of osmosis of technique that produces homogeneity:

> The tools of polysemous expression, ostentation and referentiality collapse into one set of devices . . . Referential acting involves the self-conscious design of a performance on the basis of a previous one, often by the same actors, but also based on archetypes, exemplary models or clichéd stereotypes. (91)

In the *Parenthood* DVD production notes, Howard's emphasis on unity would appear to support this analysis: 'I've had two very good experiences with ensemble casts,' he says. 'First, as an actor in *American Graffiti* and then directing *Cocoon*. Both experiences taught me that the director has to balance and coordinate the acting styles. If not, you're left with pieces of a film, not one that is complete' (2003). What Howard refers to here is not deference to culturally produced types, but the very nature of constructing a diegesis that makes sense to the viewer – disparate performers with a variety of techniques and backgrounds will need to appear as part of the same film world. Despite Mathijs's speculative claims, this process need not oblige retrogression to types, removal of nuance or the flattening of an actor's more personal-behavioural observations. Referential acting theory colonises the work of the thespian, denying their expertise by presumption of their naivety, or their ignorance of broader issues relating to acting technique and practice. It might be kinder and more generous to begin instead from a presumption of the worker's knowledge of their own craft, accepting that a majority of actors might be entirely aware of potential stereotypes in the worlds they present, and may choose to work with, ignore, or subvert them. The acting in *Parenthood* is a perfect example: a range of styles still appear as part of the same diegesis, but simultaneously demonstrate a range of character acting, with diverse personalities and behaviours rarely slotting into pre-existing character moulds. For example, Phoenix's naturalism can sit peaceably alongside Reeves's comic teenager performance (familiar from the *Bill & Ted* movies), and both manage to communicate surprising nuance. Another intriguing mix of identities occurs as many of the known actors were cast against type, such as Rick Moranis as achievement-centric parent Nathan and Martin as Gil (at the time neither were known for serious roles), or Robards (known for playing wiser and more sympathetic figures), whose stagey, classical style (Gehring 1995: 105) had to sit alongside the adept naturalist performances of actors like Steenburgen.

After *Cocoon* and then *Parenthood*, Howard would go on to direct a variety of ensembles, in *Backdraft* (1991), *The Paper* (1994) and *Apollo 13* (1995), and Ganz and Mandel departed from the male-centric ensemble work characterising the era (Hamad 2013: 104–5; Rattigan and McManus 1992: 22) for *A League of Their Own* (Penny Marshall, 1992). In the years prior to *Parenthood*, dramatic ensemble casts were usually associated with art filmmakers including Robert Altman and John Sayles, but intergenerational multicast narratives were much more rare. Howard, Ganz, Mandel and producer Brian Grazer's innovation was to explore the social network of four – and eventually five – generations in one suburban family, and in so doing, survey the conflicting motivations and desires of people at different times in their life, as well as a matrix of personality features that somehow come together to make an endlessly problematic but occasionally rewarding whole.[5]

One of the film's primary means of close listening to domestic emotional contagion is its soundtrack, and in particular Newman's score. Newman biographer Kevin Courrier suggests that the composer channelled Howard's 'unusual gift for shifting moods, from the comically endearing (*Night Shift*, *Splash*), to the unbearably sentimental (*Cocoon*, *Willow*), to the demonstrably dark (*Ransom*, *The Missing*). In *Parenthood*, Howard used a little of all three elements' (2005: 217). As Christian Clemmensen notes, 'the disparate emotional pulls in *Parenthood* required Newman to write a score that covers a significant amount of territory' (2009) as musical ideas and motifs are transposed between sentimental, comedic and suspenseful backing. Peter Travers also wrote of the film's affective symbiosis with its score, in that the music and action are not always so unified, but rather talk back to one another: '*Parenthood* prevails when the script takes its cue from the rude and rowdy Randy Newman score and packs its observations with a sting' (1989). Newman and orchestrator Jack Hayes sometimes link thematically disparate scenes by blending the affect between them, projecting from a moment of unified emotion into a contrast of emotional spaces, and then ending in more complex sequences without music, commanding no particular emotional response.[6] Kevin's party scene, with its sexual overtones of adult male shame (the stripper) subdued by Gil into harmless play (the cowboy), is followed directly by Garry's assault on his father's office, and a sentimental string score turns spiky, matching Garry's fear and anger. The strings then follow Helen bursting through the house and into Garry's room, blending his anger into her distress, and a piano intervenes against the drama of the string section, at times reflecting her trepidation (she is afraid she might find illicit drugs in the mysterious brown bag he carts around), and at times reflecting her hope that she might instead find an answer to Garry's unhappiness.

When she discovers her son's videocassettes, the score disappears; we are asked to withhold an emotional response along with Helen. Gil's sister Susan (Harley Kozak) and Grandma (Helen Shaw) arrive while Helen is watching one of the tapes, clearly gathering her thoughts, and their comic response plays against a backdrop of the unconvincing angry grunts (rather than gratified moans) of a pornographic film that seems to emphasise sexual conflict rather than pleasure. While these sexual noises continue, Grandma makes a series of remarks that demonstrate some level of awareness of the situation, and yet she ends by light-heartedly commenting, 'you know one of those men reminded me of your grandfather.' Garry turns up furious, and the sounds of the porn film are dismissed along with Susan and Grandma. Helen has to work with this strange emotional atmosphere in order to have a serious conversation with her son (yet despite herself throws in a joke that seems inherited somewhat from her grandmother's attitude: 'I guess you have these because you're interested in sex . . . or filmmaking'). Tod appears, and like Grandma he brings with him a breezy disregard for the emotional weight in the air; when Garry and Helen turn to Tod for assistance, in a way they are also agreeing to forfeit some of their heavy emotional space and let the new member of the household affect their mood. There is no music throughout Tod and Helen's conversation, or then Frank's transitional missing car scene, and the only music at the games parlour that evening is the overlaying bang and crash of a million concurrent noise-making machines, too loud to ignore and unconducive to calming a distraught Kevin or Gil. Sound and action perform their own causal dance in *Parenthood* that informs the emotional trajectory of the characters, and the film.

Helen and Garry's story is just one subplot of many in *Parenthood*'s substantial ensemble drama, and we are regularly encouraged to be considering how other family members might be responding to the action of any given scene. The attentional politics of our guidance toward narrative focal points is key to understanding any film (Moss-Wellington 2017: 43, 53), and one of the primary methods Howard, Hanley and Hill employ to achieve polyphonic perspective-taking throughout the film is the frequent use of reaction cutaways, or grabs. In a scene during which the action appears focused on a particular character and their perspective, we cut to characters who may have been forgotten, see the unfolding drama momentarily through their eyes, and adopt a plurality of perspectives which fosters a different kind of engagement, keeping us from absorption in a particular character's emotional state, or a morality that fails to take into account the many others who are implicated.

The editors will often counterintuitively show us those who are not engaged in conversation, as *People* reviewer Ralph Novak noted: 'Howard keeps the film focused on the painful-exhilarating relationship between kids and parents. One way he does it is by often showing all the participants in a conversation onscreen; the actors react as well as speak their lines' (1989: 17). This is a primary method for what reviewers identified as *Parenthood*'s 'masterstroke . . . offering the points of view of everyone in an extended and wildly diverse middle-class family' (Variety Staff 1988). Early in the film, we meet the extended family as everyone comes together for a Thanksgiving dinner at grandparents Frank and Marilyn's (Eileen Ryan) house. We have already met three of their four children, but the wayward youngest sibling Larry (Tom Hulce) arrives as a surprise, bringing in tow a black son, Cool (Alex Burrall), whom he has until now kept secret. This scene demonstrates innovative use of the cutaway: when Cool first turns up, amidst all the shock, we cut briefly to Julie's barely concealed pleasure at the unfolding family drama; during Larry's speech about his latest get-rich-quick scheme, we cut briefly to Helen and Gil exchanging furtive glances; and we cut to the reaction of Karen and Gil's two eldest children Taylor (Alisan Porter) and Kevin (Jasen Fisher) when Larry makes an inappropriate comment to his sister Susan (Harley Kozak), and once more after Gil mistakes Helen's vibrator for a flashlight during a blackout.

These cutaways effectively signal to the viewer some of the emotionally causal links between subplots in a film with limited narrative continuity. Thompson cites *Parenthood* as an example of a multiple-protagonist picture with parallel plotlines and what she sees as 'virtually no causal interaction' (1999: 248). She explains that the transition between scenes is a primary thematic device the film asks us to become fluent in when assembling its meaning: 'characters are compared and contrasted in ways which demand a fair degree of alert interpretation' (249). *Parenthood*'s model of causation is largely attitudinal and unspoken. The trials faced by each character are not primarily physical but subliminal and social, in that most pursue metacognitive goals relating to *how they think about* their role as a parent or child or sibling, especially when the reality of each role comes into conflict with other components of their self-schema. This unspoken causation is evident from the first extended family dinner scene onward, as we are primed with some of the key relationships and (often harmful) attitudes at play from the start. The film's first transition between narratives – Gil and Karen's reproval of Garry introduces a cut to Helen's subplot – performs a similar function. We are aware of the field of expectation the family has erected around Garry before he even appears onscreen, and thus we are left to wonder at the potentiality of a Pygmalion effect (or tacit expectations that shape behaviour and performance) in the extended network (c.f. Rosenthal and Jacobson 1968).

Thompson also points out that the transitional cuts during the film's setup, introducing us to each strand of the Buckman family (except Larry and Cool, who arrive later), are focused on comparison between the relative shortcomings and merits of their children: Julie's academic performance is superior to Patty's, and Kevin's emotional disturbance is not as bad as Garry's, a comparison that will reach across scene transitions throughout the movie (1999: 256, 254, 269). The interesting part of this is that the characters themselves are doing this comparative work with us, putting together a morally charged family narrative as we do, yet the story we are invited into often subsists on unwarranted judgment that speaks more to the parents' anxieties as caregivers than it does to their child's actual capabilities; the audience must locate their own reflexive distance from these comparisons. The very structure of the film invites us to speculate on the causal relationships between family gossip, collectively distributed expectations, and each individual's wellbeing.

Many of the film's primary psychological problems are explored through Gil: excessive and obsessive worrying, all-or-nothing thinking (sometimes called 'dichotomous thinking' or 'splitting'), dysfunctional perfectionism and feeling overwhelmed. A range of other problems attach to the rest of the characters, for example Garry's sexual shame, Nathan's excessive seriousness and dogma, Frank's resentfulness, Larry's addictions, Helen's defensive anger and need for control, qualities that Julie is by turn translating into her own relationship. Addressing these interior matters is the film's principle method for resolving conflicts with spouses and family members. The will to compromise is simply crowded by caustic thought processes; the film dissects pressures, internal and external, that keep us from adapting. During a later scene in which Frank seeks parenting advice from Gil and the pair manage a tentative reconciliation, Frank speaks of his aversion to the pains of parental sympathy and his realisation that the affective work of parenthood never ends – even at sixty-four, he keeps caring, he keeps assisting, despite identifying with neither of these qualities. In his own words, 'you never cross the goal lines, spike the ball and do your touchdown, never.' Sheila Benson wrote of this line: 'How many sighs will float through the audience at that moment, validating a sentiment that seems to come from one parent's very corpuscles' (1989). Indeed, the audience is able to experience the validation both men enjoy on co-authoring a narrative of their parenting trials, and if they are parents themselves, their own validation of an anxiety vocalised that we are rarely comfortable broadcasting outside of fiction.

Much of the research on family narratives and intergenerational perspective taking looks at a process of values induction during childhood and adolescence (Fivush et al. 2011), yet *Parenthood* shows the benefits of intergenerational perspective taking as they progress later into life. Both men are enriched as they push through their inhibitions to share some of their private trials that go on to form a more complex (and thereby more robust and generous) causal and moral family narrative. Robyn Fivush et al. stress the benefits of an inclusive and transactional family history, and they posit that wellbeing arises, 'perhaps because these stories provide larger narrative frameworks for understanding self and the world, and because these stories help provide a sense of continuity across generations in ways that promote a secure identity' (50). Families can co-author notions of complex multi-causality, and this is how a more realistically considerate morality comes to be embedded in the family narrative. But again, the film will not let this moment be uncomplicatedly positive. Frank still transmits some anxiety back to Gil, and lets slip a remark that he 'never should have had four' children. He does not know that Gil is currently discussing this very prospect with Karen, and his remark connects directly to Gil's own insecurities. Using a sporting analogy, Frank also holds onto his self-defeating rhetoric of winners and losers in parenthood even as he enjoys the bonding catharsis of co-confession with Gil (Novak 1989: 17).

This kind of values contagion across family narratives and networks points to the connection between ethics and affect. Our ethical standards and projections are inextricable from the emotions that mediate them (c.f. Haidt 2012), and our emotions will inform any attempts to live up to the morals we distribute amongst the family. Some of them pass subliminally, like Frank's extemporaneous 'fourth child' remark to Gil. On the other hand, when expressions of care exhausted a younger Frank to the point of resentment and avoidance, Frank became part of a family narrative as the 'shitty father' and to an extent lived up to the moral identity it bestowed – but he also has the opportunity of challenging it. Family narratives bestow moral statuses that can be negative, and we can live up to or match that negative appraisal (conferring again something of a golem effect, the damaging adverse of the Pygmalion effect), and at the same time derive from those narratives the comforts of identity consistency. Identifying our agency for identity change within these structures is a demanding task. The stresses of achieving clarity in such environments can give rise to generalised anxiety, and in order to cope we might turn to dogmatic principles, all-or-nothing thinking, or perfectionism simply because they appear to obliterate such challenges. Yet in their unrealistic reduction of complexity, they only compound our problems every time they rub against a more 'messy' reality. They can therefore be thought of as defective coping mechanisms. Ultimately the film is less concerned with proselytisation than with understanding the social and psychological impediments we face as we try to live up to that better and more virtuous version of ourselves, weighing heavily upon our minds as we proceed through our daily trials.

The Psychology of *Parenthood*

One of *Parenthood*'s most striking structural components is a refusal to separate its own gags, play and emotional release from its probing moral-psychological questions: 'Within its humorous incidents and dialogue, *Parenthood* manages to cover a great deal of moral ground' (Kupfer

1999: 92). So morals are embedded in the film's humour and humour is embedded in the film's depiction of moral quandaries. As in later suburban ensemble dramedies, satire mediates sentimentality and vice versa to achieve an affective realism: '*Parenthood*, heartfelt and howlingly comic, also comes spiced with risk and mischief. Just when you fear the movie might be swept away on a tidal wave of wholesomeness, a line, a scene or a performance pokes through to restore messy, perverse reality' (Travers 1989). Humour here is not just a coping mechanism to deal with harsh realities, but a reminder of the dimensionality of our problems so that we do not fall prey to the reductions of sentiment.

In interviews, Ganz and Mandel have reflected on the fine line between comedy and drama both in their personal lives, and in their writing work. A scene written as a drama could easily be tweaked to play as a comedy, and vice versa (Schanzer and Wright 1993: 161). There are benefits when we listen to another's emotional world and work with it, whether in telling a story or living our social lives, especially when we can find the positive affect within a tense or difficult situation. This is the 'coping' function of humour. We might read a situation as personally violating or threatening, but when we highlight its benign elements through creative analogy, humour is produced and the violation is minimised. Richard Schickel writes:

> There is something brave and original about piling up most of our worst parental nightmares in one movie and then daring to make a midsummer comedy out of them. It really shouldn't work, but it does. The movie does not linger too long over any moment or mood, and it permits characters to transcend type, offering a more surprising range of response to events. Martin, for example, gets to do distraction as well as obsession, and Robards is allowed sentiment as well as cynicism. (1989: 54)

But we can ask here: what about humour's potential misuse? What about minimising a conflict to avoid it, or to tell another loved one that their concerns are less serious than our own? At times, Gil uses humour as a deflective device to avoid dealing with Karen's concerns (about their division of labour, or whether she should have an abortion). There is some manner of affective responsibility at work here. Thompson agrees that, 'One of *Parenthood*'s strengths is that it manages to balance comedy with melodrama' (1999: 259), and this is equally what the film tells us about parenthood – the best results come when we balance genuine care for one another's emotional space with good humoured play. If Gil is learning to relinquish some of the more derisive uses of humour he has inherited from his father, then we can see Kevin, the eldest male child of his own generation, as the next in line of humour's heredity, and his attitude to play seriously fluctuates throughout the narrative. Gil attempts to introduce fun into Kevin's life with too much seriousness. He knows the kind of light-heartedness he wants to teach, and thinks of play as intrinsically virtuous, but he has no model for achieving it as, using his father as a benchmark, he has defined himself by what he will *not be* rather than what he *can be*.

Attitudes to sex – and especially sexual development – present perhaps the film's most challenging intersection of agency, morality and mixed emotion. As such, sex is perhaps the area that most requires the sense of perspective provided by humour and play. So how are concerns regarding sexual shame resolved in *Parenthood*? Garry and Tod's narrative arc represents the film's primary example of modelling healthy attitudes to sex and sexual relations between men, and deflating shame. Garry's narrative begins in earnest after Julie's relationship breaks down, and she returns home to be consoled by her mother; during their conversation, they both agree that 'men are scum.' This may form part of a necessary moment of bonding for mother and daughter, but we soon see that Garry has been standing nearby, absorbing their conversation. Until now, Garry has flown under the radar. Like Helen and Julie, the audience is jolted into consideration of the oft-silent and -absent Garry, and the attitudes expressed in their conversation become more dimensional as we see others implicated: an overheard conversation like this (in a household where it is hard to avoid one another) informs Garry's growing sense of induction into the world of male sexuality as serious, dark and shameful, and these responsibilities as his alone. The contagion of adversarial gender identities also explains part of his investment in living with his father, and why he is relieved to have Tod in his life – he finally has someone who knows his situation and is willing to talk to him about sex.

When Helen finds the pornographic videocassettes in Garry's room, she asks her son if he would like to talk to Tod. After a brief shot-reverse-shot of Tod playing nonchalantly with the toys Garry has held onto from his boyhood – and the pair's ambivalent reaction – Howard, Hanley and Hill cut forward to Tod's debriefing conversation with Helen in which Tod explains how he soothed Garry's fears that frequent masturbation meant 'there was something wrong with him, you know, like he was a pervert or something.' This is followed by Tod's marvellous line: 'and I told him, that's what little dudes do,' which at once humorously punctures the projected problem of shame, offering insight through casual understatement, and demonstrates how Tod is able to generously translate his own knowledge and experience (in this case of male puberty) into a sensitivity of language which is his own and has its own intelligence. Helen recognises this, in turn denting her classism – Helen's prior ambivalence toward Tod is, at this moment, revised. Tod's chat is effective: Garry smiles. In Tod's words, 'I never even knew he had teeth.' His personality changes, a weight is lifted, and a more playful Garry graces the remainder of the movie. *Parenthood*, by and large, deals much more openly and candidly with sexual politics than most films, using practical situations to talk about the way gender problems actually play out in our lives.

Yet this is not the end of Tod and Helen's conversation. When Helen again raises the notion of a positive male influence, Tod complicates the presumption of a man's presence as inherently good by pointing to his own adversative experience – an abusive paternal influence. 'Depends on the man,' he says, and launches into a sensitive and considered philosophical monologue about abuse. When he is done, he physically shakes the philosophy out of himself, and returns to going about his day as before. Reeves plays this gesture as comic, again displaying the kind of broad physical humour engendered by observation of teenaged mannerisms that he made famous in the *Bill & Ted* series. Humour is also part of the healing, as signalled earlier when Tod is playing with the toys in Garry's room: 'The humor is crude in that Tod is clowning around while Garry and Helen are dealing with a crisis. But the humor is also subtle in that it captures the way we cannot always tell from appearances who, or what, is going to be effective in meeting a crisis' (Kupfer 1999: 106). In pointing back to Tod's modest and laidback resilience, these gestures cause reflection: we now understand how hard won these qualities are, and so does Helen. When she thanks him, she means it, and she is thanking him for more than talking to her son. Tod has almost instinctively improved her family's relationships, and all she had to do was include him; Tod had graciously overlooked the classism that inhibited these positive relations. Helen is thankful for both his input and his patience. Wiest's performance of this single line, 'Tod. . . thanks,' is loaded with extenuatory feeling. Tod's aptitude for deep thinking is revealed when he is entrusted with environments through which it can flourish – his very different experiences of family trauma have caused him to be necessarily reflective. These differences make his perspective unique, and thereby all the more valuable in families as they come to encompass considerably divergent backgrounds.

Helen's acceptance of Tod presents the first of the Buckman parents to make a breakthrough in their psychological inhibitions to adaptability. As Kupfer has it, single working mother Helen could be considered *Parenthood*'s superior parent, emerging as the most adaptable. She is the only one who is not a fantasist: 'Helen is upset with Julie's disregard for her feelings and also is facing the weight of being a lone parent. But she is realistic – missing male companionship, distraught that Julie is throwing away college and a productive future, and upset with her son's reclusive behaviour' (1999: 102). Directly after her resolution with Garry, however, Howard, Hanley and Hill cut to Frank as he goes to polish his prize car, and finds it gone. His problems are just beginning. The next cut moves us later in the evening, and Frank brings his foul attitude to a games parlour where Gil is in the middle of dealing with his own son's crises; Frank infects those around him who are already struggling with their own anxieties. The causal network of extended family is vast and confounding, its positive outcomes come riddled with negative side effects, and its negative outcomes are often motivated from genuine care. It is, thus, perfectly natural to feel overwhelmed. The existential components of anxiety – often addressed by the characters as life's 'mess' – are perhaps the film's binding psychological concern.

In a way, *Parenthood* is interested in the difficulty of living up to narrative humanism's demands: using stories to understand social causality as realistically complex. Again, this is borne out in the film's very structure. The climaxes in each plot do not quite match up, resolutions and breakthroughs for each character occur at different times rather than being massaged into the traditional three acts that coincide epiphanies, and this is what makes *Parenthood* feel alive. Some have noted that this structure also permits sad endings to certain narratives even while the film remains positively sentimental: 'Larry's story does, in fact, end sadly, but the *film*'s ending is still upbeat and happy' (Dement 1999: 101). Its counterintuitive structural realism points to the uncertainty of parental responsibility in its unsynchronised resolutions, which often catch the characters themselves off guard. For example, Gil does not expect Grandma's rollercoaster monologue, Helen does not expect Tod's help with Garry, and Susan does not expect Nathan to appear in her classroom singing a song.[7] These minor resolutions do not follow from one another, but are staggered throughout the feature's running time.[8] Nor does *Parenthood* have the emotional trajectorial unity of most ensemble cinema. It does not start humorously before herding all of its characters as a unit through their allotted dramas and back to good cheer. The affect is blended throughout, such that the narrative never quite coalesces into any obvious way to feel about the action.

The amalgamation of positive and negative affect, humour and drama is not merely a matter of happy and comedic scenes following sad scenes and vice versa; it is the filmmakers' attempt to explore more nuanced and complex emotional landscapes, as rarely in life do we find ourselves dealing with circumstances so clearly defined by affect as they are at the movies. We live with an infinitely miscible range of emotions, blending and changing inexorably rather than following logically or separably. Attempting narrative representation of such inconsistent changes can be one aspiration of realist genres. Ganz and Mandel may have their characters crack jokes in situations of high tension to attempt to stem the negative affect that has taken hold, mixing bittersweet uplift into anger or grief or confusion, but at the same time drama intervenes unhelpfully throughout a happy occasion. At Kevin's party, children yell, scream and play, but while playing, Gil's youngest Justin (Zachary La Voy) gets his head stuck in a banana lounge and Susan and Nathan's daughter Patty (Ivyann Schwan), who finds it hard to connect with other children through play, is terrified by one of Gil's magic tricks; in the same space adults are exploring their gender role confusions, Susan and Nathan argue about childrearing, and a stripper wanders into the mix. The film registers the pains of happy occasions so common and omnipresent they usually go unremarked. For example, Ebert lists as one of the film's key observations: 'when kids at a party refuse to have the good time that has been so expensively prepared for them' (1989). When these dramas intervene, we have complex reactions to them, and here the film's reaction cutaways serve yet another purpose: blending in different emotional responses to convey a more complex affective scene, one that records the push and pull of micro emotional contagions. This all sits back-to-back with some of the film's most memorably funny moments, such as Martin's performance as Cowboy Gil, entertaining a party of children with gallows humour and bad puns. Denby writes of the depth of affective and personality detail within his comic performance: 'Martin has often used his explosive clown's skills to suggest pent-up hostility; it's fascinating to see him do it to express love . . . At the same time, he brings out the deeply foolish narcissism in Gil's drive' (1989: 79).[9] Even in triumphant comic moments like this one, where Gil's ludic sensibility comes to the fore, there is still the complicating detail of one's ego, as Gil 'turns himself almost inside out seemingly to will happiness into his insecure son' (Gehring 1995: 102).

Our own emotions are rarely dominated by one clear affective source, and then they come into contact with the emotional mix of proximate others. In parenthood and caregiving, one is required to consistently confront inconsistent affect: elders and children rarely occupy the same emotional space despite their propinquity. When Gil quits his job, he arrives home miserable to a hive of happy youngsters who covet his playful attention.

The locus of Helen's anxieties may be worlds apart from her son's, but they create between one another a formidable and contagious emotive ambiance; something dark, sad, nostalgic, and yet new to both of them. In Mary Douglas's view, 'The mixture of nostalgia and resistance explains why the topic [of the home] is so often treated as humorous' (1991: 287). This is the pivotal inextricability of narrativised affect that the suburban ensemble dramedy relies upon: beneath the happy–sad binary there is another more nuanced emotional palette that always rewards closer attention. It is one variety of storied empathy directed toward complex transactive causality, in this case acknowledging the complex ways we affect one another emotionally. At Kevin's party, Gil is able to tap into that empathy. He is clearly anxious after turning away the stripper, but he also implicitly understands the children's world of play and performs best as a parent when he is able to put himself, emotionally, in their shoes – a methodology of close listening.

We are thus delivered back to the close listening and attention to the lives of others we began with, but it is more informed and richer thanks to the information gathered through *Parenthood*'s inquiry into psychological, ethical and political multicausality and contagion. But the film is not primarily about the politics of the everyday, and it does not primarily preach sacrosanct virtues; *Parenthood* is primarily about the existential psychology of feeling overwhelmed, and this is the effect of piling love and rage, caution and abandon, tenderness and resentment, excitement and fear on top of one another. We need to find ways to accept the affective mess and circumstantial uncertainty of life, or we cyclically fail to resolve even its most trifling conflicts and challenges. When we feel no control over our lives, we also feel helpless, insignificant, and closer to oblivion (Rowe [1987] 2011); small problems tap into an overarching insecurity or generalised anxiety and become catastrophic to our sense of self (Meeten et al. 2012). When we are overwhelmed, we reach for a sense of conceptual control, but this often entails a reduction of life's mess or its ineffable causal complexity; to strive to understand complex causality is to accept that we will never master it. Our efforts to maintain models of self-control that reach beyond what we can possibly manage will produce anxiety. Generalised anxiety in turn produces understandable selfishness, as we become absorbed in a cycle of dealing with our own woes by ineffective means. If we are able to gain some perspective using light-heartedness, jokes and play, we might be able to put our anxieties aside to hear from others, and this outward-listening in itself presents a solution to most conflicts as our ire is stemmed by a contagion of empathic goodwill; even if we listen with empathy and still disagree, we are thereafter endowed with the resources for meaningful compromise. Helen and Garry's narrative provides one of the best examples of empathy contagion in the film:

> She sees Julie's marriage to Tod for the frail thing it is and doesn't hide this from Garry . . . As if his mother's self-conscious concern for her children's well-being has struck a resonating chord, Garry expresses his wish for Helen's welfare. He tells her he's glad she's going out with the biology teacher, Mr. Bowman, remarking how 'he's funny and he's the kind of guy that'd be nice to you.' The movie hints at the possibility that parental devotion and attention to children may engender in them a regard for their parents as people with lives and interests of their own. Such regard could be the seeds in children of social adaptability toward their parents. (Kupfer 1999: 108)

Likewise, the film addresses potential audience members in their late teens, and equally asks them to consider what their parents might be going through (Orndorf 2009). This reciprocal 'close listening' is a learned and learnable process that the humanities, since Niethammer and Humboldt, have attempted to cultivate and liberalise. Humanism is a kind of base level of respectful kindness we begin from in conflict resolution. So one thing that relieves our overwhelmed, existential feelings is refocusing outward to look at others in our vicinity (suburban, familial, domestic) with acceptance and humour. Providing the demonstrative care of close listening, we give one another courage to overcome the daunting nature of life's problems and attend to them not separately, but together.

As much as this humanism is a personal conflict resolution method, a storytelling method, and a politico-ethical interrogative method, it is a hermeneutic method too. While I was busy penning this close reading, I battled my own feelings of being overwhelmed in these attempts to order *Parenthood*'s multi-causal complexity into a meaningful, essayistic argument. Whenever I began to write on a scene or a topic, countless mediating factors from within the same scene or others would come flooding in, threatening to obliterate the clarity one could achieve in writing out the implications of each event. This is what led reviewers to describe it as a 'multifaceted essay in fiction form' (Rosenbaum 1989) combining 'sociology and sitcom, making it into one perceptive, delicious whole' (Benson 1989). Ebert praised, 'The complexity of the movie . . . so many scenes were thought through to an additional level. Howard and his collaborators don't simply make a point, they make the point and then take another look at it from a new angle, finding a different kind of truth' (1989). When writing about sexuality in one scene, for example, unexpected lines of dialogue and later events that speak to sexuality would always complicate any clear 'message' to be derived, simply by pointing to other circumstances that affect the one we are currently focused upon – it would simply point to too rich a multitude of causal connections, political, ethical, psychological, social. Because of its complex connections, I could never retain and record all meaningful detail arising from a single scene, a single theme. Rather than frustrating, though, this was hermeneutically exciting, an alterity and sublimity produced by realism rather than metaphor or abstraction, an ineffability that truly fulfilling narratives can provide, with so many scenes, themes, motifs and dialogues silently causal, silently drawing from each other, silently upsetting a holistic or comprehensively clarifying reading of any given moment.

Parenthood attempts honesty by investigating the relationships between so many complex social psychological concerns – politics, ethics, causation, gender, inheritance, interiority, attitudes, behaviour, pathology, contagion, suburban domesticity and so on. In so doing, it produces in the attentive viewer the overwhelming feelings that it speaks to, complicating its own ethos of close listening, and then resolves these for the viewer by asking us to accept its central challenge: to observe, to comprehend but never to master this complexity. This is how hermeneutic writing processes provide comparable humanistic work to good fictions, and it is also one reason why the final rollercoaster analogy works. It is not just that life is a rollercoaster; it is that we have no option of getting off, or having it any other way. We can also know this all along, just like we know the cliché that 'life is a rollercoaster', but fail to accept it as Gil does. We can have someone put it in front of our very faces with poems and light and play and joy – as Grandma does for Gil – but still refuse to listen. And it is not until later, when this wisdom of complex acceptance has preconsciously settled in, that it comes through and makes sense for us, as when Gil finally realises he was listening to and empathising with Grandma despite himself, and in a moment when he could despair, instead her message becomes real and changes his world. When the film itself briefly becomes a rollercoaster during the climactic school play scene, with the camera and soundtrack both adopting its giddy chaos, Howard echoes the interior fantasy of *Parenthood*'s opening scene (Gehring 1995: 105), but its attention has shifted from Gil's earlier control of the world (instructing the amalgam on his role in the daydream and dispensing assured childrearing advice) to his lack thereof. In effect, our fantasies and daydreams can signal our mental health. Our sense of interior control is parsed through fantasy and imagination, and given a socially generous nature we might instinctively let in the wisdom of others like Grandma to affect our daydreams; paradoxically, when we relinquish control over our external circumstances, we must first do so internally.

Parenthood uses its character study of loving kinship to diagnose necessary pain even in the striving of humanism. The film, for example, explores a humanistic paradox: avoidant parenting and relationship behaviours may be motivated from genuine care. Frank tells Gil that he was excessively anxious when he thought Gil had contracted polio as a child, and all that worrying conflicted with his self-schema: 'it wasn't for me,' he says. Likewise, when Tod crashes his car, Julie threatens to walk away, crying, 'I can't! I can't! This is too intense!' Both of these responses are borne from the pain of genuine care, not just affective empathy but affective sympathy, when we adopt another's goals and wellbeing as our own, the kind of sympathetic relations a family requires of us. We will then also feel their pains as our own; a load that compounds our existing troubles and can threaten to overwhelm the unprepared. Gil finally admits to his similarities with his father, as he recognises the motivating emotions of parenthood yet sees too the opportunity to respond to aversive affect differently.[10] Helen indicates her support for Julie's marriage even while she recognises from her own marital experiences the threat posed by an impulse to retreat from confrontation. Although we may push others away in times of crisis, perhaps in attempts to simply reduce the sheer quantity of concerns and complications that cloud us, we need loved ones to look past our reactionary impulses and foster this kind of empathy and support – precisely what family, at its best, can provide. In the psychology of *Parenthood*, some of our most problematic and harmful behaviours are motivated from our most genuine concerns for the wellbeing of others. Denby writes of the film's eponymous parents:

> Haunted by child-rearing theories they only half understand, vaguely resentful and vaguely guilty, mortifyingly self-conscious, they hang on to the tiller with baffled determination . . . [Howard] certainly gets onscreen, as no moviemaker before him has, the teasing, taunting complexity of child-rearing, the perversity of a job that flummoxes even the most intelligent and self-composed people. (1989: 79–80).

Part of accepting the mess of life is accepting one's own failures. With this acceptance comes new hope, and the film's penultimate rollercoaster scene emphasises the difficulty of finding hope despite fragmentation and confusion (Gehring 1995: 104). Howard, Ganz and Mandel then turn to an enduring populist trope to close the film: the hope evident in new life (105).

The final scene of the film appears to be, for the most part, a sentimental conclusive montage, showing the extended family together at a happy time – Helen has given birth to a new child – played over images suggesting each character's personal development toward overcoming their particular challenges. But there is a darkness here, too. Astute reviewers noted melancholy undertones (Novak 1989: 17; Gehring 1995: 107), suggested both in the piano score's minor changes and subtle vignettes at the edge of the frame: the existential anxieties never fully subside. The film's final image is of Karen, overwhelmed, perhaps unable to match the sentiment asked of her at the occasion, brimming with tears and turning away. Gil notices, approaches, and puts his arms around her. Where she has helped him with his anxiety throughout the picture, now he comforts her. The final images speak to the inextricability of these emotions even from the joyous times shared with one's family, the exhaustion and uncontrollability inherent in the family experience, the pain we must navigate even within hopeful new beginnings, and the reciprocity of care demanded in a family, where one's responsibilities are rarely easy to identify, but ever present. Life's bittersweet affective tightrope extends, daunting as ever, in front of us, but as long as we attempt to help each other through, we find a way.

Notes

1. McAlpine, it should be noted, is no stranger to domestic cinematography and became somewhat of an expert in lensing these environments throughout the 1980s and 1990s (Dawson 2013: 62).
2. There is some continuity in Howard's mapping of later-life existentialism distributed in familial communities from *Cocoon* to *Parenthood* (Colarusso 2011: 158), and in Ganz and Mandel's work from *Parenthood* to *City Slickers* as well.
3. Thompson writes: 'Gil, while wanting to avoid Frank's mistakes, has some sympathy for and understanding of his father . . . Gil's tossing around of pop-psychological terms suggests that he has read books on child-rearing, trying to avoid his father's mistakes' (1999: 251).
4. For evidence of these associations, see Graham et al. (2010) and Meeten et al. (2012).
5. This view contravenes many of the more negative assessments of family narratives on film (see Loukides 1991: 97–88).
6. Jeff Smith writes of film music as performing three dramatic functions: it signifies character emotions; sets an emotional tone or mood; and attempts to inspire emotion within the viewer (1999: 167). The score here blends these expressive capacities together, too.
7. The narrative disruption of Nathan's 'artless singing' is another example of the film's playful attitude toward mimetic film conventions (Gorbman 2011: 162–3).

8. It should be noted, too, that Grandma introduces another causally structural element that the film works with: she unites everyone almost imperceptibly, yet her movements and advice are such subtle narrative events that Thompson believes 'most spectators probably do not notice this motif' (1999: 258).
9. Gehring called this performative style 'populist implosion' and likened the performance to the comedy of Eddie Murphy, who, similarly to Martin, has a wild, comic hostility playing dynamically against a more light-hearted surface (1995: 102). Later, he makes a connection between Martin's physical humour and Charlie Chaplin's Tramp (108); this is a testimony to the actor's ability to combine the innocent and acerbic, the joyous and the sad. It might also be noted that Martin's comedic cowboy associations began before his typecasting in suburban contexts, especially with *Three Amigos* (John Landis, 1986), and continued long afterward in his career as a banjoist.
10. There is some circularity to the narrative structure here. Gil extends sympathy to Frank right from the opening scene, explaining that Frank had no positive model for fatherhood, being thrown out of the house at 15; his subsequent efforts, despite all of his shortcomings, were still a kind of progress, and two generations hence produced Gil, an even more caring father who is able to reflect on the generational changes that have paved some manner of progress in male caregiving.

Afterword

In my final year of writing this work, Donald Trump was elected president of the United States. Like so many others at my university and within my peer group, especially those working in some manner of American studies, I went through a brief period of crisis: what was I doing to countervail the growing influence of the alt-right at home and abroad, was my work just more intellectual dithering while Rome burned, and why should I be writing about ordinary lives in American suburbia at a time like this? What interested me, however, were the campaigning voices of intellectual left: Slavoj Žižek, John Pilger and new digital-age libertarian heroes like Julian Assange all threw their support behind the Trump presidential bid. Their reasoning? Despite the vast corporate wealth and influence that make up the American political system, Trump was somehow positioned 'against the system' and would positively shake things up (Monbiot 2016). This connected with much of what I had been reading in antihumanist scholarship: a rather simple notion that *anything* radical or transgressive is necessarily good, because the world we have at the moment is bad. In Pilger's words, 'Donald Trump is a symptom of [Americanism], but he is also a maverick . . . The danger to the rest of us is not Trump, but Hillary Clinton. She is no maverick. She embodies the resilience and violence of a *system*' (2016).

This seductive idea has become a careless new progressive politics, and we are now seeing the dawn of a major political ideology that unites the far right with leftist intellectuals (somewhat like the bipartisan libertarianism that birthed it): a request for anything destructive, no matter the cost. This is careless politics in that it values impact upon concepts, mindspaces and 'the system' more than investigating impact on people's lives. An eventual positive impact on human lives is speciously presumed, abstracted into a chimeric and unspecified future that will arise after the maligned minorities have undergone allotted violence, and paid for our distant utopia. It is a rarefied and removed ethical illogic, in that it chooses to be blind to its most basic outcomes of pain and injustice not inflicted on the philosopher himself. This is how Žižek can make absurd distinctions between humanist and antihuman terror, justifying extreme violence (that he will never be party to himself) in the name of theory (2011: 674).[1] It is time to return to some foundational principles that have stood the test of humanism's long journey through various theisms, secularisms, pedagogies, canonical protectionisms, and so on, and they are found in Karl Popper's famous summary of Immanuel Kant's humanist perspective on ethics: 'Always recognize that human individuals are ends, and do not use them as means to your end' (1945: 102). This mandates that our attention be turned to human outcomes rather than ideal or morally perfect ones like toppling 'the system'.

What I ultimately concluded was that more than anything right now, the world needs the kindness of humanism. In order not to forget the people on which our theories are predicated, or to lose sight of their lived experience, we need to tell their stories; filling this space in our theoretical accounts is what fiction, and other humanist narrative styles like humanistic anthropology (Gardner 1994: 167), can offer. Our adversarial identity politics – pointing out one another's silent and nascent bigotries, naming and shaming one another – only seems to calcify regressive positions on sexism and racism, entrenching pride in nationalism and prejudice. From Brexit to Trump, bigotry appears to have grown. Humanistic scholarship instead appeals to scholars to write of social consequence, not of villainy; the humanism of storytelling is a means by which we counterbalance any limits placed on our notions of accountability, and who we see as human and therefore equal. Humanism is regularly under fire for being airy-fairy, vague or not militant enough (Torrance 2001: 165), not offering a distinct programme for change, or eschewing interventionist political prescription (Eagleton 1983: 207). But in the aftermath of wars, periods of oppression and resistance, what remains are the stories, and if, as Jablonka and Lamb (2005) suggest, a distinctive quality of human evolution is symbolic inheritance, then we are provided a unique opportunity to learn from these stories as they accumulate – storytelling could be the greatest responsibility of all.[2]

I hope I have demonstrated that although this philosophy is unfashionable, it is feasible. I hope, too, that I have demonstrated that such a focus can be political, and generous close listening can reveal the inculcation of values – within contexts of privilege just as in contexts of disadvantage – that affects others in the world. Humanist storytelling is its own kind of ethical intervention (Moss-Wellington 2015: 119), yet Booth believes that reading the ethical language of fiction has fallen out of vogue, and our theories are forced to be indirectly ethical: 'It is practiced everywhere, often surreptitiously, often guiltily, and often badly, partly because it is the most difficult of all critical modes, but partly because we have so little serious talk about why it is important, what purposes it serves, and how it might be done well' (1988: 19). Any ethical conversation will be better informed the more perspectives and contexts it is willing to encounter, and I have tried to demonstrate what attention to a multiplicity of perspectives might look like both in narrative and in my own scholarship. Those perspectives I have included here – a mode of ensemble filmmaking, or scholarly works that inquire into human difference – in turn demonstrate their own close attention to a multiplicity of perspectives. The work of integrating perspectives treats one another's narratives as living, mutable, changeable, and thus stasis in one's own personal beliefs never seems like a viable option – that is to say, humanism is one way to never stop inquiring, to never (as in canonical humanism's inbuilt inertia) assume we have among us the unassailable end point of learning.

Suburbia, as we have seen, is a place of overlap and tension between lifeworlds; in its polymorphic nature, American suburbia has been a site of shifting perspectives and cultures, and when those lives are investigated, we might understand the transactions between classes and cultures where everyday politics are developed, and then later taken to the polling booth. I have made the case that antisuburbanism and dystopic suburban cinema often take the form of a cultural classism. Antisurbanism can present as leftwing or progressive critique of a political status quo, but it takes aim at the inheritors of a problematic culture rather than its purveyors (breaking down in its wake a historic alliance between the material interests of the working classes and the more abstracted goals of an intellectual leftwing class, often expressed through identity politics). This is why we need humanistic understanding of the broad ideologies that emerge therein – from self-destructive consumerism to outwardly destructive neo-Nazism – not just their distanced condemnation. From the outset, suburban ensembles like *American Beauty* were invested in asking questions of the lives of repugnantly intolerant characters: neo-Nazis like Colonel Frank Fitts (Chris Cooper). This goes to the heart of humanism's challenge: that there is a difference between understanding and indulging. For many of those working in fields like anthropology, collapsing the distinction between cognitive and affective empathy makes little sense – it is the foundation of ethnographic work to empathise deeply while retaining a critical perspective on the emergence of cultural phenomena. We cannot truly reject that which we do not first comprehend. If we are to condemn a culturally produced ideology, we should first understand the context in which it arises so that we also understand how it will change. How do we expect to understand and challenge the Trump phenomenon without first doing the work of empathy to understand the conditions in which it arises?

By now it is evident that I keep coming back to another central theme – the benefits of thinking generously about others. We should remind ourselves that situations of desperation produce the need for competition, and that competition will in some cases be expressed as bigotry. In a less equal world, more conflict, resentment and bigotry simply make more sense.[3] We should take aim at those with the means to relieve the artificial scarcity that creates such cultures, not turn our backs on the social echelons caught in its throes. This care *in no way* necessitates adopting *any* bigoted views.[4] These are all the problems of humanism and the abject, and point to the need for further articulation of an 'abject humanism' – that is, a humanism that accounts for the place of narrating human ill (Moss-Wellington 2018). For example, we can ask how one might attempt humanistic close readings of antisocial narratives, both fictive and non-fictive, such as those distributed by neo-Nazis like Fitts.

There are two other key areas of concern that I would like to flag for future research before closing. Firstly, the problem of abject humanism causes us to reflect on the possibilities for admitting personality variation into humanistic research; in particular, how we might account for those who have little appetite for complex cognitive tasks, for social reasoning, or those who simply do not empathically respond to others through narrative (cf. the Interpersonal Reactivity Index in Davis 1983). Any recommendation for a general ethic of narrative, for instance, must take these personality variables into account, as we cannot expect everyone to display the same aptitudes or appetites in reading narrative. This is a broader issue going to the heart of all hermeneutics, which necessarily rely on some conjecture or versions of the hypothetical audience member. Even in the more quantitative methods within audience studies, we infer general types of audiences and trends in spectatorship from gathered data.

Secondly, there is a cluster of terms – insight, nuance, subtext, subtlety, and so on – that have recurred throughout this text with limited exposition. They all express some of the narrative qualities a humanist may value, and they all describe something different about the observation of human psychological and social complexity. Humanism holds pride of place for the forward-looking vulnerability of the new (insight, imagination, discovery), for attention to micro-causal details (nuance, subtlety), and for a connotative realism that replicates the mental work of our attempts to understand social connections at the level of inference (subtext). As life itself provides no inherent tools for crafting a specific meaning from any social scenario, all of these qualities come together to create a sense of 'eudaimonic' purpose. Oliver and Raney write of eudaimonic motivations for narrative engagement as our desire to derive a sense of meaningfulness which, for some, can be more important than hedonic motivations: 'this broader conceptualization of the entertainment experience may assist in untangling the seeming paradoxes of 'sad' or 'tragic' entertainment by suggesting that greater insight or meaningfulness is the more important and sought-after outcome from consuming such fare' (2011: 1001). There can also be a selflessness in the pursuit of the eudaimonic in fiction:

> eudaimonic motivations (as we have defined them) reflect a need for greater insight into or understanding of the human condition more broadly than the fulfilment of needs focused on the self . . . Additionally, though grappling with issues of human poignancies and life meanings may be gratifying in terms of added insight, we also believe that such insight may, at times, be somewhat painful. (2011: 989)

Clearly there are some narratives that impress upon us a vast cognitive map of intentional agents, but beyond these complex connections have no case to put forward that we might read as a specific meaning or insight. Some television shows, like *Lost*, have become infamous for constructing mysteries of human interaction that are never solved – the authors not only failed to come up with a solution to their narrative puzzle, but also a 'meaning' to these instances of human interaction by which we might identify and evaluate a broader perspective (the hedonic has come at the expense of the eudaimonic). So ensemble casts and the multi-causality of multiple intentional agents are not enough to make a narrative humanistic: both can still fail to illuminate anything about human interaction, and simplify or fail to accurately represent human interaction. Our judgments of a story's level of 'insight' require another more sustained theoretical inquiry, perhaps drawing again from experimental psychology, which I will leave for another time.

The humanist hopes that exploring human nuance is more likely to achieve a longer-lasting grounding in inclusive politics and generous thinking than more militant approaches. Some of these broader questions of humanist generosity are encapsulated at the conclusion of Jim Henson's television series *The Storyteller*, written into a retelling of 'The Heartless Giant' by Anthony Minghella. The heartless giant in question discovers his long-buried empathy at the narrative's conclusion (in the form of a fragile egg), yet those he has tormented cannot forgive him for what he has done – they crush his heart and kill him. But the protagonist who found and returned the giant's heart lives on to become a storyteller himself, and amends the original narrative to highlight the villagers' capacity for mercy, negotiation and peace. One can ask if there is a reinforcing power in telling of our facility for goodwill to other living things; however, if we value realism above all, to what extent may we be selective about the spotlight we shine on human existence to retell, and hopefully reinforce, its best qualities?

Humanism was the beginning of the humanities disciplines, and there remains today a call to good-naturedness at the heart of humanities scholarship even in its more militant iterations. If, as so many of us do in one form or another, we are to insist on exhibiting generosity toward others, we would probably best achieve this by thinking generously of the people we write about; in this way, through story, we can demonstrate the world we want to live in.

Notes

1. As Patrick Stokes puts it, 'Political violence unavoidably reduces the life and body of another human being to a means to achieve a political end. There are desperate circumstances in which that becomes necessary. But in those instances one does not avoid guilt – rather one takes *on* the guilt of violence for the sake of preserving the moral life we share. Violence may become necessary, but that does not make it good, merely least-worst' (2017). There may indeed be political circumstances under which violence is both understandable and necessary, but it is far from clear that constituents of Western liberal democracies are living in one of these circumstances – although consistent theoretical focus on subject positioning, governance, and the worst abuses of power will certainly make it seem that we are.
2. Humanism, thus, is longitudinally political, and morally concerned without being moralistic.
3. The same generosity of thought could be extended to interdisciplinary antagonism between scholars attempting to make their mark in a field of limited employment opportunities.
4. We can have cognitive empathy without affective empathy, affective empathy without sympathy, sympathy without identification, and then identification without adopting the same goals as the identified. These distinctions are too often blurred.

Bibliography

Adorno, Theodore (1973), *Negative Dialectics*, trans. E. B. Ashton, London: Routledge and Kegan Paul.
Albuquerque, Sara, Marco Pereira, and Isabel Narciso (2016), 'Couple's Relationship After the Death of a Child: A Systematic Review', *Journal of Child and Family Studies* 25.1: 30–53.
Alea, Nicole, and Susan Bluck (2003), 'Why are You Telling Me that? A Conceptual Model of the Social Function of Autobiographical Memory', *Memory* 11.2: 165–78.
Allchin, Douglas (2009), 'The Evolution of Morality', *Evolution: Education and Outreach* 2.4: 590–601.
Alter, Adam L., and Hal E. Hershfield (2014), 'People Search for Meaning when they Approach a New Decade in Chronological Age', *Proceedings of the National Academy of Sciences* 111.48: 17066–70.
Anderson, Eric, Erika H. Siegel, Eliza Bliss-Moreau, and Lisa Feldman Barrett (2011), 'The Visual Impact of Gossip', *Science* 332.6036: 1446–8.
Anderson, Joseph D. (1996), *The Reality of Illusion: An Ecological Approach to Cognitive Film Theory*, Carbondale: Southern Illinois University Press.
Appadurai, Arjun (1996), *Modernity at Large: Cultural Dimensions of Globalization*, Minneapolis: University of Minnesota Press.
Appiah, Kwame Anthony (2006), *Cosmopolitanism: Ethics in a World of Strangers*, New York: W. W. Norton.
Apter, Emily (2004) 'Saidian Humanism', *boundary 2* 31.2: 35–53.
Ardery, Julia S. (1997), '"Loser wins": Outsider art and the Salvaging of Disinterestedness', *Poetics* 24.5: 329–46.
Aristotle [330 BCE] (1987), *Poetics*, trans. R. Janko, Cambridge: Hackett.
Ashe, Laura (2015), '1155 and the Beginnings of Fiction', *History Today* 65.1: 1–13.
Azcona, María del Mar (2010), *The Multi-Protagonist Film*, Malden; Oxford; Chichester: Wiley-Blackwell.
Bacon, Francis (1996), *Novum Organum*, in Graham Rees (ed.), *Collected Works of Francis Bacon, Volume 7, Part 1*, London: Routledge/Thoemmes.
Bahloul, Joëlle (2012), 'Telling Places: The House as Social Architecture', in Kathy Mezei and Chiara Briganti (eds), *The Domestic Space Reader*, Toronto: University of Toronto Press, pp. 259–64.
Bal, Mieke (1985), *Narratology: Introduction to the Theory of Narrative*, Toronto: University of Toronto Press.

Baldwin, James [1955] (1984), *Notes of a Native Son*, reissue edition, Boston: Beacon Press.
Barefoot, John C., Kimberly E. Maynard, Jean C. Beckham, Beverly H. Brummett, Karen Hooker, and Ilene C. Siegler (1998), 'Trust, Health, and Longevity', *Journal of Behavioral Medicine* 21.6: 517–26.
Barnier, Amanda, and Penny Van Bergen (2014), 'Remember when we . . .? Why sharing memories is soul food', *The Conversation*, 24 December, <https://theconversation.com/remember-when-we-why-sharing-memories-is-soul-food-35542> (5 January 2015).
Barnier, Amanda J., Alice C. Priddis, Jennifer M. Broekhuijse, Celia B. Harris, Rochelle E. Cox, Donna Rose Addis, Paul G. Keil, Adam R. Congleton (2014), 'Reaping what they Sow: Benefits of Remembering Together in Intimate Couples', *Journal of Applied Research in Memory and Cognition* 3.4: 261–5.
Barratt, Daniel (2014), 'The Geography of Film Viewing: What are the Implications of Cultural-Cognitive Differences for Cognitive Film Theory?', in Ted Nannicelli and Paul Taberham (eds), *Cognitive Media Theory (AFI Film Readers)*, London: Routledge, pp. 62–82.
Barrett, Justin (2004), *Why Would Anyone Believe in God?* Walnut Creek: Altamira.
Basinger, Jeanine (2012), *I Do and I Don't: A History of Marriage in the Movies*, New York: Knopf.
Bastian, Brock, Jolanda Jetten, and Laura J. Ferris (2014), 'Pain as Social Glue: Shared Pain Increases Cooperation', *Psychological Science* 25.11: 2079–85.
Bauman, Zygmunt (1993), *Postmodern Ethics*, Cambridge: Basil Blackwell.
Bauman, Zygmunt (2004), *Work, Consumerism and the New Poor*, Maidenhead: McGraw-Hill International.
Baumgartner, M. P. (1988), *The Moral Order of a Suburb*, New York: Oxford University Press.
Beauregard, Robert A. (2006), *When America Became Suburban*, Minneapolis: University of Minnesota Press.
Bell, Quentin [1947] (1992), *On Human Finery*, reprint edition, London: Allison and Busby.
Benson, Sheila (1989), 'Ahhhh! The Joys of *Parenthood*', *Los Angeles Times*, 2 August, <http://articles.latimes.com/1989-08-02/entertainment/ca-483_1_movie-parenthood-robards> (1 February 2017).
Bentley, Frank, and Janet Murray (2016), 'Understanding Video Rewatching Experiences', *Proceedings of the ACM International Conference on Interactive Experiences for TV and Online Video*, IIT Institute of Design, 17 June, New York: ACM, pp. 69–75, <http://web.mit.edu/bentley/www/papers/tvx119-bentley.pdf> (9 September 2016).
Berger, John (1987), *Once in Europa*, reissue edition, New York: Vintage, 1992.
Bergson, Henri (1911), *Laughter: An Essay on the Meaning of the Comic*, London: Macmillan.
Berlant, Lauren (2008), *The Female Complaint: The Unfinished Business of Sentimentality in American Culture*, Durham, NC: Duke University Press.
Berlant, Lauren (2011), *Cruel Optimism*, Durham, NC: Duke University Press.

Berry, Edward (2001), *Shakespeare and the Hunt: A Cultural and Social Study*, Cambridge: Cambridge University Press.
Best, Stephen, and Sharon Marcus (2009), 'Surface Reading: An Introduction', *Representations* 108.1: 1–21.
Beuka, Robert (2004), *SuburbiaNation: Reading Suburban Landscape in Twentieth-Century American Fiction and Film*, New York: Palgrave Macmillan.
Bierhoff, Hans-Werner, and Bernd Vornefeld (2004), 'The Social Psychology of Trust with Applications in the Internet', *Analyse Und Kritik* 26.1: 48–62.
Binford, Henry C. (1985), *The First Suburbs: Residential Communities on the Boston Periphery, 1815–1860*, Chicago: Univerity of Chicago Press.
Blair, James, Derek Mitchell, and Karina Blair (2005), *The Psychopath: Emotion and the Brain*, Malden: Blackwell Publishing.
Blegvad, Peter (1996), 'Blegvad on Blegvad', *Hearsay* 12, <http://www.hearsay-magazine.co.uk/blegvad_retro> (26 September 2016).
Bogaert, Anthony F. (2005), 'Age at Puberty and Father Absence in a National Probability', *Journal of Adolescence* 28.4: 541–6.
Bookchin, Murray (1995), *Re-Enchanting Humanity: A Defense of the Human Spirit Against Anti-Humanism, Misanthropy, Mysticism and Primitivism*, London: Cassell.
Booth, Wayne C. (1988), *The Company We Keep: An Ethics of Fiction*, Berkeley; Los Angeles; London: University of California Press.
Bordwell, David, and Thompson, Kristen (2003), *Film Art: An Introduction*, 5th edition, New York: McGraw-Hill.
Bourdieu, Pierre [1979] (1984), *Distinction: A Social Critique of the Judgement of Taste*, trans. Richard Nice, Cambridge, MA: Harvard University Press.
Bourdieu, Pierre (1990), 'The Scholastic Point of View', *Cultural Anthropology* 5.4: 380–91.
Bourne, Mark (2007), '*Junebug*: Another Time Amy Adams Enchanted Us', *Film.com*, 30 November, <http://www.film.com/dvds/story/junebuganothertimeamyadamsenchantedus/11597476/17489141> (19 May 2013).
Bowles, Samuel and Herbert Gintis (2002), 'Social Capital and Community Governance', *The Economic Journal* 112.483: F419–F436.
Boyar, Jay (1989), 'Family Ties Are Put To The Test In *Parenthood*', *Orlando Sentinel*, 10 September, 18.
Box Office Mojo [no date], 'American Beauty', *Box Office Mojo*, <http://www.boxofficemojo.com/movies/?id=americanbeauty.htm> (7 April 2016).
Boyanowsky, Ehor O, Darren Newtson, and Elaine Walster (1974), 'Film Preferences Following a Murder', *Communication Research* 1.1: 32–43.
Boyd, Brian (2009), *On the Origin of Stories: Evolution, Cognition, and Fiction*, Cambridge, MA: Belknap Press of Harvard University Press.
Boyer, Pascal (2001), *Religion Explained: The Human Instincts That Fashion Gods, Spirits and Ancestors*, London: William Heinemann.
Boyle, David (2003), *Authenticity: Brands, Fakes, Spin and the Lust for Real Life*, London: Flamingo.

Boym, Svetlana (2001), *The Future of Nostalgia*, New York: Basic Books.
Brants, Kees (2012), 'Trust, Cynicism, and Responsiveness: The Uneasy Situation of Journalism in Democracy', in Chris Peters and M. J. Broersma (eds), *Rethinking Journalism: Trust and Participation in a Transformed News Landscape*, Hoboken: Taylor and Francis, pp. 15–27.
Brekhus, Wayne (2003), *Peacocks, Chameleons, Centaurs: Gay Suburbia and the Grammar of Social Identity*, Chicago; London: University of Chicago Press.
Brenner, Neil and Christian Schmid (2014), 'The "Urban Age" in Question', *International Journal of Urban and Regional Research* 38.3: 731–55.
Brooks, Nancy A., Diana W. Guthrie, and Curtis G. Gaylord (2009), 'Therapeutic Humor in the Family: An Exploratory Study', *Humor – International Journal of Humor Research* 12.2: 151–60.
Brooks, Peter [1984] (1985), *The Melodramatic Imagination: Balzac, Henry James, Melodrama, and the Mode of Excess*, Morningside edition, New York: Columbia University Press.
Brown, S. L., and R. M. Brown (2006), 'Selective Investment Theory: Recasting the Functional Significance of Close Relationships', *Psychological Inquiry* 17.1: 1–29.
Bruner, Jerome (1986), *Actual Minds, Possible Worlds*, Cambridge, MA: Harvard University Press.
Buller, David J. (2005), *Adapting Minds: Evolutionary Psychology and the Persistent Quest for Human Nature*, Cambridge, MA; London: MIT Press.
Burch, Noël (1982), 'Narrative/Diegesis-Thresholds, Limits', *Screen* 23.2: 16–33.
Burke, Kenneth (1952), *A Grammar of Motives*, New York: Prentice-Hall.
Burke, Kenneth (1969), *A Rhetoric of Motives*, Berkeley: University of California Press.
Burkert, Walter (1979), *Structure and History in Greek Mythology and Ritual*, Berkeley: University of California Press.
Bushman, Brad J., Roy F. Baumeister, and Angela D. Stack (1999), 'Catharsis, Aggression, and Persuasive Influence: Self-Fulfilling or Self-Defeating Prophecies?' *Journal of Personality and Social Psychology* 76.3: 367–76.
Buston, Peter M., and Stephen T. Emlen (2003), 'Cognitive Processes Underlying Human Mate Choice: The Relationship Between Self-Perception and Mate Preference in Western Society', *Proceedings of the National Academy of Sciences of the United States of America* 100.15: 8805–10.
Cacioppo, John T., Richard E. Petty, Jeffrey A. Feinstein, and Blair G. Jarvis (1996), 'Dispositional Differences in Cognitive Motivation: The Life and Times of Individuals Varying in Need for Cognition', *Psychological Bulletin* 119.2: 197–253.
Caillois, Roger [1961] (2001), *Man, Play and Games*, trans. Meyer Barash, Urbana; Chicago: University of Illinois Press.
Califia, Pat (1994), *Public Sex: The Culture of Radical Sex*, San Francisco: Cleis Press.

Cantor, Joanne (2004), '"I'll never have a clown in my house" – Why Movie Horror Lives On', *Poetics Today* 25.2: 283–304.
Cantor, Joanne, and Mary Beth Oliver (2004), 'Developmental Differences in Responses to Horror', in Stephen C. Prince (ed.), *The Horror Film*, New Brunswick, NJ: Rutgers University Press, pp. 224–41.
Carroll, Joseph (2004), *Literary Darwinism: Evolution, Human Nature, and Literature*, New York; London: Routledge.
Carroll, Joseph (2011), *Reading Human Nature: Literary Darwinism in Theory and Practice*, New York: SUNY Press.
Carroll, Noël (1988), *Mystifying Movies: Fads and Fallacies in Contemporary Film Theory*, New York: Columbia University Press.
Carroll, Noël (1990), *The Philosophy of Horror, or Paradoxes of the Heart*, New York: Routledge.
Cavell, Stanley (1981), *Pursuits of Happiness: The Hollywood Comedy of Remarriage*, Cambridge, MA: Harvard University Press.
Cavell, Stanley (2004), *Cities of Words: Pedagogical Letters on a Register of the Moral Life*, Cambridge, MA: The Belknap Press of Harvard University Press.
Chamorro-Premuzic, Thomas, Andrea Kallias, and Anne Hsu (2014), 'What Type of Movie Person are You? Understanding Individual Differences in Film Preferences and Uses: A Psychographic Approach', in James C. Kaufman and Dean K. Simonton (eds), *The Social Science of Cinema*, Oxford; New York: Oxford Scholarship Online, pp. 87–122.
Chandler, Daniel (1997), 'An Introduction to Genre Theory', *Aberystwyth University Website*, <http://www.aber.ac.uk/media/Documents/intgenre/chandler_genre_theory.pdf> (24 April 2015).
Chion, Michel (1994), *Audio-Vision: Sound on Screen*, trans. Claudia Gorbman, New York: Columbia University Press.
Christakis, Nicholas A., and James H. Fowler (2010), *Connected: The Amazing Power of Social Networks and How They Shape Our Lives*, London: Harper Press.
Clark, Margaret S., and Edward P. Lemay, Jr (2010), 'Close Relationships', in Susan T. Fiske, Daniel T. Gilbert, and Gardner Lindzey (eds), *Handbook of Social Psychology, Volume 2*, fifth edition, Hoboken: John Wiley & Sons, pp. 898–940.
Clark, Margaret S., and Judson Mills (1979), 'Interpersonal Attraction in Exchange and Communal Relationships', *Journal of Personality and Social Psychology* 37.1: 12–24.
Clemmensen, Christian (2009), review of *The 'Burbs*, by Joe Dante et al., *Filmtracks*, 13 July, <http://www.filmtracks.com/titles/burbs.html> (12 December 2016).
Clemmensen, Christian (2012), review of *Parenthood*, by Ron Howard et al., *Filmtracks*, 22 February, <http://www.filmtracks.com/titles/parenthood.html> (3 February 2017).
Cohen, Brett, Gordon Waugh, and Karen Place (1989), 'At the Movies: An Unobtrusive Study of Arousal-Attraction', *Journal of Social Psychology* 129.5: 691–4.

Colarusso, Calvin A. (2011), 'Death, Rejuvenation and Immortality in Film: *On Golden Pond* (1981), *Cat on a Hot Tin Roof* (1958) and *Cocoon* (1985)', *The American Journal of Psychoanalysis* 71.2: 146–61.
Coleman, Stephen, Scott Anthony, and David E. Morrison (2009), *Public Trust in the News: A Constructivist Study of the Social Life of the News*, Oxford: Reuters Institute for the Study of Journalism.
Colson, Elizabeth (1953), *The Makah Indians: A Study of an Indian Tribe in Modern American Society*, Manchester: Manchester University Press.
Connerton, Paul (2008), 'Seven Types of Forgetting', *Memory Studies* 1.1: 59–71.
Conzen, Michael P. (2014), 'Making Urban Wealth: The Primacy of Mercantilism', in Craig E. Colten and Geoffrey L. Buckley (eds), *North American Odyssey: Historical Geographies for the Twenty-first Century*, Lanham; Plymouth: Rowman & Littlefield.
Coon, David R. (2014), *Look Closer: Suburban Narratives and American Values in Film and Television*, New Brunswick, NJ; London: Rutgers University Press.
Coontz, Stephanie (1992), *The Way We Never Were: American Families and the Nostalgia Trap*, New York: Basic Books.
Courrier, Kevin (2005), *Randy Newman's American Dreams*, Toronto: ECW Press.
Covert, Colin (2010), 'Terry Gilliam: "It's Still a Mess, the Way I Work": Terry Gilliam on Working with Heath Ledger, Seeking Movie Financing and Jumping into Massive Snowdrifts while Growing Up in the Twin Cities', *Star Tribune*, 7 January, <http://www.startribune.com/terry-gilliam-it-s-still-a-mess-the-way-i-work/80930892> (26 September 2016).
Crawford, Shelley A., and Nerina J. Caltabiano (2011), 'Promoting Emotional Well-Being through the Use of Humour', *The Journal of Positive Psychology* 6.3: 237–52.
Creed, Barbara (2009), *Darwin's Screens: Evolutionary Aesthetics, Time and Sexual Display in the Cinema*, Melbourne: Melbourne University Publishing.
Crisp, Richard J., and Rhiannon N. Turner (2010), 'Imagining Intergroup Contact Reduces Implicit Prejudice', *British Journal of Social Psychology* 49.1: 129–42.
Csíkszentmihályi, Mihaly [1990] (1991), *Flow: The Psychology of Optimal Experience*, 1st Harper Perennial edition, New York: HarperCollins.
Dabashi, Hamid (2012), *The World of Persian Literary Humanism*, Cambridge, MA: Harvard University Press.
Dai, Hengchen, Katherine L. Milkman, and Jason Riis (2015), 'Put Your Imperfections Behind You: Temporal Landmarks Spur Goal Initiation when they Signal New Beginnings', *Psychological Science* 26.12: 1927–36.
Dal Cin, Sonya, Mark P. Zanna, and Geoffrey T. Fong (2004), 'Narrative Persuasion and Overcoming Resistance', in Eric S. Knowles and Jay A. Linn (eds), *Resistance and Persuasion*, Mahwah: Erlbaum, pp. 175–91.
Darwin, Charles (1898), *The Descent of Man, and Selection in Relation to Sex*, London: John Murray.

Darwin, Charles [1859] (2003), *The Origin of Species*, 150th Anniversary edition, New York: Signet Classics.
Davies, Nick (2008), *Flat Earth News: An Award-Winning Reporter Exposes Falsehood, Distortion and Propaganda in the Global Media*, London: Chatto & Windus.
Davies, Tony (1997), *Humanism*, London: Routledge.
Davis, Mark H. (1983), 'Measuring Individual Differences in Empathy: Evidence for a Multidimensional Approach', *Journal of Personality and Social Psychology* 44.1: 113–26.
Dawson, Jonathan (2013), 'Show Me the Magic: The Adventures of Don McAlpine', *Metro Magazine* 177: 62–3.
Dement, Jeffrey W. (1999), *Going for Broke: The Depiction of Compulsive Gambling in Film*, Lanham: Scarecrow Press.
Denby, David (1989), 'Father Knows Worst', *New Yorker*, 14 August: 79–80.
de Waal, Frans B. M. (2008), 'Putting the Altruism Back into Altruism: The Evolution of Empathy', *Annual Review of Psychology* 59.1: 279–300.
Dewey, John (1958), *Experience and Nature*, Mineola: Dover Publications.
Dickenson, Ben (2006), *Hollywood's New Radicalism: War, Globalisation and the Movies from Reagan to George W. Bush*, London; New York: I. B. Tauris.
Dickins, Thomas E., and Qazi Rahman (2012), 'The Extended Evolutionary Synthesis and the Role of Soft Inheritance in Evolution', *Proceedings: Biological Sciences* 279.1740: 2913–21.
Dickinson, Greg (2015), *Suburban Dreams: Imagining and Building the Good Life*, Tuscaloosa: University of Alabama Press.
Dilthey, Wilhelm (1988), *Introduction to the Human Sciences: An Attempt to Lay a Foundation for the Study of Society and History*, trans. R. J. Betanzos, Detroit: Wayne State University Press.
Dissanayake, Ellen (2000), *Art and Intimacy: How the Arts Began*, Seattle; London: University Press of Washington.
Donaldson, Lucy Fife (2014), *Texture in Film*, Basingstoke: Palgrave Macmillan.
Douglas, Mary (1991), 'The Idea of a Home: A Kind of Space', *Social Research* 58.1: 287–307.
Dunbar, Robin (1996), *Grooming, Gossip and the Evolution of Language*, London: Faber and Faber.
Duncan, Margaret C., and Lori A. Klos (2014), 'Paradoxes of the Flesh: Emotion and Contradiction in Fitness/Beauty Magazine Discourse', *Journal of Sport & Social Issues* 38.3: 245–62.
Durkheim, Émile (1893), *The Division of Labor in Society*, Paris: Alcan.
Dutton, Dennis (2009), *The Art Instinct: Beauty, Pleasure, & Human Evolution*, New York: Oxford University Press.
Eagleton, Terry (1983), *Literary Theory: An Introduction*, Oxford: Blackwell.
Easton, Nina J. (1989), 'For Hollywood, It's All in the Family. Ron Howard's *Parenthood* Reflects the Movies' Latest Discovery: Kids and Families', *Los Angeles Times*, 30 July: 5.

Ebert, Roger (1989), review of *Parenthood*, by Ron Howard et al., *Rogerebert. com*, 2 August, <http://www.rogerebert.com/reviews/parenthood-1989> (2 February 2017).
Eitzen, Dirk (1995), 'When Is a Documentary?: Documentary as a Mode of Reception', *Cinema Journal* 35.1: 81–102.
Ekers, Michael, Pierre Hamel, and Roger Keil (2015), 'Governing Suburbia: Modalities and Mechanisms of Suburban Governance', in Pierre Hamel and Roger Keil (eds), *Suburban Governance: A Global View*, Toronto; Buffalo; London: University of Toronto Press, 19–48.
Ekman, Paul (1992), 'Are There Basic Emotions?' *Psychological Review* 99.3: 550–3.
Elias, Norbert, and Eric Dunning (1970), 'The Quest for Excitement in Unexciting Societies', in Günther Lüschen (ed.), *The Cross-Cultural Analysis of Sport and Games*, Champaign: Stipes, pp. 31–51.
Ellis, Jack C. (2000), *John Grierson: Life, Contributions, Influence*, Carbondale; Edwardsville: Southern Illinois University Press.
Elsaesser, Thomas (2009), 'The Mind-Game Film', in Warren Buckland (ed.), *Puzzle Films: Complex Storytelling in Contemporary Cinema*, London: Wiley-Blackwell: pp. 13–41.
Erikson, Erik H. [1950] (1977), *Childhood and Society*, London: Paladin Books.
Evans, Dylan (2001), *Emotion: The Science of Sentiment*, New York: Oxford University Press.
Everett, Wendy (2005) 'Fractal Films and the Architecture of Complexity', *Studies in European Cinema* 2.3: 159–71.
Fechner, Gustav T. (1876), *Vorschule der Aesthetik*, Leipzig: Breitkoff & Hartel.
Felperin, Leslie (1997), 'Close to the Edge', *Sight & Sound* 7.10: 15–18.
Felski, Rita (2008), *Uses of Literature*. Oxford: Blackwell.
Fishman, Robert (1987), *Bourgeois Utopias: The Rise and Fall of Suburbia*, New York: Basic Books.
Fivush, Robyn, Catherine A. Haden, and Elaine Reese (2006), 'Elaborating on Elaborations: Role of Maternal Reminiscing Style in Cognitive and Socioemotional Development', *Child Development* 77.6: 1568–88.
Fivush, Robyn, Jennifer G. Bohanek, and Widaad Zaman (2011), 'Personal and Intergenerational Narratives in Relation to Adolescents' Well-Being', *New Directions for Child and Adolescent Development* 131: 45–57.
Foucault, Michel [1984] (1986), 'Of Other Spaces', trans. Jay Miskowiec, *Diacritics* 16.1: 22–7.
Fraigneau, Andrew, and Jean Cocteau (1967), 'Dialogues with Cocteau', *Film Makers on Film Making: Statements on their Art by Thirty Directors*, in Harry M. Geduld (ed.), Harmondsworth: Penguin Books, 149–61.
Frank, Arthur W. (2010), *Letting Stories Breathe: A Socio-Narratology*, Chicago: University of Chicago Press.
Frank, Robert H. (2011), *The Darwin Economy: Liberty, Competition, and the Common Good*, Princeton: Princeton University Press.

Freedman, Samuel G. (1999), 'Suburbia Outgrows Its Image in the Arts', *New York Times, Section Two*, 28 February: 2.1.

Freilich, Robert H., Robert J. Sitkowski, and Seth D. Mennillo (2010), *From Sprawl to Sustainability: Smart Growth, New Urbanism, Green Development*, Chicago: American Bar Association.

Freud, Sigmund (1900), *The Interpretation of Dreams*, Leipzig: Franz Deuticke.

Freud, Sigmund [1905] (1960), *Jokes and Their Relation to the Unconscious*, trans. James Strachey, London: Routledge & Kegan Paul.

Frost, Joe, and Paul J. Jacobs (1995), 'Play Deprivation: A Factor in Juvenile Violence', *Dimensions of Early Childhood* 23.3: 14–20.

Frow, John (2007), 'Reproducibles, Rubrics, and Everything You Need: Genre Theory Today', *PMLA* 122.5: 1626–34.

Frow, John (2012), 'Avatar, Identification, Pornography', *Cultural Studies Review* 18.3: 360–80.

Fudge, Erica (2002), *Perceiving Animals: Humans and Beasts in Early Modern English Culture*, Champaign: University of Illinois Press.

Fukuyama, Francis (1989), 'The End of History?' *The National Interest*, Summer: 3–18.

Gabbard, Glen O. (1993), 'On Hate in Love Relationships: The Narcissism of Minor Differences Revisited', *The Psychoanalytic Quarterly* 62.2: 229–38.

Gadamer, Hans-Georg (1986), 'The Play of Art', in Robert Bernasconi (ed.), *The Relevance of the Beautiful and Other Essays*, Cambridge: Cambridge University Press, 123–30.

Gallese, Vittorio (2007), 'Before and Below "Theory of Mind": Embodied Simulation and the Neural Correlates of Social Cognition', *Philosophical Transactions of the Royal Society B: Biological Sciences* 362.1480: 659–69.

Gallese, Vittorio (2010), 'Mirror Neurons and Art', in F. Bacci and D. Melcher, (eds), *Art and the Senses*, Oxford: Oxford University Press, pp. 441–9.

Gallese, Vittorio, and Michele Guerra (2012), 'Embodying Movies: Embodied Simulation and Film Studies', *Cinema: Journal of Philosophy and the Moving Image* 3: 183–210.

Gallese, Vittorio, and Maxim Stamenov (eds) (2002), *Mirror Neurons and the Evolution of Brain and Language*, Amsterdam: John Benjamins.

Gardner, Cristine (1994), 'Humanism in the Narrative Voice', *Anthropology and Humanism* 19.2: 166–8.

Gehring, Wes D. (1995), *Populism and the Capra Legacy*, Westport: Greenwood Press.

Van Gennep, Arnold (1909), *Les rites de passage*, Paris: Émile Nourry.

Gerbner, George, and Larry Gross (1976), 'Living with Television: The Violence Profile', *Journal of Communication* 26.2: 172–94.

Gerbner, George, Larry Gross, Michael Morgan, and Nancy Signorielli (1994), 'Growing Up with Television: The Cultivation Perspective', in Jennings Bryant

and Dolf Zillmann (eds), *Media Effects: Advances in Theory and Research*, Hillsdale: Lawrence Erlbaum Associates, pp. 17–41.
Gilbert, Daniel T., Douglas S. Krull, and Patrick S. Malone (1990), 'Unbelieving the Unbelievable: Some Problems in the Rejection of False Information', *Journal of Personality and Social Psychology* 59.4: 601–13.
Giles, Howard, and Philip M. Smith (1979), 'Accommodation Theory: Optimal Levels of Convergence', in Howard Giles and Robert N. St. Clair (eds), *Language and Social Psychology*, Oxford: Basil Blackwell, pp. 45–65.
Gluckman, Max (1963), 'Papers in Honor of Melville J. Herskovits: Gossip and Scandal', *Current Anthropology* 4.3: 307–16.
Godfrey, Nicholas (2011), 'Going Through the Neighbourhood with Your Eyes Open: An Interview with John Sayles', *Metro Magazine: Media & Education Magazine* 170: 98–102.
Goldstein, Jeffrey H. (1975), *Aggression and Crimes of Violence*, New York: Oxford University Press.
Goodman, Lenn E. (2003), *Islamic Humanism*, New York: Oxford University Press.
Gorbman, Claudia (2011), 'Artless Singing', *Music, Sound, and the Moving Image* 5.2: 157–72.
Grabowski, Michael (2014), 'Resignation and Positive Thinking in the Working-Class Family Sitcom', *Atlantic Journal of Communication* 22.2: 124–37.
Graeber, David (2011), *Debt: The First 5,000 Years*, New York: Melville House Printing.
Graham, Aislin R., Simon B. Sherry, Sherry H. Stewart, Dayna L. Sherry, Daniel S. McGrath, Kristin M. Fossum, and Stephanie L. Allen (2010), 'The Existential Model of Perfectionism and Depressive Symptoms: A Short-Term, Four-Wave Longitudinal Study', *Journal of Counseling Psychology* 57.4: 423–38.
Greenberg, Melanie A, Camille B. Wortman, and Arthur A. Stone (1996), 'Emotional Expression and Physical Health: Revising Traumatic Memories or Fostering Self-Regulation?' *Journal of Personality and Social Psychology* 71.3: 588–602.
Greenwood, Dara N., and Christopher R. Long (2009a), 'Mood Specific Media Use and Emotion Regulation: Patterns and Individual Differences', *Individual Differences* 46.5: 616–21.
Greenwood, Dara N., and Christopher R. Long (2009b), 'Psychological Predictors of Media Involvement: Solitude Experiences and the Need to Belong', *Communication Research* 36.5: 637–54.
Greimas, Algirdas Julien, Joseph Courtés, and Michael Rengstorf (1989), 'The Cognitive Dimension of Narrative Discourse', *New Literary History* 20.3: 563–79.
Griffiths, Huw (2013), 'The Lecture as Theatre: Learning the Boundaries of Scepticism in *The Winter's Tale*', in Kate Flaherty, Penny Gay, and L. E. Semler

(eds), *Teaching Shakespeare Beyond the Centre: Australasian Perspectives*, Basingstoke: Palgrave Macmillan, pp. 87–96.

Grodal, Torben (2009), *Embodied Visions: Evolution, Emotion, Culture, and Film*, New York: Oxford University Press.

Grosz, Elizabeth (2005), *Time Travels: Feminism, Nature, Power*, Durham, NC: Duke University Press.

Gunning, Tom (2000), 'The Cinema of Attraction: Early Film, Its Spectator, and the Avant-Garde', in Toby Miller and Robert Stam (eds), *Film and Theory: An Anthology*, Oxford: Blackwell, pp. 229–35.

Habermas, Tilmann, and Susan Bluck (2000), 'Getting a Life: The Emergence of the Life Story in Adolescence', *Psychological Bulletin* 126.5: 748–69.

Haidt, Jonathan (2012), *The Righteous Mind: Why Good People are Divided By Politics and Religion*, New York: Pantheon Books.

Halbwachs, Maurice (1950), *The Collective Memory [La mémoire collective]*, Paris: Presses Universitaires de France.

Hamad, Hannah (2013), 'Hollywood Fatherhood: Paternal Postfeminism in Contemporary Popular Cinema', in Joel Gwynne and Nadine Müller (eds), *Postfeminism and Contemporary Hollywood Cinema*, New York: Palgrave Macmillan, pp. 99–115.

Hames, Jennifer L., Jessica D. Ribeiro, April R. Smith, and Thomas E. Joiner (2012), 'An Urge to Jump Affirms the Urge to Live: An Empirical Examination of the High Place Phenomenon', *Journal of Affective Disorders* 136.3: 1114–20.

Haneke, Michael (1992), 'Film als Katharsis', in Francesco Bono (ed.), *Austria (in)felix: zum österreichischem Film der 80er Jahre*, Graz: Edition Blimp.

Hannagan, Rebecca J. (2008), 'Gendered Political Behavior: A Darwinian Feminist Approach', *Sex Roles* 59.7–8: 465–75.

Haraway, Donna (1991), 'A Cyborg Manifesto: Science, Technology, and Socialist-Feminism in the Late Twentieth Century', *Simians, Cyborgs and Women: The Reinvention of Nature*, New York: Routledge, 149–81.

Hardt, Michael, and Antonio Negri (2008), *Reflections on Empire*, Cambridge: Polity Press.

Harmon, Mark D. (2006), 'Affluenza: A World Values Test', *International Communication Gazette* 68.2: 119–30.

Harvey, David (2013), *Rebel Cities: From the Right to the City to the Urban Revolution*, New York; London: Verso.

Haskell, Molly (1987), *From Reverence to Rape: The Treatment of Women in the Movies*, Chicago: University of Chicago Press.

Hasson, Uri, Ohad Landesman, Barbara Knappmeyer, Ignacio Vallines, Nava Rubin, and David J. Heeger (2008), 'Neurocinematics: The Neuroscience of Film', *Projections* 2.1: 1–26.

Hatfield, Elaine, John T. Cacioppo, and Richard L. Rapson (1993), 'Emotional Contagion', *Current Directions in Psychological Sciences* 2.3: 96–9.

Hayden, Dolores (2003), *Building Suburbia: Green Fields and Urban Growth, 1820–2000*, New York: Vintage Books.
Heider, Fritz, and Marianne Simmel (1944), 'An Experimental Study of Apparent Behavior', *The American Journal of Psychology* 57.2: 243–59.
Hentzi, Gary (2000), review of *American Beauty*, by Sam Mendes et al., *Film Quarterly* 54.2: 46–50.
Herman, David (2013), 'Cognitive Narratology', in *The Living Handbook of Narratology*, 13 March, <http://wikis.sub.uni-hamburg.de/lhn/index.php/Cognitive_Narratology> (8 September 2016).
Herpertz, Sabine C., and Henning Sass (2000), 'Emotional Deficiency and Psychopathy', *Behavioral Sciences & the Law* 18.5: 567–80.
Herskovits, Melville J. (1937), *Life in a Haitian Valley*, New York: Knopf.
Herskovits, Melville J. (1947), *Trinidad Village*, New York: Knopf.
Higgins, E. Tory, and William S. Rholes (1978), '"Saying is Believing": Effects of Message Modification on Memory and Liking for the Person Described', *Journal of Experimental Social Psychology* 14.4: 363–78.
Hirst, William, Alin Coman, and Dora Coman (2014), 'Putting the Social Back into Human Memory', in Timothy J. Perfect and D. Stephen Lindsay (eds), *The Sage Handbook of Applied Memory*, Washington, DC: Sage, pp. 273–91.
Hjort, Mette (2014), 'Community Engagement and Film: Toward the Pursuit of Ethical Goals through Applied Research on Moving Images', in Jinhee Choi and Mattias Frey (eds), *Cine-Ethics: Ethical Dimensions of Film Theory, Practice, and Spectatorship*, London: Routledge, pp. 195–213.
Hobbs, Frank, and Nicole Stoops (2002), *Demographic Trends in the 20th Century*, Washington, DC: US Census Bureau.
Hoffman, Martin L. (1981), 'Perspectives on the Difference Between Understanding People and Understanding Things: The Role of Affect', in John H. Flavell and Lee Ross (eds), *Social Cognitive Development: Frontiers and Possible Futures*, Cambridge: Cambridge University Press, pp. 67–81.
Holden, Stephen (1990), 'Problems (In Toto) Of Being Parents', *New York Times: Late Edition East Coast*, 11 February: 234.
Holland, Mary K. (2013), *Succeeding Postmodernism: Language and Humanism in Contemporary American Literature*, New York; London: Bloomsbury.
Hood, Nathanael (2015), review of *Black or White*, by Mike Binder et al., *The Young Folks*, 30 January, <http://theyoungfolks.com/review/movie-review-black-or-white/47442> (2 February 2016).
hooks, bell [1996] (2009), *Reel to Real: Race, Sex and Class at the Movies*, New York: Routledge.
Horn, John, and Lisa Cholodenko (2010), '*The Kids Are All Right* is an appropriate opener for the Los Angeles Film Festival', *Los Angeles Times*, 17 June, <http://articles.latimes.com/2010/jun/17/entertainment/la-et-kids-20100617> (22 July 2014).

Howard, June (1999), 'What Is Sentimentality?' *American Literary History* 11.1: 63–81.
Howard, Ron (2003), 'Production Notes', *Parenthood*, dir. Ron Howard, 1989, Region 2, 4 DVD, Universal Studios.
Hsu, Hsuan L. (2006), 'Racial Privacy, the L.A. Ensemble Film, and Paul Haggis's *Crash*', *Film Criticism* 31.1/2: 132–56.
Hühn, Peter et al. (2013), *The Living Handbook of Narratology*, Hamburg: Hamburg University Press, <hup.sub.uni-hamburg.de/lhn>.
Huizinga, Johan (1944), *Homo Ludens: A Study of the Play-Element In Culture*, Switzerland: Routledge.
Hume, David (1757), 'Of Tragedy', *Four Dissertations*, London: A. Millar, in the Strand, pp. 193–209.
Hunter, Albert (1987), 'The Symbolic Ecology of Suburbia', in Irwin Altman and Abraham Wandersman (eds), *Neighborhood and Community Environments*, New York: Plenium Press, pp. 191–221.
Huntsinger, Jeffrey R. (2013), 'Affective Incoherence Reduces Reliance on Activated Stereotypes', *Social Cognition* 31.3: 405–16.
Huron, David (2011), 'Why is Sad Music Pleasurable? A Possible Role for Prolactin', *Musicae Scientiae* 15.2: 146–58.
Husserl, Edmund (1962), *Ideas: General Introduction to Pure Phenomenology*, New York: Collier.
Hutcheon, Linda [1994] (2003), *Irony's Edge: The Theory and Politics of Irony*, London and New York: Routledge.
Hynds, Susan D. (1985), 'Interpersonal Cognitive Complexity and the Literary Response Processes of Adolescent Readers', *Research in the Teaching of English* 19.4: 386–402.
Ingemark, Camilla Asplund (ed.) (2013), *Therapeutic Uses of Storytelling: An Interdisciplinary Approach to Narration as Therapy*, Lund: Nordic Academic Press.
Ingold, Tim (2014), 'That's Enough About Ethnography!' *Hau: Journal of Ethnographic Theory* 4.1: 383–95.
Jablonka, Eva, and Marion J. Lamb. (2005), *Evolution in Four Dimensions: Genetic, Epigenetic, Behavioral, and Symbolic Variation in the History of Life*, Cambridge: MIT Press.
Jackson, Kenneth T. (1985), *Crabgrass Frontier: The Suburbanization of the United States*, New York: Oxford University Press.
Jackson, Michael D. (1995), *At Home in the World*, New York; London; Toronto; Sydney: Harper Perennial.
Jahn-Sudmann, Andreas, and Ralf Stockmann (eds) (2008), *Computer Games as a Sociocultural Phenomenon: Games Without Frontiers, War Without Tears*, Basingstoke: Palgrave Macmillan.
Jamison, Kay Redfield [1993] (1996), *Touched with Fire: Manic-Depressive Illness and the Artistic Temperament Paperback*, reissue edition, New York: The Free Press.

Jarvie, Ian (1999), 'Is Analytic Philosophy the Cure for Film Theory?' *Philosophy of the Social Sciences* 29.3: 416–40.
Jarvie, Ian (2007), 'Relativism and Historicism', in S. P Turner and M. W. Risjord (eds), *Philosophy of Anthropology and Sociology*, Amsterdam; Oxford: North-Holland, pp. 553–89.
Jenkins, Henry (2006), *Convergence Culture: Where Old and New Media Collide*, New York: New York University Press.
Johnson, Daniel B. (1982), 'Altruistic Behavior and the Development of the Self in Infants', *Merrill-Palmer Quarterly* 28.3: 379–88.
Johnston, Deirdre D. (1995), 'Adolescents' Motivations for Viewing Graphic Horror', *Human Communication Research* 21.4: 522–52.
Joyce, Richard (2006), *The Evolution of Morality*, Cambridge, MA; London: The MIT Press.
Jung, Jaehee, and Yoon-Jung Lee (2009), 'Cross-Cultural Examination of Women's Fashion and Beauty Magazine Advertisements in the United States and South Korea', *Clothing and Textiles Research Journal* 27.4: 274–86.
Jurca, Catherine (2001), *White Diaspora: The Suburb and the Twentieth-Century American Novel*, Princeton: Princeton University Press.
Karlyn, Kathleen Rowe (2004), 'Too Close for Comfort: *American Beauty* and the Incest Motif', *Cinema Journal* 44.1: 69–93.
Katz, Phyllis A., and Sue R. Zalk (1978), 'Modification of Children's Racial Attitudes', *Developmental Psychology* 14.5: 447–61.
Kellner, Douglas (1995), *Media Culture: Cultural Studies, Identity and Politics Between the Modern and the Postmodern*, London: Routledge.
Kempley, Rita (1989), review of *Parenthood*, by Ron Howard et al., *The Washington Post*, 2 August: D1.
Keyes, Corey L. M., Dov Shmotkin, and Carol D. Ryff (2002), 'Optimizing Well-Being: The Empirical Encounter of Two Traditions', *Journal of Personality and Social Psychology* 82.6: 1007–22.
Keyser, Cassius Jacskon (1931), *Humanism and Science*, New York: Columbia University Press.
King, Geoff (2009), *Indiewood, USA: Where Hollywood meets Independent Cinema*, London; New York: I. B. Tauris.
King, Geoff (2014), *Indie 2.0: Change and Continuity in Contemporary American Indie Film*, London; New York: I. B. Tauris.
Kozloff, Sarah (2000), *Overhearing Film Dialogue*, Berkley: University Press of California.
Kunstler, James Howard (2004), 'The Ghastly Tragedy of the Suburbs', *TED*, February, <http://www.ted.com/talks/james_howard_kunstler_dissects_suburbia/transcript?language=en#t-158164 > (13 January 2015).
Kupfer, Joseph H. (1999), *Visions of Virtue in Popular Film*, Boulder: Westview Press.
Lakin, Jessica L., Valerie E. Jefferis, Clara Michelle Cheng, and Tanya L. Chartrand (2003), 'The Chameleon Effect as Social Glue: Evidence for the

Evolutionary Significance of Nonconscious Mimicry', *Journal of Nonverbal Behavior* 27.3: 145–62.

Lamarck, Jean Baptiste (1914), *Zoological Philosophy: An Exposition with Regard to the Natural History of Animals*, trans. H. Elliot, London: Macmillan.

Lamarque, Peter (2007), 'On the Distance between Literary Narratives and Real-Life Narratives', *Royal Institute of Philosophy Supplements* 60, 117–32.

Lamb, Charles M. (2005), *Housing Segregation in Suburban America since 1960: Presidential and Judicial Politics*, Cambridge: Cambridge University Press.

Landy, Joshua (2011), 'Still Life in a Narrative Age: Charlie Kaufman's *Adaptation*', *Critical Inquiry* 37.3, 497–514.

Lauretis, Teresa de (1985), 'Aesthetic and Feminist Theory: Rethinking Women's Cinema', *New German Critique* 34.34: 154–75.

Laurie, Timothy (2015), 'Becoming-Animal Is a Trap for Humans: Deleuze and Guattari in Madagascar', in Jon Roffe and Hannah Stark (eds), *Deleuze and the Non/Human*, Basingstoke; New York: Palgrave Macmillan, pp. 142–62.

Lee, Barrett A., and Peter B. Wood (1991), 'Is Neighborhood Racial Succession Place-Specific?' *Demography* 28.1: 21–40.

Lefebvre, Henri (1968), *The Right to the City*, Paris: Anthropos.

Lefkowitz, Monroe, Robert R. Blake, and Jane Srygley Mouton (1955), 'Status Factors in Pedestrian Violation of Traffic Signals', *Journal of Abnormal and Social Psychology* 51.3: 704–6.

Leinberger, Christopher B. (2008), 'The Next Slum?', *The Atlantic*, March, 70–2, 74–5.

Levell, Nicola (2015), *The Seriousness of Play: The Art of Michael Nicoll Yahgulanaas*, London: Black Dog Publishing.

Levitin, Daniel J. (2006), *This Is Your Brain on Music: The Science of a Human Obsession*, New York: Dutton.

Lichter, John H., and David W. Johnson (1969), 'Changes in Attitudes toward Negroes of White Elementary School Students After Use of Multiethnic Readers', *Journal of Educational Psychology* 60.2: 148–52.

Liebowitz, Flo (1996), 'Apt Feelings, or Why "Women's Films" Aren't Trivial', in David Bordwell and Noel Carroll (eds), *Post-Theory: Reconstructing Film Studies*, Madison: University of Wisconsin Press, 219–29.

Littrell, Jill (1998), 'Is the Reexperience of Painful Emotion Therapeutic?' *Clinical Psychology Review* 18.1: 71–102.

Littrell, Jill (2009), 'Expression of Emotion: When It Causes Trauma and When It Helps', *Journal of Evidence-Based Social Work* 6.3: 300–20.

Long, Christopher R., and Dara N. Greenwood (2013), 'Joking in the Face of Death: A Terror Management Approach to Humor Production', *Humor* 26.4: 493–509.

Lorenz, Amanda R., and Joseph P. Newman (2002), 'Deficient Response Modulation and Emotion Processing in Low-Anxious Caucasian Psychopathic Offenders: Results from a Lexical Decision Task', *Emotion* 2.2: 91–104.

Loukides, Paul (1991), 'The Celebration of Family Plot: Episodes and Affirmations', in Paul Loukides and Linda K. Fuller (eds), *Beyond the Stars: Plot Conventions in American Popular Film*, Bowling Green: Bowling Green State University Popular Press, pp. 91–9.

Love, Ashley B., and Mark D. Holder (2014), 'Psychopathy and Subjective Well-Being', *Personality and Individual Differences* 66: 112–17.

Macek, Steve (2006), *Urban Nightmares: The Media, the Right, and the Moral Panic over the City*, Minneapolis: University of Minnesota Press.

Maner, Jon K., Carol L. Luce, Steven L. Neuberg, Robert B. Cialdini, Stephanie Brown, and Brad J. Sagarin (2002), 'The Effects of Perspective Taking on Motivations for Helping: Still No Evidence for Altruism', *Personality and Social Psychology Bulletin* 28.11: 1601–10.

Manin, Bernard (1997), *The Principles of Representative Government*, Cambridge: Cambridge University Press.

Mar, Raymond A., and Keith Oatley (2008), 'The Function of Fiction is the Abstraction and Simulation of Social Experience', *Perspectives on Psychological Science* 3.3: 173–92.

Margulis, Elizabeth Hellmuth (2014), 'One More Time: Why We Love Repetition in Music', *Aeon*, 7 March, <http://aeon.co/magazine/culture/why-we-love-repetition-in-music> (13 February 2015).

Marks, Peter (2009), *Terry Gilliam*, Manchester; New York: Manchester University Press.

Massey, Douglas S., and Nancy A. Denton (1987), 'Trends in the Residential Segregation of Blacks, Hispanics, and Asians: 1970–1980', *American Sociological Review* 52.6: 802–25.

Mathijs, Ernest (2011), 'Referential Acting and the Ensemble Cast', *Screen* 52.1: 89–96.

Mauss, Marcel [1925] (1966), *The Gift: Forms and Functions of Exchange in Archaic Societies*, trans. Ian Cunnison, London: Cohen & West.

May, Elaine Tyler (2008), *Homeward Bound: American Families in the Cold War Era*, New York: Basic Books.

Maxfield, Molly, Samantha John, and Tom Pyszczynski (2014), 'A Terror Management Perspective on the Role of Death-Related Anxiety in Psychological Dysfunction', *The Humanistic Psychologist* 42.1: 35–53.

McAdams, Dan P. (2006), 'The Redemptive Self: Generativity and the Stories Americans Live By', *Research in Human Development* 3.2: 81–100.

McCabe, Earl, and Lauren Berlant (2011), 'Depressive Realism: An Interview with Lauren Berlant', *Hypocrite Reader*, 5 June, <http://hypocritereader.com/5/depressive-realism> (2 July 2014).

McDonnell, Andrea (2014), *Reading Celebrity Gossip Magazines*, Hoboken: Wiley.

McFadden, George (1982), *Discovering the Comic*, Princeton: Princeton University Press.

McGraw, Peter (2014), 'Benign Violation Theory', *Humor Research Lab*, <http://leeds-faculty.colorado.edu/mcgrawp/Benign_Violation_Theory.html> (25 November 2014).
McGraw, Peter, and Joel Warner (2014), *The Humor Code*, New York: Simon & Schuster.
McGraw, Peter, and Caleb Warren (2010), 'Benign Violations', *Psychological Science* 21.8: 1141–9.
McHugh, Kathleen Anne (1999), *American Domesticity: From How-to Manual to Hollywood Melodrama*, New York: Oxford University Press.
McKee, Alan (2012), 'Pornography as Entertainment', *Continuum* 26.4: 541–52.
McKee, Seth C., and Daron R. Shaw (2003), 'Suburban Voting in Presidential Elections', *Presidential Studies Quarterly* 33.1: 125–44.
Meeten, F., S. R. Dash, A. L. S. Scarlet, and G. C. L. Davey (2012), 'Investigating the Effect of Intolerance of Uncertainty on Catastrophic Worrying and Mood', *Behaviour Research and Therapy* 50.11: 690–8.
Mendel, Gregor (1901), 'Experiments in Plant Hybridization', trans. C. T Druery and W. Bateson, *Journal of the Royal Horticultural Society* 26, 1–32.
Menocal, María Rosa (1987), *The Arabic Role in Medieval Literary History: A Forgotten Heritage*, Philadelphia: University of Pennsylvania Press.
Meretoja, Hanna (2017), *The Ethics of Storytelling: Narrative Hermeneutics, History, and the Possible*, New York: Oxford University Press.
Mesce, Bill (no date), 'Myth #5: Show Don't Tell', *Shore Scripts*, <https://www.shorescripts.com/screenwriting-myth-5-show-dont-tell> (15 September 2016).
Millard, Kathryn (1994), 'Beyond the Pale: Colour and the Suburb', in Chris Healy and Chris McAuliffe (eds.), *Beasts of Suburbia: Reinterpreting Cultures in Australian Suburbs*, Melbourne: Melbourne University Press.
Miller, D. A. (2010) 'Hitchcock's Hidden Pictures', *Critical Inquiry* 37.1: 106–30.
Miller, Lulu, and Alix Spiegel (2015), 'The Secret History of Thoughts', *Invisibilia. NPR. Natl Public Radio*, 9 January, <http://www.npr.org/programs/invisibilia/375927143/the-secret-history-of-thoughts> (19 November 2018).
Mintz, Steven (2003), 'The Family', in Peter C. Rollins (ed.), *The Columbia Companion to American History on Film*, New York: Columbia University Press, pp. 352–62.
Misek, Richard (2010), 'Dead Time: Cinema, Heidegger, and Boredom', *Continuum* 24.5: 777–85.
Moalem, Sharon, and Peter Satonick (2007), *Survival of the Sickest: The Surprising Connections Between Disease and Longevity*, New York: William Morrow.
Monbiot, George (2016), 'The Man in the Mirror', *Monbiot.com*, 28 October, <http://www.monbiot.com/2016/10/28/the-man-in-the-mirror> (10 November 2016).
Montaigne, Michel de (1910), *Essays of Montaigne, vol. 4*, trans. C. Cotton, rev. W. Carew Hazlett, New York: Edwin C. Hill.

Morreall, John (2009), *Comic Relief: A Comprehensive Philosophy of Humor*, Chichester; Malden: Wiley-Blackwell.

Morrison, Murray D., and Linda A. Rammage (1993), 'Muscle Misuse Voice Disorders: Description and Classification', *Acta oto-laryngologica* 113.3: 428–34.

Moss-Wellington, Wyatt (2015), 'Humanist Ethics in John Sayles's *Casa de los Babys*', *Film International* 13.1: 105–21.

Moss-Wellington, Wyatt (2016), 'Our Suburban Contempt', *Overland*, 23 November, <https://overland.org.au/2016/11/our-suburban-contempt> (23 November 2016).

Moss-Wellington, Wyatt (2017), 'Affecting Profundity: Cognitive and Moral Dissonance in Lynch, Loach, Linklater, and Sayles', *Projections* 11.1: 38–62.

Moss-Wellington, Wyatt (2018), 'Abject Humanism in Tom Perrotta Adaptations: *Election* and *Little Children*', *Sydney Studies in English* 43: 88–107.

Mousley, Andy (2007), *Re-Humanising Shakespeare: Literary Humanism, Wisdom and Modernity*, Edinburgh: Edinburgh University Press.

Mujica-Parodi, Lilianne R., Helmut H. Strey, Blaise Frederick, Robert Savoy, and David Cox (2009), 'Chemosensory Cues to Conspecific Emotional Stress Activate Amygdala in Humans: e6415', *PLoS One* 4.7: 1–14.

Müller, Hans-Peter (1994), 'Social Differentiation and Organic Solidarity: The "Division of Labor" Revisited', *Sociological Forum* 9.1: 73–86.

Murdock, George P. (1945), 'The Common Denominator of Cultures', in Ralph Linton (ed.), *The Science of Man in the World Crisis*, New York: Columbia University Press, 123–42.

Myers, David G., and Helmut Lamm (1976), 'The Group Polarization Phenomenon', *Psychological Bulletin* 83.4: 602–27.

Narvaez, Darcia (2002), 'Does Reading Moral Stories Build Character?' *Educational Psychology Review* 14.2: 155–71.

Nayak, Alpana, Takeo Ohno, Tohru Tsuruoka, Kazuya Terabe, Tsuyoshi Hasegawa, James K. Gimzewski, and Masakazu Aono. (2012), 'Controlling the Synaptic Plasticity of a Cu2S Gap-Type Atomic Switch', *Advanced Functional Materials* 22.17: 3606–13.

Neill, Alex (2006), 'Empathy and (Film) Fiction', in Noël Carroll and Jinhee Choi (eds), *Philosophy of Film and Motion Pictures: An Anthology*, Malden: Blackwell, 247–59.

Nelson, Katherine (2003), 'Self and Social Functions: Individual Autobiographical Memory and Collective Narrative', *Memory* 11.2: 125–36.

Newman, Michael Z. (2006), 'Character and Complexity in American Independent Cinema: *21 Grams* and *Passion Fish*', *Film Criticism* 31.1/2: 89–106.

Niethammer, Friedrich Immanuel (1808), *Der Streit des Philanthropinismus und Humanismus in der Theorie des Erziehungs-Unterrichts unsrer Zeit (The Dispute between Philanthropinism and Humanism in the Educational Theory of our Time)*, Jena: F. Frommann.

Noonan, Jeff (2003), *Critical Humanism and the Politics of Difference*, Montreal: McGill-Queen's University Press.
Novak, Ralph (1989), review of *Parenthood*, by Ron Howard et al. *People*, August: 17.
Nussbaum, Martha (2002), 'Education for Citizenship in an Era of Global Connection', *Studies in Philosophy and Education* 21.4: 289–303.
Oatley, Keith (2008), 'The Science of Fiction', *New Scientist* 198.2662: 42–3.
Oliver, Mary Beth (1993), 'Exploring the Paradox of the Enjoyment of Sad Films', *Human Communication Research* 19.3: 315–42.
Oliver, Mary Beth, and Arthur A. Raney (2011), 'Entertainment as Pleasurable and Meaningful: Identifying Hedonic and Eudaimonic Motivations for Entertainment Consumption.' *Journal of Communication* 61.5: 984–1004.
Oliver, Mary Beth, and Meghan Sanders (2004), 'The Appeal of Horror and Suspense', in Stephen Prince (ed.), *The Horror Film*, New Brunswick, NJ: Rutgers University Press, 242–59.
Olsen, Mark (1999), 'If I Can Dream: The Everlasting Boyhoods of Wes Anderson', *Film Comment* 35.1: 12–17.
O'Neal, Edgar C., and S. Levi Taylor (1989), 'Status of the Provoker, Opportunity to Retaliate, and Interest in Video Violence', *Aggressive Behavior* 15.2: 171–80.
Orndorf, Brian (2009), 'Reliving the Summer of 1989 Diary – Week Eleven', *Brianorndorf.com*, 4 August, <http://www.brianorndorf.com/2009/08/reliving-the-summer-of-1989-diary-week-eleven.html> (2 February 2017).
Osborne, David (1982), 'John Sayles: From Hoboken to Hollywood – and Back', *American Film*: 31–6.
Osteen, Mark (ed.) (2002), *The Question of the Gift: Essays Across Disciplines*, New York: Routledge.
Palen, J. John (1995), *The Suburbs*, New York: McGraw-Hill.
Palmer, Alan (2004), *Fictional Minds*, Lincoln: University of Nebraska Press.
Parker, Sue Taylor, and Michael L. McKinney (1999), *Origins of Intelligence: The Evolution of Cognitive Development in Monkeys, Apes, and Humans*, Baltimore: Johns Hopkins University Press.
Parry, Jonathan (1986), 'The Gift, the Indian Gift and the "Indian Gift"', *Man* 21.3: 453–73.
Patrick, Christopher J. (1994), 'Emotion and Psychopathy: Startling New Insights', *Psychophysiology* 31.4: 319–30.
Payne, Alexander (2004), 'Declaration of Independents', *Daily Variety*, September 7: S7.
Peel, Mark (2007), 'The Inside Story of Life on the Outer', *The Age*, 16 September, <http://www.theage.com.au/news/in-depth/the-inside-story-of-life-on-the-outer/2007/09/15/1189277037851.html?page=fullpage> (9 February 2015).
Pennebaker, James W., and Sandra Klihr Beall, 'Confronting a Traumatic Event: Toward an Understanding of Inhibition and Disease', *Journal of Abnormal Psychology* 95.3: 274–81.

Pennebaker, James W., and Anna Graybeal (2001), 'Patterns of Natural Language Use: Disclosure, Personality, and Social Integration', *Current Directions in Psychological Science* 10.3: 90–3.
Pepperell, Robert (2003), *The Posthuman Condition: Consciousness Beyond the Brain*, Bristol: Intellect.
Perkins, Claire Elizabeth (2012), *American Smart Cinema*, Edinburgh: Edinburgh University Press.
Peters, Chris, and M. J. Broersma (2012), *Rethinking Journalism: Trust and Participation in a Transformed News Landscape*, Hoboken: Taylor and Francis.
Peterson, Carole, Beulah Jesso, and Allyssa McCaabe (1999), 'Encouraging Narratives in Preschoolers: An Intervention Study', *Journal of Child Language* 26.1: 49–67.
Petrarch, Francesco (1989), Davy A. Carozza and H. James Shey (eds), *Petrarch's Secretum: With Introduction, Notes, and Critical Anthology*, 1347–53, New York: P. Lang.
Petrini, Carlo (1989), 'Slow Food Manifesto', *Slowfood.com*, <http://www.slowfood.com/_2010_pagine/com/popup_pagina.lasso?-id_pg=121&-session=query_session:7CA8035F076cf0C4B2RQ52996E20> (4 March 2015).
Pettigrew, Thomas F., and Linda R. Tropp (2006), 'A Meta-Analytic Test of Intergroup Contact Theory', *Journal of Personality and Social Psychology* 90.5: 751–83.
Piaget, Jean [1945] (1962), *Play, Dreams and Imitation in Childhood*, New York: Norton.
Pierson, Michele (2002), *Special Effects: Still in Search of Wonder*, New York: Columbia University Press.
Pilger, John (2016), 'John Pilger: Why Hillary Clinton Is More Dangerous Than Donald Trump', *New Matilda*, 23 March, <https://newmatilda.com/2016/03/23/john-pilger-why-hillary-clinton-is-more-dangerous-than-donald-trump> (10 November 2016).
Pinker, Steven (1997), *How the Mind Works*. New York: W. W. Norton.
Plantinga, Carl (2009), *Moving Viewers: American Film and the Spectator's Experience*, Berkley: University of California Press.
Plantinga, Carl (2018), *Screen Stories: Emotion and the Ethics of Engagement*, Oxford: Oxford University Press.
Polkinghorne, Donald E. (1988), *Narrative Knowing and the Human Sciences*, Albany: SUNY Press.
Popper, Karl (1945), *The Open Society and Its Enemies*, London: Routledge.
Popper, Karl (1957), *The Poverty of Historicism*, London: Routledge & Kegan Paul.
Popper, Karl (1963), *Conjectures and Refutations: The Growth of Scientific Knowledge*, London: Routledge & Kegan Paul.
Popper, Karl (2002), *The Logic of Scientific Discovery*, London: Routledge.
Porton, Richard (1993), 'American Dreams, Suburban Nightmares', *Cinéaste* 20.1: 12-15.

Price, Jill, and Bart Davis (2008), *The Woman Who Can't Forget: The Extraordinary Story of Living with the Most Remarkable Memory Known to Science – A Memoir*, New York: Free Press.
Price, Martin (1983), *Forms of Life: Character and Moral Imagination in the Novel*, New Haven: Yale University Press.
Prince, Gerald (2003), *Dictionary of Narratology*, revised edition, Lincoln: University Press of Nebraska.
Prinz, Jesse (2008), 'Is Morality Innate?', in Walter Sinnott-Armstrong (ed.), *Moral Psychology, volume 1*, Cambridge: MIT Press, pp. 367–406.
Puig, Claudia (2007), 'As entertainment, *Lions* whimpers rather than roars', *USA Today*, November 9, <http://www.usatoday.com/life/movies/reviews/2007-11-08-lions-for-lambs_N.htm> (4 June 2012).
Quart, Alissa (2005), 'Networked: Don Roos and *Happy Endings*', *Film Comment* 41.4: 48–5.
Radin, Paul (1927), *Primitive Man as Philosopher*, New York and London: D. Appleton and Company.
Rattigan, Neil, and Thomas P. McManus (1992), 'Fathers, Sons, and Brothers: Patriarchy and Guilt in 1980s American Cinema', *Journal of Popular Film and Television* 20.1: 15–23.
Richter, Virginia (2011), *Literature After Darwin: Human Beasts in Western Fiction, 1859–1939*, Basingstoke: Palgrave Macmillan.
Rosenbaum, Jonathan (1989), review of *Parenthood*, by Ron Howard et al., *Chicago Reader* <http://www.chicagoreader.com/chicago/parenthood/Film?oid=1057448> (1 February 2017).
Rosenthal, Robert, and Lenore Jacobson (1968), *Pygmalion in the Classroom*, New York: Holt, Rinehart & Winston.
Rowe, Dorothy [1987] (2011), *Beyond Fear*, London: HarperCollins.
Rubin, Gayle (1984), 'Thinking Sex: Notes for a Radical Theory of the Politics of Sexuality', in Carole S. Vance (ed.), *Pleasure and Danger: Exploring Female Sexuality*, Boston: Routledge & Kegan Paul, 267–319.
Rushton, Richard (2013), *The Politics of Hollywood Cinema: Popular Film and Contemporary Political Theory*, New York; Basingstoke: Palgrave Macmillan.
Ryan, Marie-Laure (2006), *Avatars of Story*, Minneapolis: University of Minnesota Press.
Ryan, Marie-Laure, and Jan-Noël Thon (eds) (2014), *Storyworlds Across Media: Toward a Media-Conscious Narratology*, Lincoln: UNP – Nebraska Paperback.
Saegert, Susan (1980), 'Masculine Cities and Feminine Suburbs: Polarized Ideas, Contradictory Realities', *Signs* 5.3: 96–111.
Said, Edward (1979), *Orientalism*, New York: Vintage.
Said, Edward (2004), *Humanism and Democratic Criticism*, New York: Columbia University Press.
Sales, Jessica McDermott, Robyn Fivush, and Carole Peterson (2003), 'Parental Reminiscing about Positive and Negative Events', *Journal of Cognition and Development* 4.2: 185–209.

Sampson, Robert J. (2006), 'Collective Efficacy Theory: Lessons Learned and Directions for Future Inquiry', in Francis T. Cullen, John Paul Wright, and Kristie R. Blevins (eds), *Taking Stock: The Status of Criminological Theory*, Rutgers: Transaction, pp. 149–67.

Sardar, Ziauddin, and Merryl Wyn Davies (2010), 'Freeze Framing Muslims: Hollywood and the Slideshow of Western Imagination', *Ziauddinsardar.com*, <http://ziauddinsardar.com/2014/09/freeze-framing-muslims> (21 May 2015).

Sarris, Andrew (1976), 'Towards a Theory of Film History', in Bill Nichols (ed.), *Movies and Methods: An Anthology Volume 1*, Berkeley; Los Angeles; London: University of California Press, pp. 237–51.

Sarton, George (1931), *The History of Science and the New Humanism*, New York: Henry Holt and Co.

Sartre, Jean-Paul (1946), *Existentialism and Humanism*, London: Methuen.

Schaller, Mark (2006), 'Parasites, Behavioral Defenses, and the Social Psychological Mechanisms Through Which Cultures Are Evoked', *Psychological Inquiry* 17.2: 96–101.

Schanzer, Karl, and Thomas Lee Wright (1993), *American Screenwriters*, New York: Avon.

Schickel, Richard (1989), 'A Typical, Terrible Family', *Time*, 7 August: 54.

Schleier, Merrill (2009), *Skyscraper Cinema: Architecture and Gender in American Film*, Minneapolis: Universityr of Minnesota Press.

Schmaal, L., and the ENIGMA-Major Depressive Disorder Working Group (2016), 'Subcortical Brain Alterations in Major Depressive Disorder: Findings from the ENIGMA Major Depressive Disorder Working Group', *Molecular Psychiatry* 21.6: 806–12.

Schudson, Michael (2012), 'Would Journalism Please Hold Still!', in Chris Peters and M. J. Broersma (eds), *Rethinking Journalism: Trust and Participation in a Transformed News Landscape*, Hoboken: Taylor and Francis, pp. 191–9.

Schwartz, Barry (1967), 'The Social Psychology of the Gift', *American Journal of Sociology* 73.1: 1–11.

Schwartz, Joel (1990), 'Antihumanism in the Humanities', *Public Interest* 99: 29–44.

Sconce, Jeffrey (1995), '"Trashing" the Academy: Taste, Aesthetics, and an Emerging Politics of Cinematic Style', *Screen* 36.4: 371–93.

Sconce, Jeffrey (2002), 'Irony, Nihilism and the New American "Smart" Film', *Screen* 43.4: 349–69.

Seigneurie, Ken (2005), 'Ongoing War and Arab Humanism', in Laura Doyle and Laura A. Winkiel (eds), *Geomodernisms: Race, Modernism, Modernity*, Bloomington: Indiana University Press, pp. 96–113.

Semin, Gün R., and Eliot R. Smith (2008), *Embodied Grounding: Social, Cognitive, Affective, and Neuroscientific Approaches*, Cambridge: Cambridge University Press.

Sennett, Richard, and Jonathan Cobb (1972), *The Hidden Injuries of Class*, New York: Knopf.

Sheehan, Paul (2002), *Modernism, Narrative, and Humanism*, Cambridge; New York: Cambridge University Press.
Sherif, Muzafer (1966), *In Common Predicament: Social Psychology of Intergroup Conflict and Cooperation*, Boston: Houghton-Mifflin.
Shiel, Mark and Tony Fitzmaurice (eds) (2001), *Cinema and the City: Film and Urban Societies in a Global Context*, Oxford; Malden: Blackwell Publishers.
Silverstone, Roger (ed) (1997), *Visions of Suburbia*, London; New York: Routledge.
Silvey, Vivien (2009), 'Not Just Ensemble Films: Six Degrees, Webs, Multiplexity and the Rise of Network Narratives', *Forum* 8, <http://www.forumjournal.org/article/view/621> (16 December 2015).
Sim, Lorraine (2012), 'Ensemble Film, Postmodernity and Moral Mapping', *Screening the Past* 35, <http://www.screeningthepast.com/2012/12/ensemble-film-postmodernity-and-moral-mapping> (16 December 2015).
Singer, Ben (2001), *Melodrama and Modernity: Early Sensational Cinema and Its Contexts*, New York: Columbia University Press.
Singer, Peter (1999), *A Darwinian Left: Politics, Evolution and Cooperation*, New Haven: Weidenfeld & Nicolson.
Sinnerbrink, Robert (2016), *Cinematic Ethics: Exploring Ethical Experience through Film*, London; New York: Routledge.
Skolnick, Arlene S. (1991), *Embattled Paradise: The American Family in an Age of Uncertainty*, New York: Basic Books.
Smicek, Melanie (2014), *American Dreams, Suburban Nightmares: Suburbia as a Narrative Space between Utopia and Dystopia in Contemporary American Cinema*, Hamburg: Anchor Academic Publishing.
Smith, Adam (2002), *The Theory of Moral Sentiments*, Cambridge: Cambridge University Press.
Smith, Jeff (1999), 'Movie Music as Moving Music: Emotion, Cognition, and the Film Score', in Carl Plantinga and Greg M. Smith (eds), *Passionate Views: Film, Cognition, and Emotion*, Baltimore: Johns Hopkins University Press, pp. 146–67.
Smith, Murray (1995a), *Engaging Characters: Fiction, Emotion, and the Cinema*. Oxford: Clarendon Press.
Smith, Murray (1995b), 'Film Spectatorship and the Institution of Fiction', *The Journal of Aesthetics and Art Criticism* 53.2, 113–27.
Smith, Murray (2010), 'Darwin and the Directors: Film, Emotion, and the Face in the Age of Evolution', in Brian Boyd, Joseph Carroll, and Jonathan Gottschall (eds), *Evolution, Literature, and Film: A Reader*, New York: Columbia University Press, pp. 231–45.
Smith, Murray (2017), *Film, Art, and the Third Culture: A Naturalized Aesthetics of Film*, Oxford: Oxford University Press.
Smyth, Joshua M. (1998), 'Written Emotional Expression: Effect Sizes, Outcome Types, and Moderating Variables', *Journal of Consulting and Clinical Psychology* 66.1: 174–84.
Soper, Kate (1986), *Humanism and Anti-Humanism*, La Salle: Open Court.

Spacks, Patricia Meyer (2011), *On Rereading*, Cambridge, MA: Belknap Press of Harvard University Press.
Spigel, Lynn (2001), *Welcome to the Dreamhouse: Popular Media and Postwar Suburbs*, Durham, NC: Duke University Press.
Stadler, Jane (2008), *Pulling Focus: Intersubjective Experience, Narrative Film, and Ethics*, New York: Continuum.
Staiger, Janet (1997), 'Hybrid or Inbred: The Purity Hypothesis and Hollywood Genre History', *Film Criticism* 22.1: 5–20, 90.
Staiger, Janet (2008), 'Film Noir as Male Melodrama: The Politics of Film Genre Labeling', in Lincoln Geraghty and Mark Jancovich (eds), *The Shifting Definitions of Genre: Essays on Labeling Films, Television Shows and Media*, Jefferson: McFarland & Company, pp. 71–91.
Stearns, Linda Brewster, and John R. Logan (1986), 'The Racial Structuring of the Housing Market and Segregation in Suburban Areas', *Social Forces* 65.1: 28–42.
Stewart, Judith Ann (1982), 'Perception of Animacy', Ph.D. dissertation, University of Pennsylvania.
Stokes, Patrick (2017), 'Is it OK to Punch Nazis?' *The Conversation*, 27 January, <https://theconversation.com/is-it-ok-to-punch-nazis-71991> (5 April 2017).
Subramanian, S. V., Daniel J. Kim, and Ichiro Kawachi (2002), 'Social Trust and Self-Rated Health in US Communities: A Multilevel Analysis', *Journal of Urban Health* 79.4: 21–34.
Sugiyama, Michelle Scalise (2001), 'Narrative Theory and Function: Why Evolution Matters', *Philosophy and Literature* 25.2: 233–50.
Sutton, John, Celia B. Harris, Paul G. Keil, and Amanda J. Barnier (2010), 'The Psychology of Memory, Extended Cognition, and Socially Distributed Remembering', *Phenomenology and the Cognitive Sciences* 9.4: 521–60.
Swirski, Peter (2007), *Of Literature and Knowledge: Explorations in Narrative Thought Experiments, Evolution, and Game Theory*, Abingdon: Routledge.
Syse, Astri, Jon H. Loge, and Torkild H. Lyngstad (2010), 'Does Childhood Cancer Affect Parental Divorce Rates? A Population-Based Study', *Journal of Clinical Oncology* 28.5: 872–7.
Taberham, Paul (2014), 'Avant-garde Film in an Evolutionary Context', in Ted Nannicelli and Paul Taberham (eds), *Cognitive Media Theory (AFI Film Readers)*, London: Routledge, pp. 214–31.
Tamborini, Ron, and James Stiff (1987), 'Predictors of Horror Film Attendance and Appeal: An Analysis of the Audience for Frightening Films', *Communication Research* 14.4: 415–36.
Tan, Ed S. H., and Nico H. Frijda (1999), 'Sentiment in Film Viewing', in Carl Plantinga and Greg M. Smith (eds), *Passionate Views: Film, Cognition, and Emotion*, Baltimore: Johns Hopkins University Press, pp. 48–64.
Tarkovsky, Andrei (1989), *Sculpting in Time: Reflections on the Cinema*, trans. Kitty Hunter-Blair, London: Faber and Faber.

Taylor, Charles [1989] (2006), *Sources of the Self: The Making of the Modern Identity*, eighth printing, Cambridge: Cambridge University Press.
Terrizzi, John A., Natalie J. Shook, and Michael A. McDaniel (2013), 'The Behavioral Immune System and Social Conservatism: A Meta-Analysis', *Evolution & Human Behavior* 34.2: 99–108.
Thompson, Kristin (1999), *Storytelling in the New Hollywood: Understanding Classical Narrative Technique*, Cambridge, MA; London: Harvard University Press.
Thompson, William Forde, Andrew M. Geeves, and Kirk N. Olsen (2018), 'Who Enjoys Listening to Violent Music and Why?' *Psychology of Popular Media Culture* 7.4: 399–606.
Thrasher, Cat, and Vanessa LoBue (2016), 'Do Infants Find Snakes Aversive? Infants' Physiological Responses to "Fear-Relevant" Stimuli', *Journal of Experimental Child Psychology* 142: 382–90.
Throop, C. Jason (2010), *Suffering and Sentiment: Exploring the Vicissitudes of Experience and Pain in Yap*, Berkeley: University of California Press.
Thwaites, Tony, Lloyd Davis, and Warwick Mules (1994), *Tools for Cultural Studies: An Introduction*, Melbourne: Macmillan.
Torrance, Robert M. (2001), in William S. Haney and Peter Malekin (eds), 'The Radical Tradition of Humanistic Consciousness', *Humanism and the Humanities in the Twenty-first Century*, Lewisburg: Bucknell University Press, pp. 164–81.
Travers, Peter (1989), rev. of *Parenthood*, by Ron Howard et al., *Rolling Stone*, 2 August, <http://www.rollingstone.com/movies/reviews/parenthood-19890802> (2 February 2017).
Treger, Stanislav, Susan Sprecher, and Ralph Erber (2013), 'Laughing and Liking: Exploring the Interpersonal Effects of Humor Use in Initial Social Interactions', *European Journal of Social Psychology* 43.6: 532–43.
Trotsky, Leon [1925] (2005), *Literature and Revolution*, ed. William Keach, trans. Rose Strunsky, Chicago: Haymarket Books.
Turner, Terence (1997), 'Human Rights, Human Difference: Anthropology's Contribution to an Emancipatory Cultural Politics', *Journal of Anthropological Research* 53.3: 273–91.
Turner, Victor (1974), 'Liminal to Liminoid, in Play, Flow, and Ritual: An Essay in Comparative Symbology', *The Rice University Studies* 60.3: 53–92.
Turner, Victor (1982), *From Ritual to Theatre: The Human Seriousness of Play*, New York: Performing Arts Journal Publications.
Turvey, Malcolm (2014), in Ted Nannicelli and Paul Taberham (eds), 'Evolutionary Film Theory', *Cognitive Media Theory (AFI Film Readers)*, London: Routledge, pp. 46–61.
Vaillant, George E. (1992), *Ego Mechanisms of Defense: A Guide for Clinicans and Researchers*, Washington, DC: American Psychiatric Press.
Val Morgan Cinema Network, no date, 'Horror Movies', *Val Morgan*, <http://www.valmorgan.co.nz/audiences/profiles/horror-movies/> (21 January 2015).
Van Bergen, Penny, Karen Salmon, Mark R. Dadds, and Jennifer Allen (2009), 'The Effects of Mother Training in Emotion-Rich, Elaborative Reminiscing

on Children's Shared Recall and Emotion Knowledge', *Journal of Cognition and Development* 10.3: 162–87.
Van de Port, Mattijs (2011), *Ecstatic Encounters: Bahian Candomblé and the Quest for the Really Real*, Amsterdam: Amsterdam University Press.
Van Vugt, Mark, and Claire M. Hart (2004), 'Social Identity as Social Glue: The Origins of Group Loyalty', *Journal of Personality and Social Psychology* 86.4: 585–98.
Varela, Charles R. (2009), *Science for Humanism: The Recovery of Human Agency*, London; New York: Routledge.
Variety Staff (1988), review of *Parenthood*, by Ron Howard et al., *Variety*, 31 December, <http://variety.com/1988/film/reviews/parenthood-2-1117793867> (1 February 2017).
Veatch, Thomas C. (1998), 'A Theory of Humor', *Humor – International Journal of Humor Research* 11.2: 161–216.
Veblen, Thorstein [1899] (1994), *The Theory of the Leisure Class*, New York: Penguin.
Veis, Greg (2009), 'Tom Perrotta On The Evolution Of Tracy Flick', *New Republic*, 16 February, <http://www.newrepublic.com/blog/the-plank/tom-perrotta-the-evolution-tracy-flick> (10 September 2014).
Wang, Qi, and Jens Brockmeier (2008), 'Autobiographical Remembering as Cultural Practice: Understanding the Interplay between Memory, Self and Culture', *Culture & Psychology* 8.1: 45–64.
Watson, J. P., and I. M. Marks (1971), 'Relevant and Irrelevant Fear in Flooding— A Crossover Study of Phobic Patients', *Behavior Therapy* 2.3: 275–93.
Wayland, Sara, and Ron Howard (2010), 'Ron Howard Interview NBC's *Parenthood*', *Collider*, 8 February, <http://collider.com/ron-howard-interview-nbc-parenthood> (2 February 2017).
Webster, Roger (ed.) (2000), *Expanding Suburbia: Reviewing Suburban Narratives*, New York: Berghahn.
Weispfenning, John (2003), 'Cultural Functions of Reruns: Time, Memory and Television', *Journal of Communication* 53.1: 165–76.
Wells, Amy Stuart, Douglas Ready, Jacquelyn Duran, Courtney Grzesikowski, Kathryn Hill, Allison Roda, Miya Warner, and Terenda White (2012), 'Still Separate, Still Unequal, But Not Always So "Suburban": The Changing Nature of Suburban School Districts in the New York Metropolitan Area', in William F. Tate IV (ed.), *Research on Schools, Neighborhoods and Communities: Toward Civic Responsibility*, Washington, DC: American Educational Research Association, pp. 125–50.
West, Joan M., and Dennis West (1999), 'Not Playing By the Usual Rules: An Interview with John Sayles', *Cineaste* 24: 28–31.
Whitehouse, Harvey (2013), 'Three Wishes for the World (with comment)', *Cliodynamics* 4.2: 281–323.
Wiewel, Wim, and Joseph J. Persky (eds) (2002), *Suburban Sprawl: Private Decisions and Public Policy*, Armonk; London: M. E. Sharpe.
Wilkie, Brian (1967), 'What Is Sentimentality?' *College English* 28.8: 564–75.

Wilkins, Kim (2013), 'The Sounds of Silence: Hyper-Dialogue and American Eccentricity', *New Review of Film and Television Studies* 11.4: 403–23

Wilkinson, Richard, and Kate Pickett (2010), *The Spirit Level: Why Equality is Better for Everyone*, revised edition, London: Penguin.

Williams, Juan (1989), 'When Horror Hits Home: The Biggest Fans of Violence Are Kids Who Live With It Every Day', 26 November, *The Washington Post*: G1.

Williams, Linda (2006), 'Generic Pleasures: Number and Narrative', in Peter Lehman (ed.), *Pornography: Film and Culture*, New Brunswick, NJ: Rutgers University Press, pp. 60–86.

Wilson, Anne E., and Michael Ross (2003), 'The Identity Function of Autobiographical Memory: Time is on our Side', *Memory* 11.2: 137–49.

Wilson, Edward O. (1999), *Consilience: The Unity of Knowledge*, New York: Vintage Books.

Wilson, Joanna (2015), 'The End of the Good Life: Literary Representations of Suburbia and the American Nightmare', *Forum* 20: 1–16.

Wilt, David E. (2003), 'Suburbia', in Peter C. Rollins (ed.), *The Columbia Companion to American History on Film*, New York: Columbia University Press, pp. 480–7.

Witherell, Carol S. (1991), 'Narrative and the Moral Realm: Tales of Caring and Justice', *Journal of Moral Education* 20.3: 237–42.

Witzel, E. J. Michael (2012), *The Origins of the World's Mythologies*, New York: Oxford University Press.

Wojcik, Pamela Robertson (2010), *The Apartment Plot: Urban Living in American Film and Popular Culture, 1945 to 1975*, Durham, NC: Duke University Press.

Wolf, Zone R. (1989), 'Learning the Professional Jargon of Nursing during Change of Shift Report', *Holistic Nursing Practice* 4.1: 78–83.

Wood, Robin (1979), 'The American Family Comedy: From *Meet Me in St. Louis* to *The Texas Chainsaw Massacre*', *Wide Angle* 3.2: 5–11.

Yan, Yan, and Kim Bissell (2014), 'The Globalization of Beauty: How is Ideal Beauty Influenced by Globally Published Fashion and Beauty Magazines?' *Journal of Intercultural Communication Research* 43.3: 194–214.

Zajonc, Robert B. (1968), 'Attitudinal Effects of Mere Exposure', *Journal of Personality and Social Psychology* 9.2/2: 1–27.

Zakarin, Jordan (2012), 'Helen Hunt, Star of *The Sessions*, Wants to Be Sex Positive', *The Hollywood Reporter*, 19 October, <http://www.hollywoodreporter.com/news/helen-hunt-star-sessions-wants-380336> (4 October 2016).

Zengotita, Thomas de (2007), *Mediated*, London: Bloomsbury.

Zillman, Dolf (1998), 'The Psychology of the Appeal of Portrayals of Violence', in Jeffrey Goldstein (ed.), *Why We Watch: The Attractions of Violent Entertainment*, New York: Oxford University Press.

Žižek, Slavoj (2011), 'Revolutionary Terror from Robespierre to Mao', *Positions: East Asia Cultures Critique* 19.3: 671–706.

Index

acting, 50–1, 108–9, 129, 130, 164, 185, 187–8, 190–1, 197, 199, 201, 207n
  referential acting theory, 190–1
adolescence, 4, 66–7, 174, 186–7, 195; *see also* teen cinema
affect, 24, 45, 47, 50, 56–2, 74, 80, 82, 92, 96n, 108, 110, 113, 131, 143, 144n, 153, 161–70, 185, 187, 189, 192, 195, 196, 197–8, 200–2, 205–6, 210, 213n; *see also* emotion
affective incoherence, 164–5
all-or-nothing thinking, 190, 195–6
Altman, Robert, 135, 191
altruism, 36, 38, 40n, 71n, 95, 99–100, 186
American Beauty, 129, 130–1, 132, 139, 140–1, 142, 144n, 148–9, 155, 162, 170, 175, 210
American Splendor, 50
analytic philosophy, 28
Anderson, Lindsay, 101
Anderson, Wes, 140, 141, 144n
anhedonia, 59, 62
animal, 17–19, 66–7, 100; *see also* anthropomorphism
animation, 5, 93, 99, 115n
anthropology, 21–3, 28, 33, 35, 36, 40n, 46, 47, 68, 118, 153, 176n, 209
  anthropology of the suburbs, 153, 176n
  cognitive anthropology, 68, 47
  evolutionary anthropology, 28, 36, 46
  existential anthropology, 23–4, 40n
  humanistic anthropology, 21–3, 209
anthropomorphism, 17–19
antihumanism, 15, 20, 26, 30–4, 40n, 50, 140, 152, 208–9
Aristotle, 13, 52, 57
art direction *see* production design

As You Like It, 18
atheism *see* religion
attention, 48, 51–3, 68, 69, 74, 78–9, 83, 102, 104, 107, 119, 130, 141, 171, 185, 187, 202, 209–11
  attentional politics 51, 193
  boredom, 64, 101, 144n
August: Osage County, 135
auteurism, 90, 141, 188
authenticity, 16, 18, 31, 60, 89–93, 159, 162
autobiographical narratives, 1, 3, 4, 50, 57, 59, 112, 115n
avant-garde, 96, 101, 110–12

badfilm *see* so-bad-it's-good
Baumgartner, M. P., 153, 176n
Beetlejuice, 138
Before Sunrise, 96n
behavioural immune system, 96n
benign violations theory *see* humour
Berlant, Lauren, 153, 161–3, 167–70
Best Man Down, 137
Beuka, Robert, 130, 133, 137, 139, 146, 148, 154, 176n
biases, 84–5, 86, 163, 164
bigotry *see* prejudice
Bildungsroman, 137–8
Bill & Ted, 191, 199
Binder, Mike, 130, 149
Black Mirror, 86
Black or White, 149–50
Blegvad, Peter, 99
Blue Velvet, 140
Boal, Augusto, 120
Bookchin, Murray, 14, 23, 35
Booth, Wayne C., 70, 121, 209
Bordwell, David, 2, 27

Boyd, Brian, 19, 36–7, 40n, 74, 98, 110, 114n
Boyle, David, 16, 60, 89, 90
bracketing, 21, 32, 202, 210–11
Brosh, Allie, 53
Bruner, Jerome S., 5, 29–30, 52–3
The 'Burbs, 138
Burton, Tim, 138
Butter, 137–8, 149

Capra, Frank, 135, 188–9
care, 7, 40n, 89, 94–5, 124, 130, 136, 141, 153, 159–60, 164, 166–7, 190, 195–7, 200–6, 207n, 211
  familial care, 76, 124, 130, 160, 164, 190, 195–7, 200–6, 207n
  see also kindness
Carroll, Joseph, 1, 32–1, 61–2
Carroll, Noël, 15, 27, 49, 66
catastrophic worrying *see* all-or-nothing thinking
catharsis, 57, 64–5, 68, 70, 140, 196
causality, 2–9, 23–6, 29, 34–9, 48–54, 61, 63–5, 102, 112–14, 120, 132, 141–2, 147, 174–5, 193–6, 200, 202–4, 207, 211–12
  multi-causality, 4, 24–6, 39, 132, 142, 196, 203, 212
Cavell, Stanley, 19, 173
Chaplin, Charlie, 86, 207n
character (fiction), 5, 19–20, 23–6, 41n, 50–1, 71n, 73–97, 99, 100, 103, 108, 113, 117, 120–1, 130, 132, 136, 138, 140–1, 143, 144n, 149, 155, 157, 160, 164–5, 167, 171–3, 185, 188, 190–1, 193–5, 197, 200–1, 205–6, 210
childhood, 65–6, 73, 79, 82, 85, 99–100, 104, 112, 123–4, 137, 144n, 149, 163, 174, 182–3, 186, 193–6, 201, 202–3;
  see also adolescence
Cholodenko, Lisa, 129, 142, 176n
The Chumscrubber, 130
Chytilová, Věra, 100
cinematography, 53, 66, 183, 206n
City Island, 155, 157, 158, 160–1, 165, 175, 176n
City of Hope, 134

City Slickers, 164, 206n
class, 31–2, 41n, 83, 87, 130, 136–9, 146–9, 151–3, 156–65, 170, 193, 199, 210
  classism, 151, 153, 159, 199, 210
  class violence, 32, 41n, 152–3, 208
  hidden injuries of class, 160
  see also wealth distribution
Cocoon, 188, 191, 192, 206n
cognitive dissonance, 53, 66, 103, 107
cognitive media studies, 27, 46, 54n, 58, 67–8, 74, 86
comedy *see* humour
coming-of-age film *see* teen cinema
competition, 36, 38, 140, 156, 211
  intellectual competition, 79–82
complexity, 4, 5, 8, 9n, 14, 16, 20–2, 23–6, 27, 29, 30, 33–4, 35, 37, 39, 40n, 45, 46, 48–51, 58, 95, 100, 104, 109–10, 111–13, 119, 122, 123, 124, 136, 141, 143, 153, 159, 173, 175, 192, 193, 196, 200–4, 211–12
  acceptance of, 26, 29, 33, 49, 50, 110, 159, 175, 204
  causality, 2–5, 8, 9n, 23–6, 29, 34–5, 39, 48–51, 112–13, 141, 175, 195–6, 200, 202–4
  character, 5, 14, 23–6, 50, 85, 89, 100, 136, 143, 200–1, 204
  ethics, 8, 9n, 14, 20–1, 25, 27–6, 29, 30, 33–5, 39, 85, 95, 110, 119, 122–4, 173, 195–6, 119, 122–4, 136, 173, 193, 202–4, 211
  human, 3, 5, 8, 14, 16, 20–2, 30, 33–4, 35, 39, 48, 153, 159
  social, 3–5, 8, 15, 23–9, 143, 193, 195, 200–1, 204, 211
  story, 4, 5, 14, 23–6, 34–5, 37, 39, 40n, 45–50, 58, 73, 89, 95, 100, 109–13, 119, 123–4, 136, 143, 153, 168, 173, 192, 196, 200–1, 204, 211
conservatism (political), 38, 75, 96, 136, 147, 155, 162, 172
consilience, 30, 34, 54
contagion (ideological), 70, 96, 168, 196, 198, 202–4; *see also* emotional contagion
The Cookout, 149

Coon, David R., 133, 136, 139, 146–7, 151, 153, 155, 157–8, 170, 173, 176n
coping mechanisms, 68, 163–4, 197
Corman, Roger, 149, 188
cosmopolitanism, 20, 33–4, 36, 74, 76, 123, 155, 166, 169, 173
crying, 71, 100, 164, 167, 184
cultural constructivism, 9n, 31, 37–8
cultural relativism *see* relativism
cynicism, 20, 138, 172, 175, 197
Czechoslovak New Wave, 100

Daisies, 100
Darwin, Charles, 39, 61; *see also* evolution
death, 59, 70, 71n, 103, 107, 144n, 166; *see also* terror management
debt, 94, 95, 97n; *see also* gift-giving
De Felitta, Raymond, 155, 160, 176n
defence mechanisms, 91, 107
depression, 53, 58–9, 114, 130, 157, 165
depressive realism, 163
The Descendants, 135
de Waal, Frans, 71n, 166
dialogue, 13, 49, 55n, 76, 83, 85, 91, 97n, 118, 134, 144n, 190, 196, 203–4
  expository dialogue, 97n
  morality in dialogue, 83, 85
dichotomous thinking *see* all-or-nothing thinking
discovery, 23, 29, 48, 59, 69, 103, 111, 113, 125, 163, 172, 185, 211–12
Dissanayake, Ellen, 57, 62, 73, 166
documentary, 4, 50–1, 86, 92, 151, 159; *see also* non-fiction
domesticity, 21, 100, 129–31, 134, 140, 142–3, 144n, 149, 155, 161–2, 170, 172–3, 181–2, 184–92, 203–4, 206n
drama *see* theatre
Duane Hopwood, 161
Dungeons & Dragons, 100

Eagleton, Terry, 75, 152, 209
early development, 60, 73, 82, 99–100; *see also* childhood
EDtv, 175
Edward Scissorhands, 138
Election, 130, 137n, 141, 143, 170, 176n

emotion, 2–3, 16, 24, 33, 41n, 49, 56–72, 74, 80, 82, 88–9, 103, 108–9, 113, 119, 121, 131, 136, 143, 153, 161–70, 172, 176n, 181, 183–5, 187–9, 192–7, 200–2, 205–6, 210
  anger, 62, 65, 67–70, 71n, 165, 185, 192, 195, 201
  bittersweetness, 184, 201, 206
  contagion, 64, 69, 181, 183–4, 192, 196, 202–4
  disgust, 71n, 96n
  excitation transfer, 63, 70, 167
  excitement, 8, 16, 26, 35–6, 55n, 56–8, 63, 70, 75, 85, 103, 167, 202, 204
  fear, 56, 65–8, 71n, 72n, 86, 109–10, 118, 125n, 154, 176, 192, 197–8, 202
  happiness, 59, 71n, 192, 200–2, 205–6
  mixed emotion, 45, 170, 182, 198, 200
  sadness, 63, 65, 69, 71n, 80, 114, 182, 184, 189, 192, 200, 202, 207n, 212
  surprise, 50, 71n, 99, 106–8, 120, 148, 162, 164, 181, 182, 191, 193–4, 197
  suspense, 56, 63, 68, 113, 192, 106–8
  see also affect; media psychology
empathy, 2, 17–21, 30, 31, 33, 35, 59, 60, 67, 69, 71, 74, 84, 88–9, 99, 113, 114, 118, 124, 161, 166, 173, 202–5, 210–13
  cognitive and affective empathy, 17, 60, 69, 74, 99, 210, 213n
The End of History?, 171, 175
The End of Suburbia, 151
Enough Said, 137
ensemble narratives, 7, 21, 25, 125, 127, 129–32, 134–6, 138, 141–2, 144n, 145n, 146, 148–9, 153–4, 157, 161, 162, 169, 170–7, 181, 185, 190–1, 193–4, 200, 210, 212
epistemology, 26, 29–30, 34, 39, 46–7, 49, 50, 119
ethics, 1–2, 5–8, 9n, 14, 17, 19, 21, 25–6, 28, 30–6, 38–9, 41n, 47–8, 51, 61, 65, 71n, 83, 85, 88, 92, 94, 101, 116, 118, 120–5, 136, 141, 155, 164, 166, 169–70, 173–4, 181, 189, 190, 196, 202–4, 208–11
  cine-ethics, 19, 47–8, 83, 122, 141, 170, 173, 190

ethics (*cont.*)
  cosmopolitan ethics, 20, 33–4, 36, 74, 76, 123, 155, 166, 169, 173
  consequentialism, 123, 125n
  meta-ethics, 6, 17, 41n
  normative ethics, 17, 31, 41n, 65
  retributivism, 125n
  virtue, 31, 181, 183, 196, 198, 202
ethnicity, 22, 32, 85, 129, 137, 147–50, 171–2
  ethnicity and American suburbia, 137, 147–50, 171–2
  see also racism
ethnography, 21, 84, 153
evaluation (arts), 7, 15, 20, 22, 26–8, 30–1, 35, 36, 51, 57, 90–1, 115n, 120, 122–3, 152, 171, 185, 212; see also *taste*
Every Day, 158
everyday, 24, 45, 75, 95, 131, 156, 172–3, 184–5, 202, 210
evolution, 1–2, 16, 19, 23, 28, 32, 35–9, 38, 39, 41, 45, 47, 52, 56, 58, 60–1, 67–8, 71, 76, 98, 101, 111–12, 116, 143, 165–6, 209
  cinematic Darwinism, 47, 54, 67–8, 98, 111–12, 101, 143
  coevolution, 15–16, 37, 39n
  Darwinian feminism, 38
  evolutionary anthropology, 28, 36, 46
  evolutionary biology, 2, 37–8, 46, 58
  evolutionary psychology, 37, 111–12
  epigenetics, 59, 116
  eugenics, 39
exaptation, 2, 37, 61
  gene–environment correlation, 41n
  hybridity, 129, 134, 143, 148–9, 161
  Lamarckian evolution, 37, 125n
  leftist Darwinism, 38
  literary Darwinism, 2, 32, 35–6, 39, 41, 45, 52, 58, 98, 101, 111–12, 143, 165–6
  Mendelian evolution, 37
  phenotypic plasticity, 37, 60
  social Darwinism, 39
  sociobiology, 1–2, 34, 37–8, 125n
  soft inheritance, 116, 125n
  spandrels, 60–1, 66, 102, 111
  superstimuli, 60–1, 66, 102, 111
  symbolic inheritance, 116, 209
  synthesis, 37
  see also Darwin, Charles; natural fallacies
existentialism, 22, 23, 40n, 45, 53, 56, 58, 66, 68, 71n, 107, 135, 141, 144n, 164, 174, 190, 200, 202–3, 206
eXistenZ, 86
extended mind, 16, 112, 168

Fair Game, 94
family, 21, 71n, 73, 76, 84, 91, 93, 105, 112, 129, 131, 133–8, 144n, 154–60, 163, 168, 172–5, 181–207
  family on film, 93, 105, 129, 131, 133–8, 144n, 154–60, 163, 172–5, 181–207
Family Guy, 136
fantasy (genre), 70, 86, 101–6, 108, 110, 114, 133, 138–40, 149, 156, 175, 188–90, 204
feminism, 31, 33, 38, 50, 83–4, 100, 118, 136, 140, 161–2, 176n; *see also* gender
  Darwinian feminisms, 38
  feminism and play, 100
film noir, 139
film theory, 8, 15, 20–1, 25, 27, 28–30, 35, 41n, 46–9, 53–4, 54n, 55n, 67, 75–6, 90, 122, 153, 161, 163, 191
  cinematic Darwinism, 47, 54, 67–8, 98, 111–12, 101, 143
  cognitive theory, 27, 46, 54n, 58, 67–8, 74, 86
  sound in film, 76, 181, 187–8, 192–3, 204
  see also auteurism; feminism
fractal narrative *see* network narrative
Freud, Sigmund, 15, 103, 107; *see also* psychoanalysis
friendship, 64, 70, 74, 86, 90, 108–9, 113, 117, 125n, 165–6, 173
Fukuyama, Francis, 171, 175
functionalism, 45–8, 93, 125n

Game of Thrones, 103, 119
games and gaming, 74, 77, 79, 86, 96n, 99–100, 105, 120–1, 189, 193, 200

Ganz, Lowell, 164, 175, 181, 189, 191, 197, 201, 205, 206n
Gehring, Wes D., 188–9, 191, 201, 204–5, 207n
gender, 31, 33, 50, 67, 83–4, 100, 109, 118, 132, 140, 161–2, 174, 176n, 187, 189, 191–2, 198–200, 207n
  suburbia and gender, 130, 134, 135, 140, 158, 161–2, 175, 176n
generativity, 4, 9n, 33, 167
genre, 4, 47, 65, 69, 81, 102, 105, 106, 108–9, 118, 129–31, 133–5, 137–8, 142–3, 149, 157, 189, 201
geography, 54n, 74, 133, 135–6, 142, 145n, 146–7, 150, 153–4, 156–8, 173
gift-giving, 94–5, 159
Gilliam, Terry, 105–6, 114–15n
Goldsmith, Jerry, 138, 144n
golem effect, 196
gossip, 19, 118–20, 195
Greenwood, Dara N., 53, 62–3, 74
Grodal, Torben, 35, 68, 102–3
group politics, 20, 75–8, 88, 101, 117, 119, 169, 190
  group cohesion, 20, 77, 81, 95, 119, 167–9
  group polarisation, 78
  ingroups and outgroups, 20, 75–7, 88, 117, 119, 169
  intergroup contact, 101
groupthink, 78, 190

Hallström, Lasse, 137
Happy Endings, 132, 141
Haynes, Todd, 136
hermeneutics, 2, 7–9, 13–41, 47–8, 65, 75, 79, 83, 92, 108, 120, 125n, 141, 203–4, 211
high place effect, 72n
history, 7, 27, 41n, 51–2, 142, 147
Hitchcock, Alfred, 69, 79–80, 105, 188
Hollywood, 33, 75, 108, 120, 134, 149, 156–8, 171, 173, 177n, 188; *see also* New Hollywood
Holofcener, Nicole, 137, 142, 158, 169
home, 83, 84, 134, 137, 138, 151, 155, 159–60, 172, 183–4, 186, 198, 202; *see also* domesticity

hope, 7, 31, 32, 34, 96, 121, 134, 156, 160, 163, 185, 192, 205–6, 212–13
horror, 57, 65–72, 73, 86, 103, 105, 134, 138, 164
horror comedy, 68, 164
House Party, 137
Housesitter, 158
Howard, Ron, 7, 88, 131, 175, 181, 183, 185, 188, 190–3, 198, 200, 203–5, 206n
'How Is Babby Formed', 77–8
How to Host a Murder Party, 86
humanism
  abject humanism, 211
  anthropology and humanism, 21–3, 209
  antihumanism, 15, 20, 26, 30–4, 40n, 50, 140, 152, 208–9
  canonical humanism, 12, 209–10
  Christian humanism, 13–14
  critical humanism, 14, 34
  high humanism, 13, 34, 40n
  human difference, 20, 23, 25, 32, 52, 56, 66, 76, 89–90, 104, 108, 124, 129, 148, 151, 162, 191, 199, 210
  human excess, 23–4, 26, 29, 33, 40n, 47, 105, 168
  humanism and science, 6, 13–14, 15, 17, 26–30, 35–6, 47–8, 50, 54n
  humanist ethics, 2, 6–8, 9n, 14, 17, 19, 21, 26, 30–6, 41n, 47–8, 65, 85, 94, 122–5, 166, 169, 174, 181, 189, 203–4, 208–11
  Islamic humanism, 14
  literary humanism, 13–15, 31, 54n, 153, 161–3
  pedagogical humanisms, 13–14, 50, 88, 92
  rationalism, 14, 29
  Renaissance humanism, 13–14, 18, 31
  secular humanism, 13, 32, 209
  see also antihumanism; posthumanism; transhumanism
humour, 53, 56, 68, 106–8, 130, 136, 138, 155, 163–4, 197–202, 203, 207n
  benign violation theory, 106–8, 197
  humour and family, 136, 138, 163, 199–202
  satire, 130–1, 138, 140, 141, 162, 190, 197
  see also irony; terror management

Hyberbole and a Half, 53
hybridity, 129, 134, 143, 148–9, 161
hyperlink narrative *see* network narrative

The Ice Storm, 132–3, 175
imagination, 3, 7–8, 17–20, 24, 28–30, 33, 35, 45, 49, 59, 61, 64, 72n, 79–80, 84–5, 98–101, 104–6, 110, 120–1, 125, 130, 133–4, 138–9, 143, 150–1, 156, 158, 161–9, 174, 187, 189, 211
    moral imagination, 17–18, 20, 29, 61, 72n, 80, 85, 98–9, 105, 110, 120–1, 165, 167, 174, 189
    see also discovery
incongruity, 66, 100, 106–7, 141
independent filmmaking, 129, 134–5, 137, 144n, 172
    Indiewood, 129, 132
In Good Company, 175
infants *see* early development
Inside Out, 93, 99
insight, 3, 24, 38, 47, 54n, 58, 71n, 74, 89, 120, 125, 163, 190, 198, 211–12
interdisciplinarity, 21, 27–8, 41, 46, 54, 94, 213
intergenerational perspective-taking, 99, 165, 174, 189, 191, 195
The Intruder, 149
irony, 16, 113, 117, 132, 136, 139, 140–1, 144n
    dramatic irony, 113
    ironic distance, 140–1
    romantic irony, 132, 140
It's a Wonderful Life, 135, 189

jargon, 75, 77
Jarry, Alfred, 96, 101
Jenkins, Tamara, 157–8
The Joneses, 139
journalism, 88, 91–3, 97n, 177n; *see also* news media
Jud Süß, 20
Junebug, 142, 145n, 155, 157, 158–60, 161, 165
Juno, 136–7, 141

The Kids Are All Right, 129, 130, 137, 142, 149, 155, 163, 176n

kindness, 20, 22, 34, 40n, 41n, 77, 141, 172, 191, 203, 209; *see also* care
Kramer vs. Kramer, 135
Kunstler, James Howard, 151
Kupfer, Joseph, 181–3, 189, 196, 199, 203

The Lady or the Tiger?, 111
language, 6, 8, 14, 18, 26–7, 32, 36, 40n, 41n, 49, 75–8, 104, 116, 119, 123, 142, 154, 160, 176n, 181, 199, 209
laughter *see* humour
Limbo, 87–8, 134
liminality, 22, 81–2, 87, 186
    liminoid experiences, 81–2, 96
linearity, 48, 52–4, 65, 103
Linklater, Richard, 96n, 137
Lions for Lambs, 97n, 132
literary theory, 2, 15, 35–6, 39, 41, 45, 52, 54n, 55n, 58, 60, 75, 98, 101, 111–12, 125n, 143, 153, 161, 163, 165–6
    literary Darwinism, 2, 32, 35–6, 39, 41, 45, 52, 58, 98, 101, 111–12, 143, 165–6
    literary humanism, 13–15, 31, 54n, 153, 161–3
Little Children, 130, 142, 155, 166, 176n
Little Miss Sunshine, 129, 130, 141, 142, 143, 155, 163, 176n
loneliness, 73–4
Lonergan, Kenneth, 142, 156
Lone Star, 134
Long, Christopher R., 53, 62–3, 74
love, 18, 56, 59, 73–4, 78, 99, 109, 125n, 159, 163, 172, 185–6, 190, 197, 201–2, 205; *see also* romance genres
Lymelife, 130, 142, 143, 157
Lynch, David, 53, 102, 140

McCarthy, Thomas, 138, 155
magazines, 93, 119
Mandel, Babaloo, 164, 175, 181, 191, 197, 201, 205, 206n
Margaret, 142, 156, 169
Mar, Raymond A., 2–4, 46, 51, 88–9, 102, 119–21
Marx, Karl, 15, 31
masculinity, 33, 83–4, 118, 140, 161–2, 174, 176n, 187, 189, 191–2, 198–200, 207n

meaning, 2–4, 8, 9n, 16, 27, 29, 40n, 48, 51, 53–4, 56–8, 61, 66, 71n, 76, 78–81, 96n, 102, 104, 111, 113, 116, 121, 125n, 132, 138, 141, 153, 155, 184, 189, 190, 194, 202–4, 211–12
media psychology, 64, 69
  cultivation, 83
  eudaimonic motivations, 58, 104, 211–12
  excitation transfer, 63, 70, 167
  hedonic motivations, 58, 65, 71n, 212
  media selection and preference, 58, 73–5, 109, 117–18
  mood regulation, 58, 60, 62–4, 68, 71n, 101, 113–14
  saturation, 83, 190
  see also cognitive media studies
melodrama, 89, 131–2, 135–6, 144n, 149, 165, 197
memory, 3–4, 49, 59, 69, 78, 98, 110, 112–14, 115n, 116–18, 133
  autobiographical memory, 1, 3, 4, 50, 57, 59, 112, 115n
  collaborative inhibition, 78
  collaborative recall, 78, 112
  forgetting, 22, 113–14, 209
  memory and family narratives, 3–4, 9n, 76, 112–13, 133, 174, 195
  see also extended mind; nostalgia
Mendes, Sam, 140
mere exposure, 80
metaphor, 16, 18, 23, 40n, 41n, 70, 141, 146, 152–3, 155, 204
metaphysics, 17, 50, 53, 99
A Midsummer Night's Dream, 77–8
Miller, D. A., 79–80
mimesis, 32, 86, 206n
Minghella, Anthony, 212–13
misogyny *see* sexism
Modern Family, 136, 164
modernity, 53, 111, 175; *see also* postmodernity
Modern Times, 86
morality *see* ethics
moral psychology, 71n, 120, 196
moral relativism *see* relativism
Mousley, Andy, 14, 31
Mr. Mom, 134

multi-causality *see* causality
multi-focalisation, 132, 143, 162, 165, 170, 174–5
multiple-protagonist *see* ensemble narratives
Mumford, 130, 138, 142, 145n, 157
music, 53, 60–1, 63, 72n, 80, 99, 104–5, 108, 109, 111, 117, 123, 132, 138, 144n, 148, 184, 186, 192–3, 206n
  film scores, 138, 144n, 184, 192–3, 206n
  music and evolution, 60–1, 111
  see also song
musical (genre), 104, 108, 132
myth, 29, 52, 81, 103, 150, 167
  comparative mythology studies, 52

narcissism, 9n, 117, 125n, 130, 171, 201
  narcissism of small differences, 117, 125n
narrative theory *see* narratology
narratology, 1–9, 15, 21, 25, 27, 29, 32–4, 35–6, 39, 40n, 45–8, 53, 54n, 108–9, 125n
natural fallacies, 17, 36, 39
Nebraska, 135
neoliberalism, 171, 176n
network narrative, 131–2, 141, 174, 191
neuroscience, 46, 50, 57–8
New Hollywood, 131, 134–5, 146
Newman, Michael Z., 25–6
Newman, Randy, 184, 189–90, 192
new sincerity *see* sincerity
news media, 1, 39n, 48, 89, 171, 177n
Night of the Living Dead, 70
No Down Payment, 146
non-fiction, 3–4, 48, 50–1, 65, 86, 92, 113, 119, 123, 151, 159, 211; *see also* documentary
nonlinearity, 48, 52
nostalgia, 16, 113–14, 133, 144n, 148, 202
nuance, 19, 21, 59, 113, 153, 159, 185, 188, 191, 200, 202, 211–12

Oatley, Keith, 2–4, 46, 51, 88–9, 102, 119–21
Oliver, Mary Beth, 57–8, 66–9, 211
oneness, 29, 68–70, 73, 93, 117

One True Thing, 135
ontology, 17, 49–51, 53, 74
openness (epistemic), 21, 24–7, 35, 39, 41n, 48, 87–8, 96n, 99–100, 103, 107, 111, 120, 124–5, 141, 149, 163, 164, 170, 174, 185, 199
optimism, 32, 163, 167
The Oranges, 130, 142–3, 155, 165
outsider art, 158–9

Parenthood, 7, 131, 164, 181–207
Passion Fish, 25
Payne, Alexander, 135, 140, 155, 170, 172
Peake, Mervyn, 103
perfectionism, 190, 195–6
performance *see* acting
Perkins, Claire, 144n, 154, 176n
Perrotta, Tom, 170–1, 176n
personality, 24–5, 57, 67, 73, 84–5, 110, 113, 129, 163, 191, 199, 201, 211
   need for cognition, 110
   need to belong, 73, 166, 169
   sensation seeking, 57–8, 61, 63, 161
   see also media psychology
persuasion, 88
Peyton Place, 133, 137
phenomenology, 18, 21, 55n, 84
philosophy of science, 13, 15, 26–30, 50
physicalism, 29
Pixar, 93
Plantinga, Carl, 41n, 46, 63, 176
play, 19, 74, 79, 82, 85–6, 96, 98–101, 105, 110, 113, 114n, 120–1, 186, 189, 192, 196–9, 201–4, 206n
   deprivation, 100
   playfulness, 86, 99–101, 105, 189, 196–9, 206n
   serious play, 98–101, 110, 198
   see also roleplay
Pleasantville, 133, 139, 175
Popper, Karl, 15, 27, 28, 52, 209
pop psychology, 36, 57, 189, 206n
pornography, 108, 186, 192, 198
posthumanism, 6, 15–17, 86
postmodernity, 40n, 140–1, 173–4
poststructuralism, 20, 40n
prejudice, 6, 20, 28, 34, 76, 85, 91, 101, 136, 151, 161, 167, 170, 209, 211

production design, 156–8, 185
propinquity *see* proximity
protoconversations, 73
proximity, 21, 57, 64–6, 87, 89, 95, 99, 108, 113, 115n, 173, 184–5, 190, 201
psychoanalysis, 27, 41n, 66, 72n
psychopathy, 59–60, 62
public relations, 51, 94
Pygmalion effect, 194, 196

quotidian *see* everyday

racism, 85, 101, 149, 161, 209
realism (film), 19, 48, 65, 94, 102, 130, 136, 139–41, 144n, 150, 156, 158, 162, 181–2, 185, 188–9, 197, 200–1, 204, 211–12
   social realism, 19, 94
   see also verisimilitude
Rear Window, 188
redemption (narrative), 4, 130, 165, 167
refraction, 45–6, 56, 78, 87–9, 96n
relativism, 13, 21, 31, 122
relief theory, 57, 107
religion, 6, 14, 16, 18, 20, 32, 57, 62, 68, 103, 105, 131, 209
   atheism, 13
rereading and rewatching, 113–14
ritual, 69, 80–2, 99, 168
   dysphoric ritual, 69, 135
   rites of passage, 81–2, 137
   see also liminality
road movies, 130, 143
Rock Bottom, 53
roleplay, 74, 85–6, 100–1
romance genres, 131, 137, 164
The Room, 77–8
Roseanne, 136, 164

The Safety of Objects, 130, 142, 155
Said, Edward, 6, 13–14, 20, 32–3
Sayles, John, 25, 87–8, 134, 149
scientism, 27–8
screenwriting, 96–7n, 164, 176n, 181
selfhood, 16, 56, 148
self–other overlap *see* oneness
sentimentality, 89, 130–1, 136, 141, 160, 161–70, 176n, 192, 197, 200, 206

A Serious Man, 130
The Sessions, 108–9
sex, 16, 22, 37, 83, 108–10, 111, 129, 133, 135, 159, 171, 172, 192, 195, 198–9, 203
  attraction, 69, 111
  sex positivity, 108–10
  sexuality, 22, 37, 83, 108, 129, 172
  sexual politics, 135, 132–3, 171, 198–9
  shame, 186, 192, 195, 198
sexism, 84, 140, 176n, 209
Shakespeare, 18–19, 77–8
Silver City, 134
The Simpsons, 136, 164
simulation, 2–5, 26, 29, 35, 40n, 45, 49, 57, 59, 65, 66, 69, 74, 85, 88–9, 98, 102, 121, 140, 174
sincerity, 136, 141, 144n
Sirk, Douglas, 136, 146
sitcoms *see* television
Slaughterhouse-Five, 114
slow cinema, 112
Slow Food Manifesto, 90
The Slums of Beverly Hills, 157–8
smart cinema, 77, 141, 144n, 154
Smart People, 155, 175
Smith, Adam, 18
Smith, Murray, 8, 54, 59, 83, 98
so-bad-it's-good, 77–8
social cognition, 27–8, 45–6, 112–13
social glue, 91, 167, 176n
social psychology, 28, 36, 69, 94, 204
Solondz, Todd, 109, 139–40, 141, 144n
song, 1, 53, 71n, 73, 81, 99, 189, 200
Soul Food, 149
special effects, 104–5
spectacle *see* special effects
spectatorship, 25, 41, 53, 55n, 70, 78, 80, 109, 163, 190, 211
Splash, 188, 192
Splendor in the Grass, 133, 137
splitting *see* all-or-nothing thinking
Star Trek, 59, n71
The Station Agent, 138
status anxiety, 130
status symbols, 32, 87, 117, 158, 176n
The Stepford Wives, 140
The Storyteller, 212–13

Strangers on a Train, 79
structuralism, 46
subtext, 87, 211
subtlety, 69, 81, 143, 149, 199, 206, 207n, 211
suburbs
  demography, 133, 148–50, 151, 157, 171–2
  environmental perspectives, 147, 151, 156, 176
  media representation, 146–61
  segregation, 147–8, 150
  sprawl, 151, 156, 176
  suburbanisation in America, 146–8
  suburbanisation in Australia, 150, 151–2
  suburbia and gender, 130, 134, 135, 140, 158, 161–2, 175, 176n
Sugiyama, Michelle Scalise, 48–9, 121
Sunshine State, 134, 149
The Swimmer, 146
symbolism, 16, 22, 71n, 80–1, 87, 89–90, 116–18, 133, 142, 146, 153–4, 158, 176n, 185, 188

taste, 32, 49, 77–8, 113, 138, 140
teen cinema, 131, 136–8, 143; *see also* adolescence
teleology, 6, 27
television, 1, 63, 74, 113, 117, 119, 131, 136, 144n, 156, 164, 175, 188, 212
  reruns, 113
  sitcoms, 136, 164
terror management, 45, 71n
theatre, 3, 18, 59n, 60, 69, 74, 77–8, 81–2, 96n, 99, 104–5, 120, 135
theism *see* religion
Thirteen Conversations About One Thing, 132, 141
Thompson, Kristin, 2, 181, 184, 186, 188–9, 194, 197, 206–7n
Three Amigos, 207
tragedy, 63, 65, 71n, 132, 135, 184, 212
transhumanism, 15–16, 60
trash cinema, 96
trauma, 3, 46, 64–5, 69, 114, 130, 135, 199
  family and trauma, 130, 135, 199
  trauma and narration, 3, 46, 64–5, 114

Troche, Rose, 109, 130
Troll 2, 77
The Truman Show, 133, 139, 144n, 175
trust, 24, 80–1, 91–3, 106, 171, 173, 175, 177n
   social trust and public health, 91
   trust in news and journalism, 91–2, 171, 177n
Turner, Victor, 21, 81–2, 99
Turvey, Malcolm, 2, 48, 54n

The Upside of Anger, 130
urbanity and cinema, 158, 176n

verisimilitude, 5, 52, 63, 102, 164
violence, 20, 62, 100, 148, 208, 213n
   class violence, 32, 41n, 152–3, 208
   screen violence, 62, 66–72, 73, 148
   see also war
virtuosity, 104, 111

visual effects *see* special effects
Vonnegut, Kurt, 114
vulnerability, 20–2, 48, 89, 96n, 142, 163, 182, 211

The Walking Dead, 120–1
war, 6, 209; *see also* violence
wealth distribution, 91, 147–8, 208
Western (genre), 134, 139
What Goes Up, 137, 155, 156
Whitehouse, Harvey, 69, 81–2, 135, 167–8, 176n
Willow, 188, 192
Wilson, Edward O., 29, 34, 37, 45
Wilt, David E., 133, 138, 156–7, 170
Wyatt, Robert, 53

Zappa, Frank, 96
Zengotita, Thomas de, 76, 89, 91, 117, 170
zombie (genre), 70

EU representative:
Easy Access System Europe
Mustamäe tee 50, 10621 Tallinn, Estonia
Gpsr.requests@easproject.com

www.ingramcontent.com/pod-product-compliance
Lightning Source LLC
Chambersburg PA
CBHW051807230426
43672CB00012B/2660